Lord of the Infrastructure

A Management Guide for IT Infrastructure Managers

By Art Carapola

Lord of the Infrastructure

Copyright © 2016, 2017 by NewVista Advisors, llc and Art Carapola

All rights reserved. No part of this publication may be reproduced, distributed, or transmitted in any form or by any means, including photocopying, recording, or other electronic or mechanical methods, without the prior written permission of the publisher, except in the case of brief quotations embodied in critical reviews and certain other noncommercial uses permitted by copyright law. For permission requests, write to the publisher, addressed "Attention: Permissions Coordinator," at the address below.

NewVista Advisors, llc
22 Indian Wells Road
Brewster, NY 10509

www.nvadvisors.com

Table of Contents

Table of Contents 3
Chapter 1   Some Initial Thoughts 8
   Why Did I Write This Book? 8
   Why You Should Read This Book 9
   *What This Book is **NOT** About* 9
   Who is the Audience For This Book? 10
   A Few Words About The Author (that would be me) 10
Chapter 2   The Basics 12
   How Did You Get Here? 12
   Is This a New Position or One That Has Been Recently Vacated? 12
   Who Do You Report To? 13
   How Is Your Job About To Change? 14
   What Will Now Be Your Key Areas of Focus? 14
   Who Are Your Customers? 15
Chapter 3   What Can Derail You? 16
Chapter 4   Starting the New Job 24
   Your Initial Assessment 24
   What Do You Do With The Information You Collected In Your Initial Assessment? 27
      Tactical Issues 28
   Strategic Issues 31
Chapter 5   IT Communications 33
   IT Newsletters 34
   Notification of Systems Maintenance Events 35
   Announcement of Major Changes to Infrastructure and Applications 36
   Monthly Dashboard Reports to Management and Business Stakeholders . 36

Frequently Asked Question Lists Should Be Published And Pro-Actively Distributed 37
Help Desk Feedback to Users Providing Ticket Results 37
The IT Intranet Site 38
A Project Communications Plan 39

Chapter 6   Budget Preparation and Management 40
How is an IT Budget Structured? 40
    Keeping the Lights On 40
    New Projects 41
    The Project Cost 42
Capital Investments Versus Expenses 45
Contingency 46
A Project Today Impacts Keeping the Lights on Tomorrow 46
Optimizing an IT budget 46
Outsourcing As An Alternative 47
Managing the Budget 48
Monthly Variance Reports 50
Handling "Unbudgeted" Business Requests 51
Vendor Selection and Management 52
The Request for Proposal (RFP) Process 56
    Adding Collateral Materials to the RFP 59
    The RFP Process Steps and Timing 60
    The RFP Timeline 61
    Bid-Leveling 61
    Notification of a Winner 63

Chapter 7   People Management 64
Be the Person They Love! 65
MBWA 66
Hiring and Retention 66
Skill Development, Mentoring, and Training 70
Generating Performance Plans 70
Employee Appraisals 72
Staff Compensation 72
Dealing with Staff Issues – Problem Employees, Conflict Resolution 74

Chapter 8   Structuring the Organization 77
Future IT Organizational Structures 79
The Infrastructure Organization Example 80
Organizational Challenge – The Storage Area Network Group 81
The Centralized Technology Aligned Infrastructure Organization 81
    Help Desk 83

    End User Services 83
    Network Services...83
    Systems Engineering and Administration...85
    Systems Operations...85
    Additional (Optional) IT Groups 86
    Extending the Organization into Multiple Sites....................................86

Chapter 9   Technology Management 90
    IT Standards 90
    Standard Operating Procedures...93
    Communicating and Enforcing IT Standards and Policies 96
    Service Level Agreements..97
    IT Processes...99
        ITIL Processes 100
    Problem Management / Root Cause Analysis....................................101
    Incident Management..103
    The Help Desk..103
        My Most Challenging Turnaround...103
        Attempting First Contact Resolution of Issues 105
    Triage of Issues and Incident Prioritization 106
        Incident Urgency (Categories of Urgency) 106
        Incident Impact (Categories of Impact)...107
        Incident Priority Classes 109
        Circumstances That Warrant the Incident to be Treated as a Major Incident 112
    Communications and Escalation for Unresolved Issues 113

Chapter 10   IT Asset Management 115
    Asset Management is a Collection of Processes 118
        Inventory of Devices..118
        Contracts & Finance – IT Cost Control & Reduction.......................119
        Software Compliance 119
    How Effective Is Your Company's Asset Management Process?.......120
    What is Your End-State Goal for IT Asset Management? 123
        Planning Your Roadmap 124
        Inventory Reconciliation 126
        Lifecycle Management 126
        IT Asset Management Tools 127

Chapter 11   Risk Management – Understanding What Can Impact or Derail Something You Are Responsible For 129
    Risk Management Process 133
    The Risk Lifecycle..134

Risk Identification *134*
Risk Categories *135*
Risk Assessment *138*
   Determining the Impact Level 139
   The Risk Summary Status Matrix 141
Risk Mitigation *143*
   Residual Risk Severity 143
   Mitigation / Remediation Activity 143
Risk Acceptance *143*
Information Security Risks *144*
Risk Documentation *145*
Risk Reporting and Review *147*
Risk Reporting Process *147*

Chapter 12   Project Management **152**
What Should Your Project Manager Be Like? *152*
Project Initiation (getting it correct up front) *155*
The Project Charter *158*
   The Project Justification 158
   High Level Project Risk Assessment 161
Project Planning *162*
   The Project Schedule 163

Chapter 13   Creating and Managing the Project Schedule **166**
Project Execution *167*
Project Status Reporting *168*
   The Weekly Dashboard 168
Project Portfolio Management *184*
   Project Scoring & Prioritization for Maximum Results 184
   Categorizing Potential Projects 185
   Building Project Scoring Models 185
   Developing the Scoring System 186
   Using a Matrix to Rank Projects 187
   Prioritize Projects Based on Plotted Scores 188
   The Bottom Line on Project Prioritization and Selection 189

Chapter 14   Operational Management **190**
Daily System Checks *190*
Change Management *193*

Chapter 15   Information Technology Metrics – A Critical Component of Your Toolbox **196**
The Case for Developing an In-Depth Metrics Program *196*
Customer Satisfaction Metrics *199*

Metrics for Analyzing What Is Driving Support Calls 208
   Break Fix Drill Down 210
Call Trending 212
Call Aging Metrics 216
   Automatic Call Distribution Metrics 218
   Volume of Tickets / Call Closure 224
   Usage Statistics 226
Messaging Services 229
Server Availability 233
Storage Availability 234
Network Availability 235
Mobile Devices 236

Chapter 16   Developing your IT Strategy 237
What is an IT Strategy? 237
The Process of Defining an IT Strategy 239
Developing an IT Strategy 240
   Engaging with the Business 240
   Identify the Gaps Using a SWOT Analysis 243
   The Actual IT Strategic Plan Document 245
   IT Strategy Summary Thoughts 248

Chapter 17   Managing the Politics of IT Infrastructure 249
The Standards Rejecter 250
The Resource Hog 250
The CYA Finger Pointer 250
The Complainer 251
The Non-Team Player 251
Last-Minute and It's YOUR Fault 253
The Change Management Failure 254
Some People Are More Equal Than Others 254
Some People Are Not 256
Home Setups 257

Chapter 18   Final Words 259
Appendix A 262
Items You Need To Have In Place 263
Some Items You Should Focus On Understanding When You Start a New Position 264

Chapter 1

Some Initial Thoughts

Why Did I Write This Book?

Having managed IT organizations for over 30 years, with the majority of that time focused on large IT Infrastructures I have long since developed a deep understanding of what's important and what is not. Managing an IT Infrastructure is a thankless job. Most people don't even realize it exists until something goes wrong. When that happens, their views are usually not very kind.

I have found that most Infrastructure Managers are literally thrown into the job with little or no training. People that were exceptional technologists are often chosen to lead an Infrastructure team. Other times exceptional Infrastructure Engineers move on to new companies to become an Infrastructure Manager.

However you became the leader of an IT Infrastructure Organization, the odds are good that you are finding yourself in many situations that no one prepared you for. This book is designed to teach the reader how to manage an IT organization and to infuse in you the information you will need to be far more successful than most. It's for those lucky individuals that suddenly find themselves in charge of IT – either a part of IT (such as the head of Infrastructure) or the entire organization (as in the CIO/CTO).

Why You Should Read This Book

Whether you are a new Infrastructure Manager or you are hoping to move up into that role, this book provides a prescriptive description of what it takes to be successful in that role. It provides a roadmap to assist you in determining what needs to be your immediate areas of focus, how to navigate relationships, manage your staff, deal with company politics and the inevitable landmines they entail. The book describes how you will build both short and long-term plans and execute on those plans. It is about managing technology and technology teams, IT budgets, Risk, Assets, and large IT projects.

This book assumes that the reader has some exposure to managing tasks or projects and possibly even small teams. Understand that there is a chasm of difference between managing a task driven team and managing an entire organization. My goal is to make that transition less painful.

This book defines major activities that an Infrastructure Manager will undertake on a day by day basis. It helps you understand how to assess the organization and technology you are now managing, the policies and processes that must be in place to manage the day to day activities, how to measure how well your organization and technology are performing, and what you need to do to make it better.

Most importantly, it is designed to alert you to the primary causes that managers get derailed from their job. If this is your first management position you will surely encounter many new situations you may not have ever thought about. New relationships, new expectations, and undefined goals all can spell doom.

What This Book is *NOT* About

This book is not designed to teach you about Networking, Information Security, Windows Networks, Servers or Desktops. In short, this is NOT about any specific technology.

This book is also not a comprehensive tutorial on Project Management. Although Project Management will be discussed in some depth, it will not make you into a great project manager if you have no previous background.

There are more detailed books and courses focused on doing that. It will provide the basics for you to function, successfully managing projects, however.

Who is the Audience for This Book?

There are several audiences for this book.

- *New Infrastructure Managers*, whether responsible for a portion of the overall Infrastructure (such as Network, Systems, Storage, End user Support or Information Security Manager) or responsible for Infrastructure Enterprise –Wide, will find this book provides a prescriptive roadmap for how to approach the new job. It will expose you to areas of IT Management I'm sure a new manager might not even know exists.
- *Those that aspire to be an Infrastructure Manager* will be exposed to the types of responsibilities that come with such a role. If you're currently interviewing for Infrastructure Management positions, this book can help you understand the types of questions you may be asked, and give you the ability to deliver a cogent answer.
- *Those that aspire to be an Infrastructure Manager in the future* will learn the responsibilities of such a role, as well as the challenges and landmines that such a role will include. The creative and financial benefits are great, but so are the stresses and landmines. This book can help you decide if Infrastructure Management is the right career direction for you.

A Few Words About The Author (that would be me)

Art Carapola is a highly-successful senior business technology solutions leader in both line management and consulting roles with demonstrated global experience formulating and delivering complex transformation initiatives for financial services firms. Art has managed global Infrastructures in as many as 26 countries supporting thousands of staff members. He has managed IT staffs as large as 400 people.

Art has extensive experience as a senior IT executive (in C-level roles) and partnering with C–level executives and senior business partners to synthesize strategies, develop long-range plans, and lead change.

He has demonstrated successes in organizational and complex technology transformations providing domestic and global enterprise companies with a sustainable competitive advantage and ability to restructure, innovate, be proactive with regulators, and navigate through distress.

Art has an outstanding client-centric focus on building technology organizations that foster exceptional relationships with key internal and external parties driven and rewarded by achieving shared business goals.

Art's career is built on the premise that technology is the change agent & transformational lever that allows organizations to lead.

Art is a creative thinker and catalyst for new ideas with a strong record of fostering technology innovation, pushing the limits for adoption, and understanding both the impact and opportunity of emerging and disruptive technologies.

Art is an outstanding organization and team leader with experience in leading cross-cultural global teams in as many as 25 countries, in high-growth fast-paced environments.

CORE COMPETENCIES

- IT Tactical, Long Range & Strategic Planning
- Strategic Relationship Building and Influencing
- Complex Program & Project Management
- IT Governance, Portfolio Prioritization & Rationalization
- Risk Management, IT Audit, & Regulatory
- Organizational Consolidation, Improvement & Mentoring
- IT Infrastructure Engineering, Implementation & Operations
- Emerging Technology
- Application and Data Migration and Management
- IT Infrastructure Optimization, Consolidation
- IT Service Management
- Business Process Reengineering and Digitization

Chapter 2

The Basics

How Did You Get Here?

One of the most important questions you need to answer for yourself as soon as you embark on your journey to becoming "Lord of the Infrastructure" is "how did I get here?" That sounds simple enough, but in reality, it's far more complicated than "because of my great technical work and commitment to the company". Here are a few questions that you should think about when answering this question:

Is This a New Position or One That Has Been Recently Vacated?

It's a Newly Created Position - If this is a new position you need to understand why it was created. This includes who created this position. Was it your immediate manager or several levels higher? Whoever created this position has some vision of what they want from it – and that vision is not always communicated very well.

Occasionally I have seen situations where an essential component of leadership was missing from an organization, such as the Head of Infrastructure or Head of Application Development. Those organizations operate without leadership, like a barge floating down the river without any tug boats to guide it.

In such a situation your job will likely include making a large number of changes, defining processes, generating reports to see how improvements are progressing – all while dealing with the inevitable push-back from your new staff – who will recite the well know chant "That's not how we do that". (More on all of this later).

Vacated – If you find that this is NOT a newly created position, you need to understand exactly what happened to the last person in your role.

Was your predecessor fired or was it a resignation? If the last manager was fired, why was that person fired? (This is hugely important to understand – don't make the same mistakes!). If the person left the job for another position try to learn what drove that decision – was it more money, closer to home, a more substantial role OR was it an impossible manager or customer base, or being career blocked?

Who Do You Report To?

Another important question to consider is who do you report to? Are you buried six level down in a behemoth corporate structure, isolated from where real decisions are being made or are you in a fully empowered position that will chart the course of IT and how it drive the business results? Are your immediate manager and your second line manager in the same building as you or are they halfway across the country?

The answers to these questions will provide your first level of guidance on how to execute in your role.

- If your predecessor was fired, find out why and make sure you have conscious plans to ensure you don't make that same mistake
- If it's a new role, spend considerable time understanding the goals and expectations of both your manager and the business in general.
- Face to face communication with your management and peers is vitally important so develop a plan for ongoing meetings either in the

same room, via Video Conferencing or by you getting on a plane and flying out to meet once a month at a minimum.

How Is Your Job About To Change?

The most significant change that any new IT manager will face is transitioning from a person tasked with the goal of *TECHNICALLY* providing the most effective and efficient IT Infrastructure or Application environment to one whose job is now primarily the management of that technology and the teams that support it.

Your staff must include those technical subject matter experts that will design, build and maintain the systems. This is usually the most difficult transition for a new IT manager – letting go of the technology tasks. I've seen this bring down new managers again and again.

What Will Now Be Your Key Areas of Focus?

Your job is now focused on how the technology you are responsible for meets the needs of the business and hopefully drives it to greater success. This means you will interact more closely with business management than ever before. In most cases, the IT manager must build a set of plans (Tactical Plan for short-term initiatives – Strategic Plan for long term direction). The strategic plans are usually socialized with the major business leaders in the organization to ensure you are well aligned with their direction and needs and to get their concurrence on your agenda.

You will focus on optimizing the cost/benefit ratio of the technology you deploy, the alignment of technology initiatives with business plans and direction, operating within allocated budgets, sourcing and retaining the best technical people, representing your organization in the interaction with the business and other technical peers.

Some of the skills that are needed for this role include:

- Budget Preparation and Management
- People Management, including development, staffing, mentoring and dealing with issues
- Technology Management – this includes such things as standards, policies, etc.

- Operational Management — Ensuring high availability and optimizing the value investments in IT provides to the organization. Change Management and Asset Management are part of this group of activities
- Project Management — you will now need to focus on cross-functional management
- Risk Management — understanding what can impact or derail something you are responsible for

Who Are Your Customers?

You must know who your customers are. Also, you must make sure that each customer understands your views of your organization and your overall direction and is satisfied with both the direction and results. As an IT manager, you will definitely have a wider range of customers than when you were a technical contributor.

As an example — If you are Head of Infrastructure for an organization:

- Application Developers and Application Product Managers are your customers. They need you to provide servers, storage, and network to host their applications
- Business Leaders are your customers. In many cases, Business leaders own segments of the infrastructure, or they own the applications that the App development teams are creating
- The entire staff is your customer — You provide End User Support, network connectivity, desktop and laptop systems, remote connectivity, wireless, telephones. Any individual can escalate an issue to the point that provides you with boatloads of grief.

Chapter 3

What Can Derail You?

I can probably write a book on just this question. Actually, lots have been written about the causes for the derailment of IT Managers. Here are some common causes you should be aware of:

Not building connections to your peers, business leaders, and upper management – One of the most important factors for your success will be how well you connect with those you will work with. As such, one of your first activities should be to meet with your peers and the business leaders that your organization supports. Discuss their assessment of your organization, its strengths, and weaknesses. Ask them what your organization doing right and what is it doing wrong. Is there anything additional that your group could do that would enhance their ability to carry on their responsibilities, even if it is currently outside of your mandate? Most importantly, this cannot be a one-time thing. Maintain the connection by meeting often. Set meetings to discuss common goals. Sit together for lunch – or better yet, get out of the office and go to a restaurant. You don't need to turn people into lifelong friends, but you should feel perfectly comfortable together.

Inability to influence - Influencing others, either up to more senior management, across to your peers or downward to those that work for you will be essential to your success. I've spent considerable time and effort working to understand how to develop the skills to influence people and gain their support. There is no magic here. To a large degree, it depends on people's perception of your integrity, credibility, and skills. Here are a few things to consider:

- *Never ever ever lie!* - This is my number one measure of a person. You can fix a lack of specific skills, however, most real managers realize you can't fix a lack of integrity. Once you are labeled as a liar you are done.
- *Have your facts straight.* - If you absolutely know the answer, then reply to a question. If not, don't be afraid to say "I can't answer that right now, but I will get you the answer by the end of the day (week, etc.). " Make sure you give the person SOME response by the deadline you set for yourself, even if that response is "I'm still working on that answer but it will take a bit more time".
- *Prepare "elevator speeches" for those questions you expect to be asked.* An elevator speech is a very short canned answer – named after the tendency to be asked questions when you're trapped in an elevator. Question "So John, I hear your team is developing a new remote access capability. What's that all about?" You should be prepared to respond with the details: Why you're doing it, what it means to the users, what issues it solves, when it will be available, what the economics are (saves this much or costs this much extra but gives us these benefits), what would the result be if you didn't do this.
- *Be dependable* – If you say something will happen by a certain time or date, make sure it happens or make sure you've prepped people for (communicated) the delay
- *Be prepared to justify your requests* – If you are looking for something – budget to buy something, additional headcount, etc. – have the justification for your request fully prepared and ready to go before you make that request. There will be more on this later.

Bottom line it comes down to the following – if someone asks you a question, make sure you are fully prepared to answer it. If you answer a question, build your reputation so that people believe the information you communicated is correct and truthful. Essentially, you are knowledgeable, credible and have high-integrity.

Difficulty leading your team (ability to influence, build and maintain a team, role modeling) - How well you manage your team will also be a major factor in your success in your new role. You cannot underestimate the level of this challenge. Whether you were promoted from within or brought in from the outside there will always be someone on your team that believes to the core of their being that they should have been given your job. Only your actions and your team's successes will address this over time. Some things to keep in mind:

- *Hire the Best of the Best of the Best* – I know, easier said than done, but you might be surprised at the number of people that won't hire someone smarter than they are. Make sure you hire the smartest most enthusiastic people you can find for every role you have available. I have always been the most successful when every person on my team is smarter than I am in their specific technical focus. Don't let critical roles remain unfilled for extended periods of time.

- *Listen to your team and make sure they feel comfortable challenging you and telling you when you're wrong!* – I always try to hire the best and smartest in their field and make sure they know I expect them to tell me when I am going down the wrong path. That has saved my butt more often than I like to think about. This also gives the subject matter experts the understanding that their opinions and contributions are respected and that they still have some level of control over their area of responsibility (remember that person who believes he/she should have gotten your job?)

- *Empowerment* – Understand what level of empowerment you can push down to your team.

As an example, in one of my roles where I had End User Support and the Help Desk in my organization, I learned an important lesson in empowerment. We had standards for desktop software (which was installed on every PC) and optional programs that were allowed (such as Photoshop) but were restricted to only those that absolutely needed them. There was a defined process to get these optional programs, which consisted of approval by a person's senior manager and approval by me.

At one meeting, someone from our Help Desk pointed out to me that I had never rejected a request from someone that had their senior manager's approval. That person recommended that I be taken out of the process and that, once the requestor's senior manager approved the request, the Help

Desk would be empowered to supply the software. That was a great recommendation and it encouraged us to look at other processes that could be simplified.

There are similar stories across virtually every aspect of the IT organization. The bottom line is not to inject yourself into the individual activities unless your contribution delivers some real demonstrable value.

- *Make sure you credit your people for their work!* – Praise your team and individual staff members publicly whenever possible and appropriate. If someone outside of your organization praises an accomplishment, instantly respond with praise those on your team that did the heavy lifting. Your team will quickly resent you if they believe you took credit for a success that they completed and you had little to do with. Don't see this as a lost opportunity to look great to the broader organization. The fact that your organization is running well and is having success will directly reflect on you.
- *Reward exceptional performance* – When someone goes above and beyond, take it past public praise and reward them. It doesn't have to be a huge reward like a major bonus (unless that is warranted). It can be something small but meaningful. If one of your team needed to work the weekend and missed some family event, reward them by offering to pay for dinner for the staff member and his/her spouse. Give someone an extra day off. Refer to these as "Spot Awards", since they are given on the spot of the extraordinary event.
- *Deal with personnel issues quickly and firmly* – If you have a personnel issue don't hope it goes away. It never will. Start documenting what you are doing to address the issue as soon as you become aware of it. Document every conversation where the issue was discussed – with everyone, including HR. Don't suffer under the delusion that, if things go very wrong, an unethical HR person will place the blame on you for something that HR told you to do. Retain all EMAIL concerning this person in a separate EMAIL folder. Create a separate file to hold all backup information. Bring HR into the discussion as early as possible and work with them to either put the staff member on the right track or manage them out of the business. (Much more on this later)
- *Be a mentor for your staff* – Become the "Go To" person for your staff. Help them work past issues. If you don't have the skills to work

through an issue, arrange for them to get help from another employee or outside person. Own the problem and always try to help your team member improve their skills or work through challenges.

Issues with honesty (Betrayed Trust) – I already mentioned this in the "Ability to Influence" category. Hopefully, I don't have to say a whole lot here. Again, this is my number 1 hot button. You can fix incompetence, but you can't fix a basic lack of honesty. If you get the reputation of being a liar, you might as well start looking for another job.

- Never lie and don't tell half-truths either.
- Don't purposely omit information that you know is important to a conversation
- Don't conveniently forget things you have said or committed to

Isolation of your department from other groups – It's not unusual for a technical group to isolate themselves from other teams or the business. How many times have I heard "It's the network, not the server" OR "It's the server, not the network". Considering how understaffed so many IT departments are today, it's not surprising to see how many will become inwardly focused in performing their specific routine tasks to the exclusion of all else. The result of this is situations such as an application team asking for major infrastructure environments a week or two before their application go-live date or the infrastructure group not being connected to general user disconnect.

Unable to think strategically – When you move from being a technology specialist or subject matter expert to becoming an IT Manager, your focus shifts from the more immediate tasks of designing and operating an IT environment or Application to one that includes projecting where you will be taking technology over the foreseeable horizon. You become the person that must ensure the technology that is deployed is well aligned with the long-term goals of the business. Those long-term company business goals drive your definition of the long-term target architecture and IT Strategy for your environment. You must ensure that your IT activities are all designed to evolve the technical environment into that long-term vision. Making this transition is essential to your success.

Strategic differences with management – It is so easy to find yourself in this situation. It can be as simple as a management change somewhere above you. You can't win this sort of battle. If you find yourself in this situation make one attempt to present your direction and then embrace the decision. If that doesn't work for you, it may be time to move on. Don't be afraid to make this decision.

Failures to delegate – New managers very often find themselves overwhelmed by the tasks before them. They often jealously hang on to some portion of their old responsibilities as a type of physiological anchor to their technical past. In addition, the new manager is often overwhelmed with new tasks that could and should be delegated to subordinates. To avoid this landmine you should embrace the delegation of work to your team. Certainly, unless there is a demonstrable lack of skilled manpower, you should reassign any of your previous responsibilities if you were promoted to your new position.

Failure to staff effectively – So often I have heard a team leader say "I have the headcount, I just don't have the time to go through the interview process". The reality is that you must make filling your open positions your top priority. Days do turn into weeks and months, and soon you will find that headcount pulled from you because someone else has a greater need. Failure to fill open positions will also be a cause of resentment within your organization. It's hard to ask someone to work lots of overtime hours when you have the ability to add more heads and are not moving on it.

Resistance to change or the "not invented here" syndrome – Another common challenge is the resistance to embracing new concepts, technologies or ways of performing a task. Whether this is the result of a person or team just being stuck on the status quo, OR if this is a person or group that just thinks that no person or the team could be smarter than they are, this is a fatal flaw. The most successful managers are those that drive change into the organization. Be that person

As a corollary to your not being the "not invented here" person, you should learn to recognize this in other people. I once had a manager that just was a complete contrarian. (We actually called him something completely different than that – extra points – what did we call him?) I eventually learned that whatever recommendation I made would be rejected by him and he would instead select an opposing solution, no matter how insane it was. It wasn't hard to decide to put the BEST solution (our recommended solution) as the one (or one of a very few) that my team rejected. He fell for it every time. We had our best-recommended solution and he could claim ownership. Guys like this always end up getting fired, so just wait him out.

Over-confidence, defensiveness or arrogance – These are all personality flaws that you should avoid. Nobody wants to work with a jerk.

Unwillingness to seek or accept feedback – Feedback will be essential to your success. New York City's former Mayor Koch used to go around asking people "How am I doing?" This became a sort of trademark for him. The citizens of New York City always felt they had someone that wanted to know about and address their issues. For Koch, he had a direct line into what the people of New York were thinking, what bothered them, and what they really felt he needed to address. As an IT manager, your understanding of your customers' assessment of both you and your organization is essential.

Don't wait for that assessment to be brought to you – you need to go out and actively seek it. Infrastructure Managers must develop communications plans outward to your customers to tell them what you are doing. In addition, in as many situations as possible, you should elicit customer feedback through surveys (help desk incident resolution survey, etc.) On an annual basis, the entire customer base should be asked to fill out a survey describing their satisfaction with your services and what they need to be changed.

I can give lots of examples of where this has gone wrong. In most cases, the story ends with the person unwilling to accept feedback getting fired. A good example is a recent office build out and headquarters relocation for a New York City Financial Services firm. The Head of Real Estate pushed back on any input from anyone – whether that was IT or the individual business unit stakeholders. The net result was that a huge number of items needed to be torn down and rebuilt. Costs quickly got out of hand. By the time the move was completed it costs almost twice what had been budgeted (which was already many tens of millions of dollars), the project was about 6 months late, and everybody had an issue with something in the new location. What do you think this manager's chances are of surviving in his position?

Poor response to a crisis - How well or poorly you respond to a crisis will be one dimension where you will be assessed with great prejudice by all involved – your management, your peers and especially your users. This is truly one area where you must shine from day one, simply because the inability to calmly and effectively lead your organization back into full systems availability could mean the difference between a minor bump in the road and the business failing.

Imagine for a second if you are responsible for supporting a Trading Floor at a financial institution. If the network goes down and the market decides to crash at the same time, the losses could be calculated into the many m of dollars per minute,

What are the steps you must take to respond to a crisis? It obviously (on the crisis, but let's assume the worst.

- Assemble a team to resolve the crisis. You should have plans beforehand to understand who will be engaged depending on what issue arises
- Communicate with the impacted stakeholders – better to over-communicate than to under communicate
- Have escalation plans in place – know when to escalate and to whom
- Have periodic status update calls – get everyone together on a call every hour, half hour, 15 minutes – whatever is required to make sure the extended team is well synced up.
- Don't wait to bring in help – Bring in the vendors sooner rather than later, especially if you have support contracts in place with them.
- When the crisis has been resolved, communicate that broadly, thanking everyone for their patience and thanking those that participated in the resolution for their help. Explain in simple language what happened, why it happened and what you have done (or are doing) to ensure it doesn't happen again.

Chapter 4

Starting the New Job

Your Initial Assessment

When you first start in a new IT Management Position it is important to make a dispassionate assessment of your organization from your new management perspective. If you were promoted to your new position, the most difficult part of this will be the need for you to separate yourself from your past role as a technologist on the team in order to develop a dispassionate assessment. As an example, if you were previously a lead engineer in the Networking department, now promoted to head of networking for the company, your tendency will be to automatically assess the technology at a minimum as being in great condition. (A simplistic example admittedly) This would be a mistake.

One of your key goals in this assessment will be to determine if there is anything in your new organization that needs fixing. There is a huge amount of information available online today discussing the top priorities of IT for the year, for the new CIO or CTO, for the organization undergoing change, ad infinitum. You will learn that most IT problems will fall into four generic areas:

- *Business Satisfaction with IT* – Most information you will see publishe on Business Satisfaction will immediately start circling the drain about Technology Alignment with the business. I'm not saying is not important, but it is only one dimension of business satisfaction. Poor business satisfaction is more likely to start from simple dissatisfaction with the most basic services your organization is providing such as the Help Desk and desktop support, the availability of the Internet and how well wireless works. Once the business staff loses confidence in those parts of your business, they will be much more critical of your performance in the business specific or business automation components.

- *Budget Issues* – Issues within IT can often be driven by the IT budget. The inability to deploy sufficient resources to meet user demand, such as for End User Support, poorly defined projects that spin out of control and exceed all budget and schedule projections, unbudgeted initiatives and capital expenditures are all issues for you to watch for.

- *Organization, People, etc.* – Insufficient staffing, lack of skill sets, poor morale, poorly defined organization, roles and responsibilities all can contribute to poor IT performance.

- *Effectiveness in Running Projects* – What is the IT organizations success rate in running significant projects, such as large software and hardware deployments, data center migrations, new network deployments, etc.?

Your assessment will almost always find issues you need to address and nothing here should scare you away. The challenge will, of course, be to define an achievable plan to address whatever is found. Each of these subjects will be reviewed in detail later in the book.

Your assessment should include:

- *Customer Satisfaction* - Your assessment should first be focused on what your customers think of your organization. Also, include peer technology organizations in your review.

- *Basic Technology* - How current is the technology, how well aligned is it with both company direction and industry trends?

- *Technical Operations* – This is about how well the technology is performing. What is the availability of each of the key technology towers (network, servers, printers, desktop), how well is the end user support operation delivering services to end users (first contact call closure rate, the number of calls, the number of repeat calls)? What is the utilization of the technology (network and server utilization percentages)

- *Processes* – Are there well-defined processes for major activities? Ask your customers if the processes your organization has in place meets their need or are overly complex.
- *Policies* – This includes standards in place, operational policies, service level agreements, etc. What is in place and what is not? Are they sufficiently robust? Are they too draconian?
- *Commitments* – What contracts are in place and what do they cost? If possible, get copies of all contracts that fall within your area of responsibility. This area will include:
  - Contracts – this is everything from contracts with carriers that include such items as burst rate charges, end dates, and termination fees, to contracts with outsourced support organizations (Printer support, desktop support), to data center colocation contracts (SLAs, renewal notification dates, holdover clauses, etc.). Make a file of the contracts and a calendar of important dates and set up automated alerts. The Legal and Finance departments can help you with this.
  - Service Level Agreements – Your organization might have Service Level Agreements (SLAs) in place with your customers. In addition, your vendors likely have service level agreements with you. Get copies of all of the SLAs that exist and make a file of them. Read them, understand them and makes sure all are being met.
  - Budgets – I am including the budget as one of your commitments since this is one of the key areas you will be measured against. It is a commitment to the company.
- *People* – get the last performance evaluation and whatever portions of the personnel files that are available to you for each member of your staff. Review these in detail. If you were promoted into your position you may find that some of your staff, who you have always enjoyed working with, have issues you will need to understand and deal with, some may be professional development, and others may be

personnel issues that will require an ongoing partnering with your HR team.
- *Applications* – What applications does your organization support? Are you just providing the platform (servers) and pipes (network) or do you have development or support responsibilities for the application? Does the application have any special characteristics that need to be taken into consideration if you are planning to virtualize servers or move to a new data center with higher network latency (e.g. further away and less expensive)? Understand what is running in your environment and what your role is to ensure that application is successful.

What Do You Do With The Information You Collected In Your Initial Assessment?

Once you have collected the information about your organization you need to put it to use. If this were an IT audit (which is essentially what you are doing), the auditor would come back to you with a series of *Recommended Actions* (recommendations) as well as the impact of not doing them in the organization. The list is usually separated into short-term (tactical) and longer term (strategic) recommendations. Your goal should be to develop this type of list for yourself.

Here are some examples of things you should be looking for:

Tactical Issues

Tactical Issues in Running An IT Department	
Issue	Reasons & Mitigation Plan
Lack of conformance to policies, such as equipment and software standards	<ul><li>Do Policies and Standards exist? If no, develop equipment and software standards</li><li>Review and tighten the Standards Exception Process</li><li>Investigate WHY staff is using Non-Standard systems and software</li></ul>
SLAs are not being met	<ul><li>Insufficient resources</li><li>Team skill sets are insufficient</li><li>Policies and Process no in place or not being followed</li></ul>
Poor Perception of IT by Users	<ul><li>Poor communications with users</li><li>No IT communications plan</li><li>Poor to no Help Desk ticket follow-up</li><li>Need to improve staff skills or resource levels</li><li>Need better-defined processes</li></ul>
Low first-call closure rate on the Help Desk	<ul><li>Skill Issues at the Help Desk</li><li>Lack of tools</li></ul>
Significant number of repeat user call issues	<ul><li>Root Cause of issues not being found - Develop a Root-Cause Identification Process that focuses on the most common issues</li><li>Investigate if Metrics are in place to identify repeat issues</li><li>Replace problematic equipment if the issue is limited to a specific User</li></ul>
Most important issues not resolved first	<ul><li>Definition of Incident Severity Levels</li><li>No or poor incident triage</li><li>Help Desk Processes are lacking</li></ul>

Tactical Issues in Running An IT Department	
Issue	Reasons & Mitigation Plan
Software patching is not current	- Lack of Policies or lack of conformance - Systems Management Administration Tools not in place
Multiple unplanned outages	- Look at Policies and Procedures - Human error issues? Skill set issues? - Change Management Issues? - Recurring issues not being addressed? - Root-Cause Analysis for incidents not being done or results ignored
Low network utilization	- Opportunities for consolidation of circuits? - Over-specification of circuit bandwidths?
Low systems availability	- Human error or skill set issues - Poor Policies and Processes - Systems not properly patched and updated
Team Skill Gaps	- Provide formalized training to current staff - Bring in new staff with deep targeted skills - Separate (fire) low performers
Unfilled headcount	- Focused effort to fill open slots

Tactical Issues in Running An IT Department	
Issue	Reasons & Mitigation Plan
Manual equipment "Build" process delays fulfillment of requests and is responsible for numerous setup errors	<ul><li>Ensure there are well-defined standards that can be implemented in an automated "image-based" build process</li><li>Create processes to build machines using a network-based image and which include provisions to keep the image up to date</li></ul>
Back-level software	<ul><li>Investigate Process and Strategy for keeping software current</li><li>Are software support contracts in place?</li><li>Address one-off users with individual upgrades</li><li>Develop plan to upgrade standard software packages</li></ul>
Unlicensed software	<ul><li>Determine extent of the unlicensed issue</li><li>Determine if unlicensed software is necessary or can be removed</li><li>Work with senior management and Finance to secure funding to purchase required software that is unlicensed</li><li>Work with vendors to purchases licenses</li></ul>

Strategic Issues

Strategic Issues in Running An IT Department	
Issue	**Reasons & Mitigation Plan**
IT Technology and services are not properly aligned with Business Objectives	Develop a strategic plan that is driven by the business strategy and individual business unit goals
Application Software selection is driven by the business units and there are multiple applications delivering identical functionality to different business units	Engage the business units to collapse applications into a single set of standards. Work with them to help standardize data definitions and structures, charts of accounts, etc.
There are no defined standards Policies and Processes	There is no single aspect of good IT management more important than defining and enforcing standards, policies and processes. These should be a number one priority and become part of the strategic plan.
IT uses a broad range of tools that are not integrated together	Develop a strategy of application integration, either leveraging the current application set or by evolving to a new set of integrated applications in the future
There is a lack of measurement and metrics in IT	Develop a comprehensive set of metrics that drives IT improvement. Ensure that all organizations are involved and embrace the concept going forward
Multiple Organizations have overlapping responsibilities	Lack of organizations strategy and clearly define roles and responsibilities. Develop an organizational plan.

Strategic Issues in Running An IT Department	
Issue	**Reasons & Mitigation Plan**
Server Deployment is haphazard with no specific vendor or configuration defined	Develop a server strategy (as part of equipment standards) that defines server types, virtualization and physical server criteria, deployment configuration processes and update and patching policies
No Disaster Recovery Strategy is in place	Develop an IT Disaster Recovery Plan in cooperation with the Business Continuity Organization. If no Business Continuity Group exists, then drive the Disaster Recovery Strategy and Plan from IT
There are no staff sourcing, retention, separation or succession strategy or plans in place	Develop strategies and plans in this area. Socialize the plans with HR and then within IT.

Chapter 5

IT Communications

There are few places where the saying "Perception is Reality" applies more substantially than it does for IT. The big issue you will need to contend with is that IT Infrastructure is essentially an invisible service until something goes wrong. At that point your organization will become the object of incredible focus – all directed at "what went wrong". You literally will not be given the opportunity to communicate all of the wonderful things that have continually gone right (until this failure).

The only way to address this inevitable situation is to proactively communicate the success. You should communicate to everyone – up, down and across. In each case the message should be crafted to accentuate the positive (successes), and also to address (explain) the failures or incidents and to communicate what has been done to ensure that the negative incidents are not repeated.

You must communicate . . .

> To your staff
>
> To your customers
>
> To the outside world

How must you communicate about your organization?

- IT Newsletters
- Notification of Systems Maintenance Events
- Announcement of major changes to Infrastructure and Applications
- Monthly Dashboard reports to Management and Business Stakeholders
- Frequently Asked Question Lists should be published and Pro-actively Distributed
- Help Desk feedback to users providing ticket results and also eliciting feedback through satisfaction surveys

IT Newsletters

IT Newsletters are regularly distributed publications that are designed to communicate a variety of information on a periodic basis. Some of the types of information you may want to include are:

- Some IT Metrics since the last newsletter. This may include information on systems availability, performance against IT goals (call resolution times, etc.), number of calls, user satisfaction results since the last newsletter
- Explanations of outages and what's been done to ensure they don't happen again
- IT Schedule of Events, such as user training, IT upgrades
- New Technology Updates
- Restatement of Policies
- Tips for users
- Contact info for specific types of questions
- Awards to IT Staff members
- Web links that may be useful to the staff

Notification of Systems Maintenance Events

Whenever IT will be modifying the environment in a way that will impact the user, either through a period of unavailability or through a change in how the system or an application will operate, the user base should receive several notification messages in an EMAIL to ensure they will be able to manage through any impact. You should create a template that defines the categories of information that needs to be communicated, so these are easy to generate and nothing gets left out. The notification should minimally cover:

- What is happening and when
- What impact the user will see – such as the unavailability of a service like EMAIL, remote access, file services, the reboot of their desktop workstation, etc.
- What they will need to do to ensure that their environment will not be damaged such as close all applications, log off of your PC but do not shut it down, etc.
- When this will be done and when the systems will be back online and functioning properly
- Who to contact if they will be adversely impacted by this systems change.

A notification of a system event should be sent out for such activities as software patching and upgrades, DR Tests, systems changes, etc.

It's important to note that these Systems Maintenance events should always have gone through the Change Management Process that you have put into place. Also, they MUST be well communicated within your own organization. The Help Desk staff should be well briefed on what is happening and who to call if they experience user issues at the start of business after an update has been applied to the systems. Any peer technology organizations that may be impacted by the updates should also be briefed on the changes and should be required to sign-off on the change request.

Note that you may get push-back from a business or technology group on your changes or schedule. This should have long been resolved in your Change Management Meetings (part of the change management process) but you may find these things coming up once the broad notifications go out. As an example, you may find an investment group within your organization (Investment Banking or Private Equity) that is in the middle of working on a deal and they cannot lose the systems for a Saturday or Sunday afternoon. If they come back at you with such an issue you need to relent and reschedule (in the event you haven't figured that out yourself)

Announcement of Major Changes to Infrastructure and Applications

As a subset to the Notification of Systems Changes, the Announcement of a Major Change to Infrastructure and Applications is a broadly communicated announcement to the organization. In this particular case, however, this change can have serious ramifications that must be well understood.

As an example, an upgrade to an application, or the standardization of several applications into one standard may have ramification to other applications that interface into something being changed. Also, you may find that staff members from around the business have developed local functionality (such as a spreadsheet) that pulls information from a centralized application or database and then process it locally for a report. Those people must be given the most time possible to hear about the change, assess what they need to do to continue working after that change is made, and to make whatever updates are necessary in their world to adjust to the after-change environment.

As such these major changes must be communicated well in advance of any actual change. I'm talking about months here. Your team should be prepared to support the organization with some level of resources to explain the changes and even help the users make changes to their world to make the update transparent.

Monthly Dashboard Reports to Management and Business Stakeholders

A Dashboard is a report that provides a multi-dimensional status of a particular subject or activity. Within the Infrastructure Department there are two types of Dashboard reports that you will typically need to create; the monthly Operational Dashboard, which covers results of the operational activities such as the Help Desk, Systems and Network operations, Customer Satisfaction and so on. The second type of report is the Project Dashboard, which provides a periodic update on the status of an individual project. You will have a Project Dashboard Report for each of your major projects and possibly another one that covers a bunch of smaller projects. Project

Dashboards are usually updated and published on a weekly basis. Both of these reports will be covered in painful detail later in this book.

Both reports are characterized by having a front page that summarizes the detail in the rest of the report. They also make use of the typical RAG (Red-Amber-Green) highest-level status indication wherever possible. This allows senior management to review the front page and then drill down to any of the areas that are not in "Green" status.

Frequently Asked Question Lists Should Be Published And Pro-Actively Distributed

This is relatively self-explanatory. The IT FAQs are used to provide answers to common issued the Help Desk may need to address. In addition, FAQs should always be used when major changes to the environment are planned.

Help Desk Feedback to Users Providing Ticket Results

Communicating with users that have been experiencing issues is a critical function that must be a cornerstone of your End User Support Strategy. In this particular case, when a Help Desk ticket is closed you should communicate with the user that opened the ticket. The communication typically comes in the form of a user survey, but it also includes ticket closure info. Minimally the communication consists of:

- Identification of the support ticket (Ticket Number, Issue Identification, Time Opened, Time Closed, Technician Assigned, etc.)
- Ticket Closure Info – What was done to address the user issue, if the Technician states that the resolution was to the satisfaction of the user, any other comments
- Contact Info To Escalate – Basically a statement that says, if the resolution was not to your satisfaction, if you have additional comments, or if you just want to discuss this issue with IT management, please call (name, phone)

37

- Customer Satisfaction Survey - A short survey that collects information about the user's experience, the results that IT delivered and the overall satisfaction with the process and resolution.

The IT Intranet Site

Every IT organization should have an internal Intranet site that allows users to get information, make requests, etc.

Minimally, this site should contain:

- Archives of
    - IT Newsletters
    - Notification of Systems Maintenance Events
    - Announcement of major changes to Infrastructure and Applications
    - Monthly Operational and Project Dashboard Reports
    - Frequently Asked Question Lists
    - Templates for documents, spreadsheets, and presentations
- Copies of all IT Processes and Procedures

Ticketing Portal

In addition, a well-designed IT Intranet site will include a web interface into the Help Desk Ticket System which allows users to:

- Submit Help Desk tickets without calling the Help Desk – a benefit to both the users and to your team.
- Look up the status on any of the Help Desk tickets they have submitted

Training Schedule

There should be a section of the IT Intranet site that provides information about any Computer related seminars or training that are either available in-house or through outside providers

A Project Communications Plan

Just as you need a plan for communications to the broad user base, you will need a communications plan for each of your major projects. This will be covered in more detail in the Project Management portion of this book.

For the time being, the following should be components of your Project Communications Plan:

- A list of Periodic Communications that will be made (Newsletters, Announcements, etc.) and the target audience
- A list of meetings that will be held, who will be participating in those meetings and what the goals of the specific meetings will be

Chapter 6

Budget Preparation and Management

IT budgets will always be the least attractive part of your job as an IT manager. That said, creating and managing your budget will be one of the most important parts of your job and will definitely be one of the key responsibilities in which your performance is measured. There will constantly be pressure to reduce operating expenses and to provide the right balance between operational priorities, incremental innovation, new functionality (projects) requested by the business and initiatives that are IT driven.

How is an IT Budget Structured?

IT budgets are typically broadly structured into two pieces (1) Keeping the lights on – operations and maintenance and (2) New Projects.

Keeping the Lights On

Keeping the lights on can best be described by asking the question: "If I didn't do a single **_new_** thing in IT and just kept what is in place today operating, what would I need to spend money on?"

What exactly would go into the "Keeping the Lights On" portion of the budget? You would include such items as:

- Network circuit costs
- Telecom costs (Voice environments, Telephone and Wireless phone contracts, Video Conferencing, etc.)
- Equipment leasing costs
- Equipment replacement costs or costs of planned expansion of current environments where equipment is not being leased. (Servers, PCs, Printers, storage equipment, network equipment)
- Equipment maintenance costs (service contracts and a budget for on-off calls)
- Depreciation of assets on your books.
- Software costs (contracts and new purchases)
- Costs of services, such as Market Data, Video, Data, EMAIL, etc.
- Costs of outsourced facilities – such as data centers, business continuity seating (if an IT item), etc.
- Cost of supplies for such items as printers, PCs, etc.
- Cost of operational personnel (Desktop Techs, Network and Server Engineers, etc.)

Note that items in this category will be operational items that would have a negative impact on the business if not funded.

Getting the information on what is or should be in your budget should be easy enough. Your first stop should be the finance department. Ask for a spreadsheet of the ledger entries for those cost codes assigned to your organization. That will tell you what you are currently spending, who you are spending it with and what the timing of those payments are.

New Projects

Most broadly, new projects can be considered anything that does not qualify as a "Keeping the Lights On" item. This would include anything from adding technology to create an application development lab that does not exist today, to performing a broad software or hardware upgrade of all PCs in the enterprise, to building a new data center and migrating to it. Projects can be relatively small or they can be massive, involving multiple departments.

e are some examples of what is a project and some examples of what is NOT a project

Project	To-Do (Not a Project)
<ul><li>A business wide upgrade of workstation software</li><li>The deployment of a major application, such as a Financial System or CRM system</li><li>Adding network circuits between sites</li><li>Moving the business to a new facility</li><li>Rebuilding a floor</li><li>Migrating to a new Data Center</li><li>Upgrading major pieces of software, such as a Database</li><li>Migrating to a new service provider</li><li>Deploying wireless connectivity or cellular enhancement in a building</li></ul>	<ul><li>Provisioning a new user with a workstation and/or phone</li><li>Installing a new software application on someone's PC</li><li>Repairing a wireless access point</li><li>Weekly or monthly patching of workstations and servers</li><li>Installing a corporate "home system" for a staff member</li></ul>

It's important to be able to differentiate between projects and to-dos. Aside from the difference in how you approach these tasks in real-life, they are treated very differently in the budget. To-Do items are part of your "Keep the Lights On" Budget and Projects are not.

There will be much more information on structuring and running projects later in this book, but for the moment we will look only at the budget portion of the project.

The Project Cost

It will obviously be necessary to develop a projected cost for the project and, once approved, this will likely become the project's budget. I know that was a pretty obvious statement, but it needs to be stated because it means that anything you miss when developing the cost must be brought to your management for approval as a budget variance.

OK, let me say this again in case you missed it or don't understand it – ANYTHING you miss when preparing the initial project cost must be brought to management when that cost arises in the project to get their approval for a budget variance. The reason for my emphasis here is that this surprise to management is not a good thing, not for the project, not for the IT Organization, not for the company, and, you guessed it, <u>ESPECIALLY</u> not good for you. It doesn't matter who missed the cost, as far as management is concerned YOU are responsible for the overrun. Maybe you didn't ask enough questions.

I have managed lots of projects over the years and, as a Project Manager, getting a clear, complete and accurate articulation of the costs from the technical contributors on a project has always been one of my more difficult tasks. My best advice to you is to ensure that every cost you are being told to put in a budget is backed up by a valid quotation from the vendor.

Also, be exceptionally wary of budget numbers that are incredibly even numbers. If you ask for a budget for network equipment and you're given a number like $1 million, ask to be provided the backup for that projection – a vendor quote. One million dollars is fine if the actual costs come in at $923,000, but not when they come in at $1.35 million. As a good example of this, I had a situation where we were building a Disaster Recovery Data Center. The budget I was asked to provide for the networking gear was $787K because that was what the cost of the last identical data center cost. The actual quotation we later received (as in after the budget was set) was $1.077 million dollars. The reason was (1) The original order had additional equipment for a separate project that drove a greater discount off the list and (2) The new environment was not quite 100% the same as the first data center. Don't depend on past purchases to develop budgets for projects today. Trust but verify!

There are so many things to keep in mind when developing a project cost. Here are a few questions you should ask that may uncover hidden costs:

- Will the purchase of new equipment, such as network equipment, require consulting services from the dealer/integrator for configuration, staging, etc.?

- Will equipment being added to an environment have a resulting need to add licenses to centralized management software? Remember the basic utility software too, such as PDU management and DCIM. What about such utilities as Virus scanning software and other tools?
- If the project includes adding external circuits, ensure you have the costs of both the monthly recurring and any non-recurring costs to bring the circuit into your technology room. This must include circuit installation costs from the carrier, the cost of providing conveyance inside the building (conduit, riser sleeves, internal cabling from the point of demarcation, etc.)
- Will upgrades or relocations require that you pay for both the old and new environments simultaneously? Typically you can't shut down the old one until the new one is successfully in production. For example, if you are moving to a new office you may need to pay for two server rooms, two sets of circuits to a data center, additional (swing) devices like servers and printers until both locations are in place.
- Will adding an application to the environment require a new physical server? What about the expansion of centralized software? Does the new application increase network traffic and will result in your needing to increase the bandwidth of certain WAN links?
- Will the project require new skills in your organization? If so, can these skills be added by training current staff (training costs) or will they require adding new staff members? Ask this question for all departments including the Help Desk, End User Support (desktop support), the Server team, etc.
- How will the changes to the environment impact the "Keep the lights on" portion of your budget next year? Are there ongoing vendor support costs (Cisco Smartnet as an example)? Is there an ongoing cost for additional staffing or additional network circuits?
- Will the environment be of sufficient size that it will impact your electrical costs in the data center (Note – some data center operators charge for electricity by the circuit, so if the project requires that you add a new cabinet with a primary and redundant power circuit for that cabinet, this can raise your power cost by several thousand dollars per month, even if there is only 1 tiny server in the box)

- If the change requires a new office to be set up, or it is to support a large influx of staff will you need to add End User Support personnel to deal with the change?
- Has the cost of very small items, such as patch cables and other consumables, been accounted for? These items can quickly add up to something very substantial.

So, with all of this said, and understanding that you will get questions like:

"Hey, I was thinking we should upgrade all of our PCs to the latest version of Windows. What will that cost?"

... just thrown at you in the hallway, what should you answer? Well, I would suggest an answer like:

"There are many variables that can impact the cost so I couldn't possibly give you an answer that would be accurate here. Let me take a look at it later today (Note: or whenever you believe you would have time), and I will come back with a good ballpark figure for you that is at least defensible."

Note, in this answer I didn't say "I have no idea" and I did not blow-off the answer entirely. The goal is to ensure that the person asking the question knows that you cannot provide an answer that is in any was actionable or fit for decision-making purposes, but given sufficient time you can.

Capital Investments Versus Expenses

When preparing a project budget, you will need to develop a comprehensive set of costs that are properly divided between capital and expense. At the most basic level, this would appear simple enough - equipment costs, facility build-out costs, software purchases in most cases, and so on would be capital costs. Items like services to be performed – equipment movers, supplemental technicians, etc. – are considered expense items. Work with your Finance department to properly allocate expenditures.

Capital	Expense
Equipment Purchase	Temporary staffing
Facility Build-out	Moving Services
Software Purchase (most)	Travel, lodging and food expenses
	Additional space to house temporary staff
	Conversion of data

45

Contingency

Once you have completed your entire project budget (expense and capital), you should always add a contingency budget line at the bottom of the sheet. I always use 10% as the contingency figure. This money is obviously for the items within the project that just cannot be accurately predicted.

A Project Today Impacts Keeping the Lights on Tomorrow

It is important to note that a project you are implementing today will have an impact on successive years "Keeping the Lights On" budget and activities. As a very simple example, if a project this year required buying a few servers and a network switch, those items would have depreciation impacts in successive years, as well as maintenance cost impacts. Also, depending on the number of items being added to the environment, they may have support personnel impacts too.

These future impacts should be fully articulated in any justifications that you present to management for this project. I often develop a 5-year cost assessment for every new initiative. This clearly will expose the ongoing (future) "keep the lights on" costs that result from a project initiative.

Optimizing an IT budget

This is a huge subject that I can only touch on here. For so many years one of the strategic tag lines for IT has been "doing more with less". To a certain extent that is true, although I don't know many IT budgets that have noticeably shrunk.

The question is, where do you start when you need to do more, but your budget is not going up? There are places to look in almost every area:

Network – I almost always find network environments have room to be optimized. As an example, market data circuits just tend to magically spawn into more and more circuits. I'm sure an analysis will find that many services are lightly used and can be combined with other services that will meet the user's information needs. The same is true with ring-down circuits. As time goes on, counter-parties are added and dropped. On PRI circuits, the slots allocated to the dropped ring-downs are often not re-allocated. The number of PRIs goes up, while the utilization goes down.

Systems – If Server Virtualization has not yet become the deployment strategy of choice for most application deployments, it should be considered.

Data Center – Unless you're running a monster environment (in which case you are likely not reading the right book), building and running your own data center is not a good thing. You cannot approach the cost efficiencies of a large colocation site. If you currently utilize data centers or server rooms carved out of your office space, consider the advantages that a colo will provide. That said, colocation sites can cost can vary widely depending on what they provide and how they charge. Consider for a moment a real-life example of two data centers. One data center uses "Metered Power", where the user area has the electricity it consumes measured. The data center operator charges what it is billed by the power company (Per Kilowatt Hour), with a multiplier that is designed to account for an amortization of the common utility fees for cooling. A second data center uses "Circuit-Based Power", where the user area is charged for the maximum amount of power that a circuit can deliver (set fee). In this example, for a 100 KW site I migrated from a circuit-based location to a metered-based location, the metered power site costs about $25K per month, while the circuit based power site costs over $100K per month, and amazingly the circuit based site had one-third the space and less than one-third the amount of equipment. Understand the alternatives here – they have a huge budget impact.

End User Support - End user support is a huge cost area in every organization and one where cost containment is always challenging. It's hard to find a short term cost reduction without impacting the quality of services, however by implementing a longer-term strategy you can drive costs down. First, by ensuring there is highly skilled staff supporting the users you will optimize the effectiveness of the team and hence their efficiency. By deploying tools such as ticketing systems and call analysis tools you will focus your team's efforts. Finally, by developing a deep set of End User Support Metrics, you will understand where there are repetitive issues where you need to understand the root cause to fix it forever. More will be said about optimizing this area later.

Outsourcing As An Alternative

One question you are sure to hear over and over is "Can this be outsourced?" The obvious answer will always be "that depends". We've already built a case for outsourcing the data center. Other parts of the environment are not so clear cut.

The obvious question you need to ask is "why would I outsource this function"? In most cases, the answer is to reduce costs. So I ask "how is this outsourced group going to provide the service at a lower cost AND make a profit?"

- For End User Support the answer is usually they will provide low skill staff that is paid low wages and few benefits. Service levels are impacted negatively. Also, since the outsourcer's staff is onsite full time there are inevitable jealousies that they are singled out to not get the benefits and are paid less than actual employees of the company
- Printer and Copier support vendors will consume much of your time pitching their services. Their pitch will always be all-inclusive "we'll service your printers and ensure you never run out of toner cartridges for less money than you can do it yourself." Of course, this is never true. Understand the hidden costs, such as monthly copy or print page allocations, and how much each extra page will cost you. You'll find that the actual cost is much different than what you budgeted for.

Understand that the cost of a function is the cost of a function. Unless there is some unusual cost associated with a full-time employee (such as an unusually generous benefit), or there are some very high cost and high-value tools that will dramatically improve the efficiencies of a function (and are amortized among many clients) there is no way for an outside firm to provide the same level of service as you AND make a profit for less money than you are paying.

Managing the Budget

More often than not I see IT managers that are completely oblivious to the current status of their budget. This is obviously a huge problem and one that will eventually catch up to and derail that person's career. IT managers are measured in many dimensions, but budget management is very close to the top of the list.

Managing the budget isn't difficult and it certainly will make your life easier if you can intelligently answer budget questions when asked about it. You need to understand the following:

- *What's in your budget and what's not* – How often in my career has someone come to me and said: "I need to buy this (whatever it is)".

For big items, I check that group's budget and find the money isn't there. After we go through the inevitable –"It's there, I budgeted for it last year – remember?" - we find that the money has been spent on a variety of unbudgeted items. Understand what is in your budget and what you may be putting at risk if you spend the money on unbudgeted items. Also, use the lessons (as in mistakes) to do a complete job of preparing next year's budget.

- *What is the timing of your spending?* – Understand if a large budget line item is designed to be spent all at the start of the year, or at the end of the year or linearly throughout the year.
- *What monies are coming from the business?* – Most likely some projects and some operational activities will be directly paid for or charged back to the business. You must understand what they have paid for and ensure that (1) if they ask you for some service or expenditure that is not within that funding, you make sure they will give you a variance to spend the extra money and (2) manage the costs allocated to their budget carefully as they will not be very amused if you charge costs not related to their business or over-run the budget allocation without their knowledge and permission.
- *What monies can be moved around?* – If you find you are overspending in one area but under-spending in another, you must understand what monies are fungible – able to be reallocated among different budget accounts. You obviously can't spend expense money on capital (or visa-verse). You also usually can't spend money coming from a business unit on expenses for another business unit. You may be able to move allocations within your direct organization (such as from Network to End User Support).
- *Be prepared to justify or lose your budget* – In a larger organization, you will find there are periodic budget reviews (quarterly, semi-annual, etc.). These reviews are designed to understand how every organization is utilizing their budget and make adjustments as required. You need to be prepared to respond to such situations as "Every group needs to give back 10% of their remaining money" or "we see you have only spent 10% of this budget account's money. Explain how the remainder will be spent for the rest of the year or lose it".

This is where the timing issue comes in. The bottom line for this budget event – you should know what budget you absolutely need to maintain to keep everything you have committed to running and what you can give up.

e prepared to discuss how you can scale back your activities and what t it will have on the organization. As an example, scaling back a project or putting it on hold until the next year to save money this year.

- *The later you try to fix your budget, the more painful it is to fix.* If you realize in February that you have an unbudgeted $10,000 spend in a $120,000 budget that is otherwise spent evenly across the year (say $10,000 a month), you can fix things by cutting back $1,000 per month for the remaining 10 months. Probably doable with a little pain. If you ignore this until November and still plan to make your budget number for the year, you cannot spend any money in December. An overly simplified example to demonstrate that you should address budget issues as soon as you learn about them.

Monthly Variance Reports

You should ask for a Monthly Budget Variance Report from your company's finance department. In its simplest form, a Variance Report tells you how much is in the budget by budget code, how much has been spent and how much is left (or has been overspent). You need to see this and understand it and what is behind it. Keeping a close track on the budget spending will allow you to take any required corrective action before you get into trouble.

Some of the questions you need to be able to answer include:

- Why is spending off? Are there budgeted headcount that has gone unfilled for some number of months? What is being done to fill that headcount?
- If spending is not happening in a linear fashion (equal amounts of a line item each month), is it due to expense timing? For example, a line item for maintenance could be consumed in the first quarter because that is when the maintenance contracts renew. Another example may be a major budgeted capital expenditure which is not planned to be made until the last quarter. Be prepared to explain that when questioned by finance.
- Are you overspending in certain areas because of increased demand by the business or unexpected issues? How will this overspend be funded?
- Do you have groups within your organization that are not spending according to plan?

- If the numbers look especially different from what you would expect them to be, ask the finance department for the backup to the report, essentially what items were charged against what accounts. I have seen many situations where items were mistakenly applied to the wrong accounts and really screwed up the allocation of funds.

Reviewing the monthly variance report can give you great insight into how your organization is performing against the plan. The money aspect of the review is important of course, but understanding where overspending or under-spending is equally valuable. Your staff may not always be completely transparent about how well they are managing their responsibilities, however, their spending will give you another point of reference.

Handling "Unbudgeted" Business Requests

You will undoubtedly be faced with many "unbudgeted" requests from the business. These will range from relatively simple items that you can easily cover to relatively significant requests, such as the deployment of a large business application or a new office. The most important advice I can give you is to never agree to these larger requests without clearly stating that these will not be covered by your current budget. Also, again as I have said previously, never fall into the trap of even mentioning a wild ballpark range of estimated cost before you have reviewed what is being requested and calculated a potential cost.

Your response should be that you'll communicate that cost when you have a good understanding of the project, translate those costs into the required budget and will begin working on the project once the money has been approved and you have a budget code to charge to. You will be pushed hard to start work before everything is approved and in place, but resist being the nice guy.

The request should be analyzed as you would for any project. Where the budget exists, in your IT budget or in the business' budget, really doesn't matter much, as long as you have full control over the budget. **To clarify what I mean by this, you should be fine having your spending on any budget represented in a consolidated project budget, but do not give approval rights to your spending on a project to people outside of your direct reporting chain.** They will not understand the details of what you need to do and will only slow down your progress if you need to wait for their approval to commit to spending.

or Selection and Management

Vendor Management is a discipline that enables organizations to control costs, drive service excellence and mitigate risks to gain increased value from their vendors throughout the deal lifecycle. Vendor management is not negotiating the lowest price possible. Vendor management is constantly working with your vendors to come to agreements that will mutually benefit both companies.

At many companies, the CIO has de facto responsibility for managing IT vendors, but the day-to-day reality is that individual departments, technology platform owners and project offices manage vendors for their local needs, tapping into corporate procurement and legal staff for some of the tactical contracts and pricing analysis. That can work in smaller companies with a small number of vendors, where the CIO or head of infrastructure can manage the information. This will be too much of a challenge in a larger environment.

Vendor management enables you to optimally develop, manage and control vendor contracts, relationships, and performance for the efficient delivery of the products and services you contracted for. This can you help meet your business objectives, minimize potential business disruption, avoid deal and delivery failure. It also ensures more sustainable multi-sourcing, while driving the most value from your vendors. The goal is to select the right vendors; categorize vendors to ensure the right contract, metrics, and relationship; determine the ideal number of vendors; mitigate risk when using vendors, and potentially establish a vendor management organization that best fits the company.

Although the ability to manage vendors effectively enhances the business perception of IT effectiveness and helps IT Management achieve success, few people have actually been formally trained in managing these relationships.

Here are some best practices to consider in developing your vendor management selection and approach:

- Establish a Vendor Selection Process - The vendor management process begins by selecting the right vendor for the right reasons. The vendor selection process can be a very complicated and emotional undertaking if you don't know how to approach it from the very start. You will need to analyze your business requirements, search for prospective vendors, lead the team in selecting the winning vendor and successfully negotiate a contract while avoiding contract negotiation mistakes.

- *Document the process early on* - This would include RFPs, Proposals, demos and negotiations.

- *Determine the model of Vendor Management you will use* - Is there a dedicated resource for this function or an actual Vendor Management department?

- *Set the parameters of the relationship* - Determine up front how you will help each other be successful.

- *Categorize your vendor relationships into buckets* - You will soon see if you have multiple relationships for resources, network equipment, PCs, etc. Reduce this number as much as possible to gain control and reduce costs.

- *Come Together on Value* -. Vendor management will focus quality for the money that is paid, not on simply negotiating the lowest overall price. Most often the lowest price also brings the lowest quality. If you want a high-quality product or solution, you should be willing to pay more in order to receive it. If the vendor is serious about the quality they deliver, they won't have a problem specifying the quality details in the contract.

- *Scrutinize the Prospects* - Once you start to look at individual vendors, be careful that you don't get blinded by the "sizzle instead of the steak." Depending upon the size of the possible contract, they will pull out all the stops in order to get your business. This may include a barrage of overzealous salespeople and "consultants". Just because they send a lot of people in the beginning, doesn't mean they will be there after the contract is signed. Understand who will be part of the long-term team supporting your account and get to know them well before committing to a vendor.

- *Ask the right questions* - As you begin your vendor search, ask some questions that will help you eliminate the more obvious misfits. For example, is the proposed material, service or outsourcing project within the vendor's area of expertise?

- *Remain Flexible* - Be wary of restrictive or exclusive relationships. For example, limitations with other vendors or with future customers. In addition, contracts that have severe penalties for seemingly small incidents should be avoided. If the vendor asks for an extremely long term contract, you should ask for a shorter term with a renewal option. Tie-down renewal cost escalation as much as possible.

On the other hand, you should be open to the vendor's requests also. If an issue is small and insignificant to you but the vendor insists on adding it to the contract you may choose to bend in this situation. This shows good faith on your part and your willingness to work towards a contract that is mutually beneficial to both parties.

- *Seek to Understand Your Vendor's Business Too* – I'll use that horrifically over-used term "the win-win" situation. You don't win if your great deal puts your vendor out of business. I have actually worked for one huge multi-national firm that just did not get this simple fact and often put their vendors out of business. If you are constantly leaning on them to cut costs, either the quality of their work will suffer or they will go out of business. The partnership aspect of vendor management includes your contributing knowledge or resources that may help the vendor better serve you.

Once you have selected your vendors, here are some best practices to ongoing management of the relationships:

- Collect information throughout the relationship - Understand how the vendor is delivering against commitments and Service Level Agreements. Address issues along the way as they arise. Have your data already when it is time to renew contracts.
- *Share Information and Priorities* - The most important success factor of vendor management is to share information and priorities with your vendors. Providing only the necessary information to the vendor at the right time will allow a vendor to better service your needs. This information may include usage forecast information, new technology deployments, changes in design and expansion or relocation changes, just to name a few.
- *Balance Commitment and Competition* – Your goal in vendor management is to gain the commitment of your vendors to assist and support the operations of your business. Conversely, the vendor is expecting a certain level of commitment from you. Include the incumbent vendor

when looking to make a future purchase but get competitive bids, especially for the larger procurements.

- *Allow Key Vendors to Help You Strategize* – In many cases, I have found that the vendors of some key pieces of technology are better suited than my internal staff to contribute to strategic discussions. The reason is obvious; the good vendors are well informed about the manufacturer's technology and product roadmaps. The vendors are often the experts in their business area and you can tap into that expertise in order to give you a competitive advantage.

- *Build Partnerships For The Long Term* - Vendor management values long term relationships over short term gains and marginal cost savings. Constantly changing vendors to pursue the lowest price for each purchase will end up costing you more money in the long run. Other benefits of a long term relationship include trust, preferential treatment and access to insider or expert knowledge.

- *Monitor Performance* - Once the relationship with the vendor has begun, don't assume that everything will go according to plan and executed exactly as specified in the contract. The vendor's performance must be monitored constantly in the beginning. This should include the requirements that are most critical to your business. For example shipping times, quality of service performed, order completion, call answer time, etc.

- *Communicate Constantly* - The bottom line in vendor management best practices is communication, communication, communication! Don't assume that the vendor intimately knows your business or can read your mind. A well established and well-maintained line of communication will avoid misunderstandings and proactively address issues before they become problems.

Why Vendor Management

The time, money and energy used to nurture a positive vendor relationship cannot be measured directly against the company's bottom line. However, a well-managed vendor relationship will result in increased customer satisfaction, reduced costs, better quality, and better service from the vendor. When and if problems arise, rest assured that a well-managed vendor will be quick to remedy the situation.

A Vendor Management Office

A Vendor Management Office (VMO) is an internal unit within an enterprise that is charged with evaluating third-party providers of goods and services, supervising day-to-day interactions and managing longer-term relationships.

With a vendor management office, your goal should not be to create a firewall between IT and the vendor, using a procurement group as a proxy, but to be smart and consistent within the enterprise about managing multiple aspects of any vendor relationship

In some cases, an IT vendor management office is established to create and monitor vendor relationships with regard to IT, including establishing the organization's proper mix of IT outsourcing and insourcing opportunities and setting vendor risk management policies.

Vendor management typically involves numerous oversight duties for a CIO or IT executive, including negotiating and then monitoring the length and substance of contracts; keeping tabs on new technologies; maintaining contact with current vendors and reaching out to vendors with which the organization has not yet worked.

The Request for Proposal (RFP) Process

If you're running an infrastructure function you will most likely find yourself in a position to purchase a substantial amount of hardware and software. Unless you're in a very small shop, you need to approach the purchases by surrounding it with a pretty rigorous process. You must never put yourself in the position where your actions in this area can be questioned. In addition, significant dollar purchases must be able to survive an audit. The generally accepted way of approaching these large purchases with a defensible high-integrity process is by issuing a ***Request For Proposal***.

A request for proposal (RFP) is a solicitation, often made through a bidding process, by an agency or company interested in procurement of a commodity, service or valuable asset, to potential suppliers to submit business proposals. It specifies what the customer is looking for and establishes evaluation criteria for assessing the proposals. The RFP outlines the bidding process and contract terms, and provides guidance on how the bid should be formatted and presented.

The RFP will always spell out very clearly what you are trying to purchase and what your expectations are for associated services, warranty and so on. The RFP is distributed to a number of acceptable vendors of the product or service providers. Those providers are instructed to respond to the RFP with a proposal delivered back to you at a specified date and time. The time is usually "by 5 PM" on a specified day.

An RFP will minimally have the following sections:

- *General Information* – usually this section contains introductory information, such as company description, the number of employees, markets served. Typically very boiler-plate.
- *Project Purpose and Description* – In this section, you should provide as much detail as possible about the project in general and the work to be performed or products to be supplied by the winner of this RFP. Although you need to present your desired solution, you should include language that encourages respondents to propose alternate and more effective solutions.
- *Project Scope* – The project scope defines the bounds of the project. As an example, if you are requesting proposals for an upgrade of a Cisco environment, this section may include language that limits the scope to a single facility or geographic region. It may also be used to specifically exclude something. In our Cisco example, this may say "except for the IT testing labs", if there was some reason you didn't want to switch out equipment there.
- *Details of the RFP Process Schedule* – This defines the timing and milestones for YOUR schedule to provide the RFP, get responses, make a decision and notify the respondents of the decision.
- *RFP Proposal Delivery Requirements* – The proposal delivery requirements would include information on the form of the response as well as the materials you want to be delivered as the response to the proposal. Some ideas for what goes here include:
    - *Table of contents for the RFP Response Proposal* – This defines exactly how you want to see their response structured
    - *Any collateral material you want to be completed by the respondent* - (usually a spreadsheet used to simplify bid-leveling, a non-disclosure statement, a company information document, etc.)

- *The materials that must be delivered as part of the RFP response* – this usually includes some number of paper copies of the proposal, so you don't have to duplicate responses from multiple vendors and distribute them, an electronic copy of all materials being delivered, etc.)
- *The details of the purchase* - This includes hardware, software, services and ongoing support

- *The desired purchase and implementation schedule* - The Request for Proposal should provide the timeline for the RFP process as well as the project itself. Although the actual implementation schedule is determined after the project starts, any major milestones that are known should be articulated here along with typical timings for milestones that are still in flux (define which are hard dates and which are not). These may include:
  - Request for Proposal Timeline:
  - All proposals in response to this RFP are due no later than 5 pm EST (date).
  - Evaluation of proposals will be conducted from (start date) until (end date). Respondents will be notified if any additional information is needed during this period.
  - The winning bidder will be selected on (date).
  - Upon notification, the contract negotiation with the winning bidder will begin immediately. Contract negotiations will be completed by (date).
  - Notifications to bidders who were not selected will be completed by (date).
  - Project Timeline:
  - Project initiation phase must be completed by (date).
- *Proposal Evaluation Criteria* – in this section you must describe what criteria you are using to evaluate proposals. If there is a minimum acceptable answer to any of the criteria, you should articulate that fact here. Evaluation criteria can include such factors as Technical Expertise and Experience, Organizational Experience, Proposal Overall Suitability to the Requirements, Support and Warranty Provisions, and of course Cost.

- *Terms and Conditions* – The terms and conditions spell out the details of the business relationship you are willing to enter into.
- *Questions* – The process to ask questions about the RFP and how questions will be managed. As an example, in some companies, any question that gets asked by any of the vendors will be answered and that question and answer will then be distributed to all of the vendors working on an RFP response. Other companies do not distribute answers. That is entirely up to you – there is no standard here.
- *Contact Information* – This section provides the contact information (Name, phone, email, address, etc.) of the designated company person that will be the single point of contact for respondents during the RFP process. This section should also include the preferred method of communication between the parties and have a disclaimer such as "*only communications that occurs or is confirmed in writing is considered valid in this RFP process.*" This prevents a vendor from having a conversation with you and then claiming you gave them an extra week to deliver a proposal, or that you exempted them from some requirement of the RFP process.

Adding Collateral Materials to the RFP

There are several documents that typically are included in the initial RFP package that the respondent is required to fill out. Some of them are your typical business legal documents, but a few are designed to ensure that you are able to analyze the responses in a logical fashion, compare the results and identify the best overall solution. Here are the usual documents:

- *Non-Disclosure Agreement* – Yep! You find this baby everywhere. You can get a copy of your company's non-disclosure agreement from your legal department or outside lawyer if you don't have a legal department. Often the legal department will modify the standard non-disclosure to be more specific to this RFP.
- *Intent To Bid* – You may include an "Intent to bid" form. This is a rather simple document that just confirms that a company is interested in responding to your RFP. This serves two purposes. (1) You know who to expect responses from on the RFP response date (in case you need to stick around late to wait for one) and (2) It lets you know early on if some of the folks you distributed the RFP to are not interested in pursuing your business. You may need to add

additional companies to your RFP distribution if you find you won't receive sufficient responses.

- *Response Information Tables* – I always include spreadsheets with my RFPs that include multiple tabs of single column items that need to be filled in by the respondent. These items should reflect the items you are purchasing, unit prices, support that is included in the price, etc. Once all of the RFPs are received back, I put the vendor response columns side by side into a new spreadsheet and can easily compare those items that are important to me.

The RFP Process Steps and Timing

The RFP process consists of a few well-defined steps:

- RFP is created, checked and approved for release to vendors
- RFP Distribution Date – this is a hard date that all vendors receive the RFP simultaneously
- Non-Disclosure and Intent to Bid forms are due back
- Period where questions can be sent you and get answered
- RFP Response Due Date
- Optional day where the respondents come in and present their proposal and answer questions
- Bid-Leveling
- Award Decision
- Award Notification

The RFP Timeline

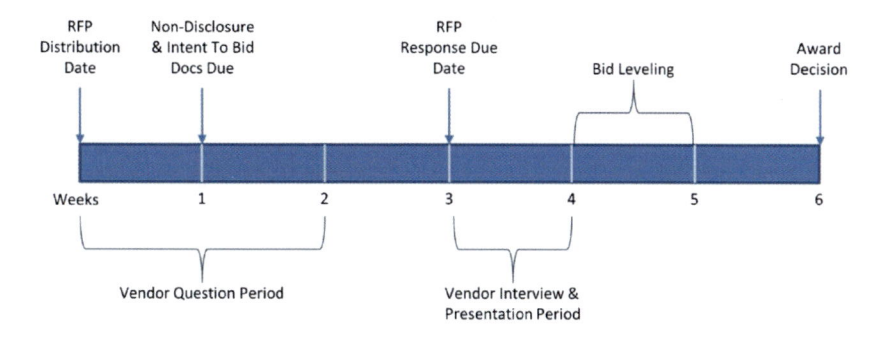

The RFP Process Timeline

Bid-Leveling

In order to make a well-informed and defensible decision that is truly the best of the proposals that were returned, you need to perform a process called bid-leveling. I have seen bid-leveling processes that are all over the map, ranging from those that simply take the bottom line cost number on a proposal and compare them, to those that inspect every component price and normalize the quantities of each item. The more detail you include in you bid-leveling process, the better your decision will be.

As an example of both the good and bad forms of bid-leveling, I will use a recent RFP for a structured cabling project at a new headquarters construction project in New York City. The RFP and bidding process was managed by the head of Real Estate and the consulting project managers that he brought in. Together they represented the single most incompetent group of people I have ever worked with.

The responses to the Structured Cabling RFP, which by the way was nothing more than a set of drawings with notes defining the requirements, were leveled by the consulting project managers. When the results came back I found that the numbers were all over the place. Vendors that were typically the low-cost providers had the highest cost numbers and those that usually weren't even on the map came in the lowest. I asked to see the proposals.

I found that the numbers being used for comparison were simply the total cost numbers that were on each proposal. There was no attempt to compare what was being provided within the context of the price. The excuse I was given by the consultants AND the head of Real Estate was that it didn't matter what was in the proposal, it only mattered what was in the RFP and if the vendor didn't deliver that for the price being quoted they simply wouldn't get paid. Obviously, you don't want to get into a business arrangement with these clowns. The issue here, of course, is that the vendors spell out clearly in their RFP response/ Proposal what they are selling you and, once you sign the agreement, ***THAT*** is what you have agreed to purchase, not what you put in the RFP.

As I drilled down into the proposals themselves I found that one vendor had two different numbers quoted as the total cost on two different pages of their proposal. Neither the vendor could explain what drove that difference in cost, nor could the folks evaluating the proposals explain why they picked the number that they chose of the two. Actually, they didn't even pick up on the fact that there were two numbers.

The deeper I drilled down, the more issues I found. I quickly realized that the different vendors all had a different amount of cable quoted for the project. The differences were as much as 50% or several hundred thousand feet between proposals. Considering the cost of copper, that amounted to a huge difference in cost.

The answer to this sort of issue is to determine what the most accurate (or logical) quantity of an item is and to normalize the proposals around that number. In other words, if you decide that the right number of feet of category 6A cable is 500,000 linear feet of cable, then adjust every one of the proposals to 500,000 feet and make sure every contract is written to charge only for the number of cable feet actually used. Adjusting the quantities and types of items in the proposals the vendor proposal costs converged into a normal spread of numbers – some of the vendors traditionally a bit more or less expensive than others, but not the huge spreads we were seeing.

The process for bid-leveling is relatively clear:

- Take a look at what the various vendors are proposing in terms of quantities, etc. and normalize the proposals around your best estimates of the actual quantities you will use
- Check that all vendors are using the manufacturers and components you have designated – sometimes they will slip in a cheap alternative to get the job.

- Make certain you can calculate the unit pricing for everything you will want to buy and compare those unit prices among the respondents. You should also get a written clarification in the project that you can purchase additional units of anything for these unit prices. As an example, for structured cabling, you would want a fixed price for additional cable drop locations – price for a 2-pack, a 4-pack, and a 6-pack of data drops. A price for coax drops for TVs, individual printer drops, and so on.
- Look at the charges for individual components of pricing. If the overall best proposal appears to be charging too much to test or label a cable, go back to them and tell them they need to get those individual prices in line.
- As I previously stated, you should create a spreadsheet that captures the main items (quantities, costs, etc.) that you will use to determine the winning proposal. This makes normalizing and comparing vendors a snap.

Notification of a Winner

Once you have selected a vendor, bring in the legal team to get a contract in place as soon as possible. NEVER EVER just sign that line at the end of every proposal that says "to accept this proposal just sign on the line below and return two signed copies." Make sure that the lawyers have reviewed the agreement, made any necessary changes and gives you the approval to sign it (or sends it to the designated person that will sign it.

Don't inform the losers that they have lost until you have a signed contract in place with the winner. This is always uncomfortable since you will be getting calls constantly from them, but you need to keep the alternatives available until you have a signed deal.

Chapter 7

People Management

If you're new to people management you will surely find this is the most substantial change in responsibilities since you moved on from your technical contributor days. This will consume a very substantial portion of your time. Your "People Management" activities will include:

- Sourcing and Retention
- Skill Development, Mentoring, and Training
- Generating Performance Plans
- Employee Appraisals
- Staff Compensation
- Dealing with Staff Issues – problem employees, conflict resolution

Make no mistake about it; this is the one area I most often hear was the biggest surprise to new managers. Once you have been doing this for some time you will find that, while it is incredibly time-consuming, it is relatively clear cut and manageable.

At the most basic level, staff face time is part of the job. Employees should always know what is expected of them. They should hear about issues sooner, rather than later and never at the appraisal for the first time. You should listen to what they have to say. Praise in public but criticize in private.

An important concept to use in dealing with your staff is what is called effective listening. Like everyone in life, your staff wants to know you are listening to them. Effective Listening is a technique that will make it clear to those you are speaking with that you are listening and they were understood, increase their trust in you and maximize the information you get from the discussion. Some of the key points of effective listening:

- Maintain Eye Contact and stay relaxed
- Don't interrupt the person you are taking to
- Wait for the person to pause then ask clarifying questions
- Ask questions that cannot be answered by yes or no. Keep the conversation going
- Feedback what you have heard to ensure you received the message the person was intending you to hear
- Don't jump in and try to prematurely impose your solution to their issue

Be the Person They Love!

Your success at People Management also benefits significantly by your personal interaction with your staff – no matter how many people are on your team. As an example of how **_NOT_** to do this, I once had a Network Manager working for me that managed completely from behind his closed office door. He was able to access everything he needed to access remotely and could summon any member of his team on a minute's notice, so he stayed in his office by himself unless he needed to interact with someone.

His staff didn't like him and didn't respect him. He wasn't considered one of the team. He had no personal connections with his staff and they frankly weren't interested in one with him. He failed and was eventually replaced. He failed at the few technical positions he had after that and eventually left technology altogether and went on to a job where he didn't have to work with others.

I had another manager working for me that was the ultimate people person. He was always out with his staff or with the users. If there was a major issue, he wasn't sitting in his office waiting for the phone to ring with an update –

he was with the team working on the problem adding whatever value he could. He never asked his team to work above and beyond what could be expected without being there as part of the team. If the team was working huge hours through the weekend, he was there with them; even if the only support he could add was to rip up the boxes of equipment they were deploying and get it to the trash.

This man's staff loved him and would do anything to make the team succeed. They knew he was always on his side and would fight for them when he needed to. Since he had such spectacular staff support, his team was able to succeed at some exceptionally audacious goals.

Who do you want to be like?

MBWA

There is a technique called MBWA – Management By Walking (or Wandering) Around. No matter how high in the organization you get, MBWA should be a philosophy you follow. MBWA will give you a great sense of how things are going. You will hear about issues before they become so large that someone feels they must bring them to you. They are also an opportunity for you to give some mentoring advice to the more junior members of your staff. Best of all you will find that the staff will begin to feel so comfortable talking to you that staff communications will never be an issue.

Hiring and Retention

Hiring and retention are NOT an HR issue. If your plan is to build a world-class IT group, you need to take the bull by the horns and own this. Your goal is to have the best person in each slot as possible.

My philosophy has always been to hire people that are smarter than I am, certainly at their specific responsibilities at a minimum. I want my staff to be independent thinkers but team players. What I mean by that is they must be the type of person that will tell me when I'm wrong. The "yes-man" (or "yes-woman") has no place in my organization. That said when a decision is made I expect everyone to fall into line, embrace the decision and work as hard as necessary to make it a success.

When you have built an organization of smart, competent technologists that are perfectly capable of running their functional responsibilities independently (whether an individual contributor or team leader), you can step back a bit and delegate more responsibilities downward. Understand that this is the only way you will be able to scale your organization. You will never be able to successfully run a 400 person organization if you need to be involved in every decision.

Now that I have outlined the personality profile of the types of people I hire let's move on to what and how to get them. I'll start with the "Captain Obvious" statement. In order to have a world-class IT organization, you need to understand what key technologies constitute your environment and have the skills in place to engineer and operate it. You need at least one "star performer" for each technology.

IT is interesting in that IT professionals are not only motivated by money, but also by the challenge of developing a complex cutting-edge technology environment. Your technology becomes part of your sales pitch as much as your salaries and benefits will. IT is also a high-stress environment where any event that causes an interruption of service or productivity immediately enters the realm of "blame", with any resulting anger being directed at your staff. Employees are on-call virtually 24 x 7 to address incidents and issues with little regard for work/life balance. It takes a special type of person to want to do this. Understanding the motivations that drive candidates for jobs is as important as understanding their technical competence.

Some skills are more difficult to source than others. Information Security, database design and management, storage management, server virtualization and networking skills are some of the most difficult to find.

Sourcing is always more difficult without a good job description. This document should be carefully written to describe the skills needed as well as the roles responsibilities and expectations. When developing a job description, work with your company's HR department to add the necessary boilerplate information about the company, benefits, and educational requirements that need to be included. You must personally define the responsibilities and required skills.

Don't try to go it alone in sourcing staff. You will never succeed. It's great to get referrals from your friends and coworkers, but you must put everyone through the same rigorous selection process. Recruiters can and will help you identify candidates but make no mistake that they work for themselves, no matter how many assurances they give you about their selection process and validation criteria, and especially how they "partner with you". They have only one goal – fill your role and get a commission. Retained Recruiters are better than contingency recruiters because of the financial relationship. Contingency recruiters will bury you with candidate paperwork – much of which bears little to no relevance to your job specifications.

When you have selected someone as the candidate to move forward with you must check their references. Obviously, a candidate will only give you the names of people that will say great things about them. That means that you need to use your network to find people that know your candidate, outside of the managed hiring process that is happening with the recruiter.

When checking references have your list of questions prepared before the call. Minimally you need to ask about:

- The candidate's technical proficiency
- Validate the successes that are being claimed on the resume. Did the candidate actually complete what is being claimed? Are the successes individual or was the candidate a minor part of a large team? I know someone that would "lean into" team group photos and then claim he was part of that team that achieved incredible results. Don't get fooled by people that claim the successes of others was their own.
- How does the candidate perform in the type of environment he/she will be hired into? Is the candidate great in an ongoing maintenance and operating environment, but is being hired into a major redefinition of the technology, or alternately is the candidate a change-agent being hired into a maintenance job?
- How well does the candidate perform under stress?
- Has the candidate traditionally be available off-hours (if this is a 24 x 7 job) or is the candidate a 9 to 5 person?
- How has the candidate functioned within the team environment that he/she is currently in?
- Test why the candidate is leaving their current job. Is the reason they are looking to move on as they described or are they one step away from getting fired?

You should add your own questions to this list. Don't fall into the trap of making both the personal interview and the reference check an event where all that is accomplished is you describing the job and asking if this is something the candidate wants to do and is capable of doing.

Retaining your staff is as important as filling the roles in the first place. There are a few simple rules to follow here:

- *Hire people that you believe will stick around* – take a look at the candidates work history. If they have stayed at previous jobs for some number of years the likelihood is that they will stay at your company too. Steer clear of people that spend a few months to a year or so at each position unless you are hiring a consultant.
- *Make sure you can develop a career path for a new hire* – you can hire someone to fill a role, but if the role does not have any chance for career advancement, you will eventually lose your staff member. Work with each employee to develop a demonstrable career path for them and a plan of training and experience that will help them achieve those goals.
- *Tailor retention to the individual worker* – While money is the motivator for many people, those top rated "A" players are often more concerned with challenging work, personal and professional growth opportunities, work/life balance, and workplace flexibility
- *Find out what is driving underperformance* – People whose performance drops dramatically are often dealing with outside distractions. Skill issues may require coaching or training. Personal issues such as divorce, health issues, mortgage issues, etc. can take a toll on a staff member. Providing the support they need in these situations can help salvage the situation and drive significant increases in staff loyalty.
- *Understand how your managers are managing* – Why does one person think that a company is the best place in the world to work while others think they died and went to hell? Most often this is due to the differences in how individual departments are managed. Understand how your group managers are managing their staff, and if they are embodying the values you want in your organization. Get them the training they need to make their departments a place their staff members will want to work.

Skill Development, Mentoring, and Training

Another dimension of your People Management responsibilities will be Skill Development, Mentoring, and Training. This essentially exists in two components (1) The "Personal Development" portion of the staff member's Performance Appraisal and (2) the fulfillment of that requirement in the form of an associated activity to develop that person professionally.

How aggressively this is managed is very dependent on the organization. In some companies, the responsibility is placed on the employee to locate appropriate development venues, propose it to management and once approved, complete the activity. This may be taking technical development course, attending seminars or conferences or other similar types of activities. In companies that pursue this more aggressively, this is often tracked by HR or some other professional development group. You may get periodic (monthly or quarterly) reports summarizing each of your team member's professional development activities and be expected to work with them to meet their goals.

Whatever type of company you work for, it is in your interest to make sure that your team receives the appropriate training. From your perspective, this will increase the value of each staff member to the group. From the employee's standpoint, it not only increases their knowledge but also it helps fulfill the creative thirst for knowledge that most likely initially made that person choose IT as a career in the first place. Also, it communicates to the employee that both you as his manager and the company overall have his ultimate success in mind.

Beyond the more formal training and skill development events, don't lose sight of the value of mentoring as a skill development tool. Every interaction you have with your staff is an opportunity to mentor them. The more senior you become, the more value your mentoring will have to the employee. This process is also valuable in building the bonds between yourself and your team that engenders the loyalty you need when faced with more challenging situations.

Generating Performance Plans

Every member of your team should have a performance plan in place that articulates your expectations of that person. Most companies have some form of a standardized format for employee Performance Plans, so you will need to work within the bounds of your company's structure. That said, there are certain things you should be sure to include.

- *Cascading Corporate Goals* – Great companies will articulate their annual corporate goals to the staff. Broad goals can include such items as "Improving the company's web presence" or "Automating the Company's Work Processes". They can also be broader statements like "reduce internal expenses by 10%". These types of corporate goals should be considered top level goals for your organization and you should try to develop objectives for each of your staff members that help drive the success of these higher-level company goals.

- *Technical Service-Level Objectives* – Individual contributors will have goals that align with Service Level Agreements/objectives/commitments (however your frame them) for their function. These may include such items as "Call Response Time" or "Time to Call Resolution" for desktop technicians. For systems or network teams they may include things like "Ensure that systems availability meets or exceeds Service-Level Commitments". Response times, first call resolution rates, staff satisfaction levels are all metrics on which staff can be measured.

- *Personal Development* – Most Performance Plans for technical staff include some form of personal development. "Staff member will take at least one course in X-technology focused on Y". "Staff member will attend networking equipment conference". This is designed to provide a continued investment in the staff member, which both improves that person's skill set and helps in retention of important staff members.

- *Interrelationships* – This area includes such things as teamwork and collaboration, etc.

- *Areas for Development* – Pretty much everybody has something that they can do better. This is your chance to articulate those areas that need improvement or you would like to see changed and discuss it with your staff member. If this Performance Plan is a problem staff member, you should include timing where you will sit down and discuss performance improvements on a shorter-term basis than waiting for a year.

Employee Appraisals

I will repeat again, an employee should never hear about a problem at the appraisal for the first time. With that said, the appraisal is the one time per year when you are formally communicating your analysis of the employee's performance since the last appraisal. Different companies have different schedules for appraisals. Most do this once per year. Some companies appraise staff more often. At one company where I worked, we appraised our staff THREE TIMES A YEAR! Think about that for a minute. I had several hundred employees on my team worldwide and I needed to manage three appraisal cycles each year. We actually never got out of appraisal mode.

The appraisal should be structured in the exact same form as the Performance Plan – usually, the categories are the same. I always strive to praise the successes as much as I articulate the failures; however, the failures are where most of the conversation will take place.

If you plan to give someone a VERY bad appraisal, you should bring the HR department into the discussion before you give the appraisal. Have them review your appraisal of the employee and get their reading of whether you are saying anything that either you can't say by law, or might come back to haunt you in the future. Also, for very bad appraisals it might be wise to have a member of HR present when you actually give the appraisal to the employee, especially if there are consequences for lack of improvement.

In most companies, the employee is required to sign the appraisal. If they will not, or if they want to read it over first, give them the time they need, within the bounds of your company policy. Also, most companies allow the employee to have a copy of their appraisal. (check with HR before you start the process)

Staff Compensation

Compensation . . . truly one of the more difficult parts of managing people. Here are some basic observations I have made over the years:

- Pretty much nobody thinks they are being paid enough money
- Pretty much everybody thinks they are worth more than every one of their peers
- People's expectations for bonuses and raises are almost always unreasonable in relation to their contribution

- You will NEVER get true gratitude in return for the raise or bonus you were able to get someone, no matter how much you had to fight the system to get it for them.

I know this seems like a dark and dismal assessment of people, but if you haven't seen it yet, you will. With all of this said, you still must be the champion for your team when it comes to their compensation.

Work with your company's HR department or Compensation group to benchmark the salaries for people in the same or similar jobs for companies in the same industry of about the same size in your geographic location. You now have numbers to compare your pay scale against. If there is a significant difference, you have the start of a case to adjust some salaries. Certainly, at a minimum, you need this information to know what to pay new hires.

As an example, if your company is in the Financial Services industry in the New York City area, and employs about 2,000 workers, then you would want to compare your jobs to a similar company. In actuality, you probably want at least two or three comparable companies to get a range.

There are several important things you can and should do to manage compensation fairly.

- Force-rank your team members from the absolute best of the best to the worst of the worst. This is an actual annual required exercise in many companies. At some companies, the goal is to see who is on the bottom and replace them with high-performance individuals. A person I once worked for said that even if you are managing a team of Einsteins, some will be more Einstein-like than others. The meaning was that even in a department of all outstanding performers, it is possible to rank them. It's amazing that I am quoting this manager here because he personally was a very low performer and pretty much his entire organization hated him. We voted him off the island almost every week.
- Ensure that there is a tight coupling between a person's performance plan and their appraisal. What were their results against goals? This will be used as a component of the rankings.
- For pay modifications (raises), understand what the range of possible changes could be and what level of latitude you have. In a company where the staff is grouped into salary "grades" or ranges, your discretion on the size of raises may be limited. In some instances, a

staff member's salary will have reached the top of his or her range and very little can be done to get additional money (of substance). My best advice here is to be open, honest and direct in these situations. Work with your employee to explore options to move into a higher salary grade, if possible.

- Is your organization funding the bonus pool so that every person that meets their objectives can receive their full target bonus, or have they reduced the overall pool by some percentage due to business reasons? What latitude do you as a manager have to move dollars around within your department?
- BE FAIR! Whether you are talking about salary adjustments or bonuses don't allocate the dollars as if you're running a popularity contest. Don't reward old friends or staff that followed you from your last job, at the expense of the rest of the team.

Dealing with Staff Issues – Problem Employees, Conflict Resolution

It would be spectacular if your organization functioned without any staff problems, but this is never the case. You will see attendance issues, drinking and drug issues, staffs' personal and family problems impacting their performance and possibly distracting your whole group. These are in addition to the normal skill or other technical performance issues you will need to deal with. The best advice you can get is not to let any of these issues go too far before addressing them.

Addressing issues early can be handled by having a brief and non-threatening talk with the person. It could be as simple as the statement "Hey John, I see you're getting in pretty late every morning. Is there some issue I should know about?" John may have a great answer, like "I need to get online every morning at 5 AM to check status on the systems, so I don't get out of the house until 9 AM." Or maybe he is just up until 1 AM playing online games.

If an employee problem is serious, bring HR into the conversation. They will help you understand how to proceed. If it is a personal issue where the employee needs some outside support, the company may be able to help with therapists, doctors or other services. They will also tell you what information to collect if the situation cannot be recovered.

The best advice you can receive overall is to keep a file on every member of your team. Both the good and bad should become part of that file. If you receive a note from a user that praises a staff member, put it in his file. Same goes for complaints.

Most important is that any discussions you have with problem staff members should be well documented. Just write a brief note that describes when the discussion took place and where and what was discussed. Any specific directions, timings or consequences should very specifically be noted.

It is important to be open, honest and direct when appraising an employee. I have seen, and unfortunately inherited, many situations where employee problems were glossed over in the appraisal process. The net result is always the same – when you try to address an issue the employee always points to years of great performance appraisals from their last manager and tries to change to conversation to why you are an issue. Glossing over issues is not good for anyone. If the employee knew there was an issue, that person could potentially address it, as opposed to letting it fester for years. It's also not fair to the new manager, who now has a terrible issue to contend with because you were incapable of confronting the issue on your watch. Make no mistake about it, that fact will come back to haunt you in the future. Performance appraisals must also always be part of each employee's file too.

Sometimes an issue you need to deal with is a conflict between two or more staff members. If there is an actual issue where one person is at fault and the other is complaining about it, you must deal with this quickly. Perform a quick investigation, get the facts, have a discussion with the person at fault getting a commitment to fix the problem and then talk with the other person explaining what has been done to address the issue.

Often the conflict is more about roles and responsibilities or other issues where there is a difference of opinion or personality conflict, as opposed to any clear issue or fault. For these situations, you need to first speak with each one alone to understand their side of the argument and then meet with them together to see how you can resolve their differences.

Over the years I have used several techniques to get people or teams to work together more effectively. At one job I had two major office locations where the IT teams just could not stand working with the other team. I instituted a staff swapping program where I would switch out one member of each team with one from the other team for a month at a time – enough time to make them start identifying with the folks from the other location. Within a year that issue was solved forever. On a more local basis, I would ask people in conflict to have lunch together once a week. (yes, I paid for it) This virtually always worked.

Chapter 8

Structuring the Organization

It's impossible to overestimate the importance of clearly defining roles and responsibilities both for the individual and often more importantly, in the organizational context. You should know that structuring an IT organization is a complex activity with many nuances. This book will only touch on the subject as an introduction and with some basic guidance for the Infrastructure component of the organization. The reader is encouraged to continue with additional in-depth research focused on your specific type of company and user environment.

IT Organizations can be aligned in several different ways. The basic organizational structures are:

- *Technically Aligned* - Grouping technology and other capabilities into competency centers based on IT function, IT processes and expertise related to activities such as application development and security management.
- *Business Unit Aligned* - Focused on lines of business, products and/or geographic structure. Grouping together the people whose work is dedicated wholly or mostly to specific organization units in the enterprise as a whole and/or whose work relates to specific

geographic locations of enterprise activities, sometimes supported by a centralized IT organization for those things that are "shared."

- *Business Process Aligned* — Integrated business process or service teams, aligned with end-to-end enterprise business processes and/or business information requirements, grouping together the people responsible for executing related processes/services or sustaining a business information asset.

How you define the structure of your IT organization will depend on technology's role in the organization. Understand that there is no single right way to design the IT organization and the structure of IT must evolve with changes to the organization. When you design your organizational structure you must take the three foundational factors into account:

- The Roles and Organizational Structures of Line Management – This refers to Technically Aligned, Business Aligned, or Business Process Aligned Organizational Structures
- The Roles and Structures of Service Delivery – These roles include IT Capability (the traditional role of IT providing services like a utility), Competitive Services (where IT delivers services like an outside provider, charging for what you receive), and Business Value (where IT becomes more fused with the business itself and is a consideration in all strategic business decisions).
- Governance Roles and Structures – This refers to Centralized, Distributed and "Enabled" governance models

Future IT Organizational Structures

Gartner Inc., the Research and Consulting organization, has identif that the role of IT within organizations is changing rapidly. This is causing CIOs to re-examine the role of IT in the organization and the part they will play in it.

Today, the CIO's goal is not just to "run" IT, but also to ensure that the business achieves strategic value from the technology investments the company has made. Gartner has identified four dominant futures for IT in the organization. They are not mutually exclusive and may exist in combination:

IT as a Global Service Provider

In this scenario, the IT organization is an expanded and integrated shared-service unit that runs like a business, delivering IT services and enterprise business processes. It is virtually or fully centralized, focuses on business areas and business value, adopts a marketing perspective, capitalizes on its internal position and delivers competitive services.

IT as the Engine Room

In this scenario, IT capabilities are delivered rapidly at market-competitive prices. The IT organization succeeds by monitoring technology and market developments, and building expertise in IT asset optimization, sourcing and vendor management, and IT financial management. It delivers ongoing cost improvements, looks for new ways to deliver the same IT capabilities for less, and is highly responsive to changing business needs.

IT "is" the Business

In this scenario, information is the business's explicit product or at least is inseparable from its product. The business is structured around information flow (not process or function) and the IT organization innovates within the value chain, rather than just enabling the supporting services found in every business.

Everyone's IT

In this scenario, business leaders and individual contributors use information and technology aggressively to break through traditional business perimeters and drive ambitious collaboration. The focus is on information, rather than echnology. Highly mature businesses embrace this divergent model for its collaborative and innovative potential. This model works in non-traditional situations such as dynamic businesses, startups and R&D/entrepreneurial/community ventures.

The Infrastructure Organization Example

The previous discussion about IT organization was pretty high-level and somewhat focused on larger organizations. Taking the discussion down to the level of a real IT Infrastructure Organization in a small to medium size company, most I have seen have adopted the Technology Aligned, IT Capability model, with some variation around governance (centralized versus Business Unit alignment). This usually works well within the infrastructure organization as Infrastructure services are most efficient when centralized in some fashion.

Stated again, you must review your organizational structure to ensure that it is best structured to support the needs of the organization AND it is sufficiently detailed to clearly define the roles and responsibilities of the departments and the individuals. If there is one thing you don't want within your organization, it is a turf war between two or more of your managers. Conversely, you don't what to find there are segments of the environment with no defined owner.

It is kind of surprising that this could happen within an organization such as IT infrastructure, but it happens more often than you might imagine. Let me give you some examples of where things can go wrong:

Organizational Challenge – The Storage Area Network Group

Storage Systems can be part of the Systems group or it may be a standalone organization. That depends on the scale of the storage environment or the particular organizational philosophy of the management. Either structure has worked well for many companies.

Most people use the word SAN (Storage Area Network) to describe both the storage devices themselves (Such as EMC or Hitachi storage frames) and the network as a single entity, but they are not. There are two distinct pieces of the environment – the storage systems and the network connecting them together. The Storage Area Network (SAN) is a fiber optic network fabric designed to support the storage systems. It connects the various storage systems with the network and servers that use the storage systems. This network may exist as a completely separate network connecting only to the servers and storage, or it may utilize the primary IP network going to the servers and the Wide Area Network for replication of the data.

You can see how this SAN is sometimes a battleground for ownership. Will this SAN network be managed by the Systems or Storage team or will it be managed by the Network team? The fact is, this is a network and requires the skills and capabilities of the network staff. In addition, in many/most cases this network is integrated with the broader IP network and must be configured holistically for such items as Virtual Networks and Quality of Service (QoS).

For these reasons, the better choice would be to place ownership of the Storage Area Network within the Network team. The exception would be if the environment was large enough that a completely separate Storage Network was being deployed, in which case the Storage or Systems team would build a SAN Network group within their organization, focused specifically on this network.

The Centralized Technology Aligned Infrastructure Organization

Most organizations have their IT organization defined into two major functional groupings; IT Infrastructure and Applications. These two major groupings are then subdivided into a number of smaller groups focused on specific technologies or services.

For the IT Infrastructure organization, the subgroups are most often:

- Help Desk
- End User Services
- Network Services
- Systems Engineering and Administration
- Systems Operations

Note that in many companies the Helpdesk and End User Services are one organization. In addition, network services is again subdivided into such groups as Local Area Network (LAN), Wide Area Network, (WAN), Telecom, and sometimes network based services such as Market Data Services.

A typical organization chart for this Centralized, Technology Aligned Infrastructure Organization is shown below:

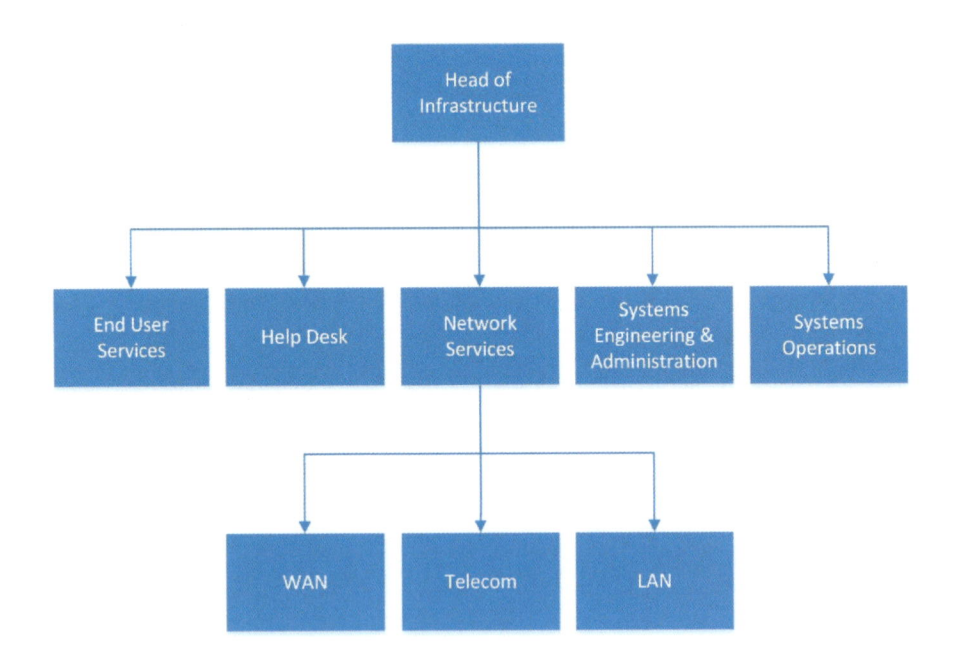

```
                          Head of
                       Infrastructure
                              |
    ┌──────────┬──────────────┼──────────────┬──────────┐
    │          │              │              │          │
End User    Help Desk      Network       Systems     Systems
Services                   Services    Engineering & Operations
                              │       Administration
                   ┌──────────┼──────────┐
                   │          │          │
                  WAN       Telecom     LAN
```

Help Desk

The Help Desk is the first point of contact between the users and IT. It should be defined as the single entry point for all user communications into IT. While the Help Desk is often the place where the most junior IT staff starts out, that is not the best decision. As the first point of contact between users and IT, especially when the user needs assistance in resolving an issue, the staff should be skilled at resolving the issues presented to them.

Staffing for the Help Desk is usually driven by a metric such as the number of user calls per Help Desk agent. This makes the case for a well-developed metrics program especially important.

End User Services

End User Services (EUS) is sometimes referred to as Desktop Support. This is the team that is dispatched to the user location to address issues or provides services that are requested by the user. This will include Break/Fix activities as well as deploying new or replacement technology to a user location. EUS is considered second tier support in that they will take over user issues that cannot be fixed at the help desk. The EUS team is responsible for all of the equipment, client-side applications and local software that operate at the user's location.

Staffing numbers for the EUS team depend on many factors, but one of the most important drivers is the compliance with the standards. The more homogeneous the environment, the more productive the EUS team will be. The number of EUS technicians is usually driven by some user metric, such as 1 technician per 75 users (exact number will vary by company)

Network Services

Network Services has overall responsibility for the various pieces of communications technology in the organization. In all but the smallest of organizations, this will minimally consist of Local Area Networking with the company facilities, Wide Area Networking and Telecommunications (Voice Communications). More than other organizations, the Network Services group's technologies are broad and relatively divergent.

The staff in Network Services needs to contend with technologies as varied as Ethernet networking, Optical Networks – both internal fiber optic communications and external fiber based optical networks such as dark fiber networks, SONET networks, Voice Communications equipment, etc. In some companies, the Network Services group is also responsible for network security, or minimally the implementation of network security architectures that are defined for them.

Network Services is also typically the organization with the greatest number of vendors that produce recurring charges, such as the carriers that supply the external circuits. As such, Vendor Management and cost optimization skills are essential in this group.

Minimally, the Network Services group contains three "Sub-groups" or functions:

- *Local Area Networking* – Focused on the internal networks within facilities. Their responsibilities include all wired and wireless communications and often the network configuration of larger Conferencing systems.
- *Wide Area Networking* – This function has the responsibility for the connectivity between company sites, between company sites and vendors or customers and to outsourced locations, such as data centers. It is this organization that is responsible for the largest recurring dollar spend in all but the smallest organizations. The wide area networking group also needs to deploy the tools required to measure network utilization and capacity and proactively manage bandwidth to ensure the required level of network performance are maintained.
- *Telecommunications* – The Telecommunications function is focused on Voice communications. It is responsible for wired telephone systems, wireless/mobile (cell) phones, audio conferencing and sometimes Video Conferencing.

In some firms, there are additional specialized voice communications systems, such as in Financial Services, where Traders use specialized telephone systems that include "Turrets" at trader positions. These are most simplistically specialized telephone systems with a large number of preset connections between users at different companies. Environments like Turret systems will require very specialized skill sets.

Beyond the standard three Network Services sub-groups, some firms will have these additional organizations within the Network Services function:

- Market Data Services – this organization is focused on providing "services" that ride in on the Network circuits. Examples of Market Data Services would include Bloomberg, Reuters, and many other similar services. The people within this function are responsible for sourcing the services, arranging for the appropriate licensing based on the number of user seats receiving the service and managing those licenses. Client side support of market Data Services is provided by the Help Desk and End User Support.

Systems Engineering and Administration

The systems engineering and Administration team are responsible for designing, implementing, administering, monitoring and tuning the IT servers and systems software that comprise the infrastructure that runs the applications that support the business.

These responsibilities are very broad and include such functional areas as:

- Entitlement Systems – such as managing Active Directory User accounts
- Messaging Systems – which include EMAIL, Instant Messaging, and mobile based messaging services
- Knowledge and collaboration systems such as SharePoint
- Storage Systems – in this example Storage Systems is considered part of the Systems Administration group. Storage Systems can also be broken out as a separate function in larger organizations.

Systems Operations

The function of the Systems Operations Manager and the team is to perform the ongoing operational processes defined for the environment. These would include such items as:

- Systems Management – The Systems Operations function is responsible for ensuring that the required updates and patches to their environment are kept up to date and that known exposures are addressed as quickly as possible.
- Data Backups and Restores
- Demand Management or Capacity Planning
- Disaster Recovery Planning and Testing

- Management processes, such as Change Management

Additional (Optional) IT Groups

The following IT organizational functions are optional groups that would typically only be found in larger organizations.

Information Security

The Information Security function may or may not exist in every company as a separate IT function or organization. In some small organizations, this may be handled by one or more individuals within the Network Services organization. In larger organizations and in those organizations with specific risks, such as Financial Services companies, this function may be supported by one or more individuals in one of the other functional groups, or it may be a separate group onto itself. In larger organizations, this is clearly a separate function that is staffed according to company size and the mandate of this group.

It's important to note that the IT Information Security function may not reside within IT at all, but instead externally in a broader security function or another group.

Project Management Office (PMO)

The Project Management Office (PMO) is most often seen in larger companies, but it is effective in any size organization that has a number of simultaneous initiatives in a process that need coordination. The PMO typically assigns one or more Project Managers to each of the separate initiatives and coordinates the activities among the different projects at a higher level.

IT Audit

In larger organizations, a separate group is created that provides an ongoing review and auditing function of the various IT activities. This group monitors the finances, project performance, and IT risks and controls that exist within IT. This function most often exists within organizations that must conform to specific agency compliance requirements.

Extending the Organization into Multiple Sites

This organizational discussion has so far focused specifically on the centralized technology aligned model. While that model works well in the majority of situations, there are instances where it must be modified or flexed to accommodate the realities of the business.

The most common need to broaden the organizational design is where there are multiple physical sites or locations within the organization. Here are some examples of multiple sites you may need to address:

- Multiple small to very small sites, such as a retail organization with several hundred stores either domestically or worldwide.
- Multiple medium to large sites or offices locally, such as a number of large domestic offices
- Multiple sites that may be either domestic or internationally based

Multiple Small to Very Small Sites

This situation is characteristic of a company that has retail locations. Unless you plan to develop a large field service workforce, you are best served by engaging an outside services organization that has the personnel and geographic scope to effectively support your needs. This has implications beyond just how you get a technician to a site. It also should impact how you architect the systems, the network, and the overall IT Security environment to ensure that the technical personnel in the field can accomplish their work with a minimum of systems permissions. Put another way, you must assume that the technical staff that is working for your field services partner will try every possible method to break into your systems and cause havoc. Don't assume for a second you are hiring "good guys".

Multiple Medium to Large Sites Domestically

In the situation where you have multiple medium to large sites domestically (25 people and up), you can best manage the organization by extending the technology aligned organizations into these additional sites. As an example, you would have End User Support and Network Services organizations in each of the other facilities, reporting into the same manager as those in your primary site. Choose the location with the most skilled staff as the Headquarters location for that function. In my specific case, the organizational design that was head and shoulders above any other that I built had the End User Support organization located in New York and the Network Services organization headquartered in the Midwest. New York network personnel reported into the Midwest Network Services Manager and all End User Support personnel reported into the New York EUS Manager.

In the smallest of locations, where local IT personnel cannot be justified, you should engage a local service provider to deliver day-to-day support, such as break/fix, software installs, and new equipment installations. If you have a more major requirement, like deploying a new server or network equipment, you can fly in the right staff to do the job.

Multiple Sites That May Be Both Domestically and Internationally Based

If you find yourself in this type of organization you will find that, in addition to the spacial or geographic separation between you and your users, there is also a significant time separation. This adds a significant complication to your organizational structure.

Like the case of multiple domestic sites, you must staff the remote sites using the same parameters as you would for your main location – End User Support, Network Services, etc. The staffing, of course, is based on the technology deployed at those locations.

The big difference, in this case, has to do with the required local management and empowerment. In the case of domestic offices, the greatest time difference between offices will be 3 hours (for US based companies). When your responsibilities include international offices, this number grows to 12 hours worst case. That requires you add two things to your organizational structure for the larger and distant offices.

1. You will need to put someone in charge as an IT site manager. That person could be the most senior of the technical staff you deploy to that location or it could be an actual site manager when the remote office is so large that you have a larger number of IT staff working there.
2. Your staff at the remote location will necessarily be in a matrix management environment. All members of these remote offices will report to more than one manager. The technical personnel (EUS, Network, etc.) will report to the overall manager of that function. In addition, they will report to the site manager for this remote location. The site manager will report to the Head of Infrastructure, but also to a local business manager at the site.

If you have a large number of remote offices you may consider adding a "Manager of Regional Office Technology" to your organization. The remote Site Managers would report this person and this Regional Office Manager would report into the Head of IT Infrastructure.

As I noted, the Site Managers would also report into some local senior manager at the remote office. This is usually a senior business leader at that location. Together, the Site Manager and the local business manager will manage daily prioritization of activities which are tactical in nature.

Chapter 9

Technology Management

IT Standards

The manageability of your technology environment will depend on, to a large extent, how well you are able to define and adhere to a set of standards. You need to define your standards across the entire IT environment, including the different types of Hardware (server, desktop/laptop, storage, network, etc.), Software, Peripherals, Operating Systems, Network Protocols, Development Languages, Telephony and Conferencing

This will undoubtedly be one of the more challenging efforts you will undertake in transforming your organization. That said, the resulting impact on the efficiency and effectiveness of your team will make this well worth the effort.

What will your organization look like of you don't define or enforce standards? It isn't pretty for sure:

- Not managing the standardization of the user workstation platform can cause havoc when deploying a new application or an application upgrade. Different processor speeds, different memory configurations, and disk capacities, as well as different operating system versions, can all cause programs to crash or behave badly. Imagine that Monday morning after a deployment as the End User Support team needs to "debug" issues on a multitude of users whose machines no longer work – each for a different reason.

- Different types or levels of software on different machines can cause all sorts of issues. Issues that may have been corrected on a later version will be present on the older versions. Security exposures may exist and put the entire organization at risk.

- Different Applications being used for the same function in different organizations may appear to work well at a purely functional level (availability, alignment with the user requirements, etc.), but they may cause more business related issues at a higher level. As an example, multiple financial systems is the usual CIO's nightmare. You can almost be guaranteed that multiple financial systems will result in differences in the charts of accounts. You can also guarantee that the different systems will define data points differently, such as how profit and loss are defined by two different departments. The amount of effort that goes into taking results from different departments and integrating them into a single report is often astounding. Another common application where we see multiple products existing in an organization is CRM. Same types of issues.

- There is a clear budgetary impact of not defining and enforcing standards. At the most basic level, you will lose the price advantage of the single large purchase. You will need to purchase support for a multitude of different pieces of hardware and software, increasing the overall cost. Finally, your support of the mixed environment will be more complex, slower and ultimately will require more staff and skill sets than a homogeneous environment.

So, what should you do if you move into a new position and find that you have a heterogeneous environment (often referred to in the industry as a complete mess)? Get started ASAP to standardize it! It is the only way to build a well-run IT environment and frankly, to save your job.

Choosing standards – In some cases, choosing standards will be a trivial exercise. A good example might be selecting Microsoft Office as the standard Office productivity platform. A slightly more difficult issue will be that ongoing quasi-religious war . . . Apple vs. PC. Do you select PC only? Apple only? PC with some Apple in managed deployments where they are specifically needed (imaging, video, and web design)? You can see how this starts getting a bit more complex.

I have always grouped standards into five classes of items:

- *Absolute Standards* – This will include such items as PC vs. Apple; standard model of desktop and laptop (including hardware specs like memory and disk storage); office productivity suite; standard browser, virus scanner, pdf reader, zip/unzip, and EMAIL program; Printers (both personal and shared); Network Operating System; standard server platform; and so on. If you are talking about user workstation equipment, this would include those items that EVERY person gets, whether they need it or not.

- *Non-Standard Standards* – These are items that are on our list of supported products, but not every user will get them. There is usually some form of process defined for someone to request an item on this list and get it approved. Some great examples of this include Adobe Photoshop or Adobe Illustrator. Google Chrome might be on this list if you chose Microsoft Edge or Internet Explorer as the standard Browser. A simple process for this group may be the authorization from a person's manager or senior executive. The help desk would have a small inventory of each item on this list and would assign a copy once the approval is received.

- *Special Requests* – This group is, for the most part, undefined and taken on a one-off basis. This would include such items as a specialty piece of software, such as physical security software, specialized Risk software, etc. In some cases, something that starts in this category will later become part of the non-standard standards – meaning anyone that later wants a similar type of software will need to use this previously reviewed, approved and supported version. This category is one where most organizations find the IT staff has no previous experience or skills to support it.

- *Don't Care* – The "don't care" category includes items that have no meaningful impact on the operation of the IT environment. This might include such items as scanners, small specialized printers, like label printers, mice, keyboards, etc. If someone wants something you place in this category and is willing to pay for it, the Help Desk is empowered to place the order and get the item installed.

- *Not allowed* – There are some types of equipment of software applications that you will specifically place on the "not allowed" list. An example of this might be personal hotspots or connecting a personal wireless router to the network.

However you decide to categorize the technology that you will see in your organization, you should have some clearly articulated process and selection criteria that you will use to defend your choices. (You will absolutely be challenged on anything you decide to limit, reject or place on the "Not Allowed" list.

Here are some good criteria for you to use during you "selection" or "decision making" process:

- Fitness for purpose
- Adoption by the industry
- Percent of the organization that will need this
- Criticality of the item to the business
- Reliability
- Manageability
- Scalability
- Skill set requirements
- Outside Support Availability
- Ease of upgrade or migration to the standard
- Level of Customization Required

Standard Operating Procedures

The need for defined and documented Standard Operating Procedures cannot be overstated. You will undoubtedly find this to be one of the more challenging aspects of managing an IT organization. IT Policies must flexibly address an ever-changing technology landscape, and therefore must be reviewed and updated at least on an annual basis. If you happen to work in an industry that is required to comply with various Federal regulations and International Standards (such as Sarbanes-Oxley, COBIT, ITIL, ISO 27000, ISO 2000, HIPPA and PCI to name a few), a comprehensive set of well-defined policies is a requirement.

Beyond the regulatory aspect, IT Policies are essential to your successfully managing your IT environment. They will define what types of hardware and software can be used in the organization, the processes for adding or removing users, adding accounts, the acceptable use of company assets, how to report security incidents and so on.

Here is a typical set of Policies your organization must create.

- Acceptable User of Information Technology Resources Policy
- Desktop Computer Standards Policy (IT Infrastructure Standards)
- Software License Compliance Policy
- EMAIL Use Policy
- Cell Phone Policy
- Password Policy
- Internet Use Policy
- Bring Your Own Device (BYOD) Policy
- Mobile Security Policy
- Mobile Data Synchronization Policy
- Wireless Network Policy
- Technology Incident Notification and Escalation Procedure
- IT Security Incident Reporting Policy
- IT Security Standards and Policy
- Information Privacy Policy
- New Equipment Request Procedure
- New Employee Setup Procedure
- Employee Termination Procedure
- EMAIL Account Request Form
- Change Management Procedure
- Data Center Access Policy
- Equipment Disposal Policy
- Records Management and Retention Policy
- Software Installation Request Procedure
- Event and Media Support Request Form
- Interactive Video Room Scheduling and Support Procedure

- Macintosh Support Procedures
- Inventory Control Procedure

While this list is extensive you should not be concerned. You should first look to see what IT Policies already exist in the organization when they were written and last updated and when and how they have been communicated to the staff. In most organizations I have been to, I have found that at least one of these areas was significantly lacking. (Either no policies or they haven't been updated in years, or they haven't been properly communicated to the staff).

As a hint here, if you find your organization has few documented policies you can purchase IT Policy template packages from a number of sources. These template packs will help kick-start your policy definition process, but should never be used "out of the box". Your policies must always take your specific organization into account.

Aside from the obvious checking a box on certification reviews (not meant to denigrate the certification process), there is a real demonstrable need to have these policies AND to make certain that every member of the staff knows that they exist. As mentioned above, these policies help you to create a manageable IT environment – that's the "when things go well" part of the explanation. The converse of that is the "when things go bad" scenario. When a staff member, be it a member of YOUR specific organization or the broader user base, uses the equipment in a fashion that violates the company rules or even just some societal rule of good behavior and the organization needs to take some action, you must have some documented policy that the HR department and lawyers can point to that defines that the behavior was against company policy. In addition, you need to have some documented acknowledgment that the user in question was provided with a copy of the policy and acknowledges that he/she read and understood it.

When developing your IT Policies you need to include the organization that owns the particular area of technology in the definition process. They are best positioned to point out flaws or omissions in the policies. Also, having the owners of the technology be part of the policy setting effort instills a sense of ownership in that team, making them more likely to enforce the standards and policies and more able to explain the rationale to users that may have questions or challenge the policy.

Once a policy has been agreed to and signed off on by the team that is creating it, the policy should move onto receiving the approval of business management. In many organizations, there is an IT Steering Committee that typically consists of senior business management. That committee should review the proposed policy, along with the data and rationale that drives it. They will provide feedback to your group to adjust the policy as required, and then provide their final approval for the policy. Once that final approval is received the policy transforms from something created by and for IT to a policy business decision owned by all of the departments. This is now communicated to the staff, including a statement that this has received Senior Business Management approval.

Communicating and Enforcing IT Standards and Policies

Standards and Policies are worthless without the proper enforcement. Make no mistake about it, you will be challenged constantly on both. In order to make this work, you need to be able to deliver a rational and articulate argument on why the standards and policies are in place and why they need to be enforced. That said, you will need a commonsense approach to making exceptions. There will be circumstances when someone cannot do their job without utilizing a piece of technology that is not on your standards list. You should include a process for vetting the reasons why people are asking for a standards or policy exception and receiving the proper approvals to get that exception.

Enforcement of the standards should follow these steps:

- Clearly, document your standards and policies, distribute them to the business and get a signed confirmation back that they were received and understood
- Document the reasons behind the standards, what they are there to achieve or to prevent and what the consequences of not having them in place would be
- Get the approval of senior IT and business management for the standards and policies and communicate the fact of their approval to the users when the standards are distributed
- Provide periodic re-distribution and communication of the standards, always with a returned signed confirmation feedback to ensure the staff keeps them in mind and any changes are communicated
- Develop simplified processes for purchasing the items covered by the standards

- Ensure that the standards are updated periodically and re-communicated to stay relevant to changes in the business, the technology or legal implications.
- Create a commonsense approach to approving exceptions to the standards

Standards and policies should be distributed to the business on no less than an annual basis. Also, whenever there is a meaningful change to the policy, it should either be communicated to the business in its entirety or there should be an "all-hands" email explaining the change and pointing to the policy on the company internal Intranet website.

I will restate this for emphasis - Communications of standards and policies should require a positive verification and acknowledgment that the recipient received the communication, read the document and understood the document and agrees to comply with the policy. There should be a contact person designated for any questions or concerns. The acknowledgment by every member of the staff with signature must have a "required by" date associated with it. As with any other vital company policy, such as compliance, signed verification of receipt, understanding, and agreement to comply with the policy should be a condition of employment.

Service Level Agreements

Service Level Agreements will be part of your life. Particular aspects of the service – scope, quality, responsibilities – are agreed between the service provider and the service user. If you become the new Infrastructure Manager ask for copies of the service level agreements that your organization has entered into. There will be two types to collect:

Services TO YOU from Equipment vendors and other service providers – These are relatively straightforward and consist of such things as Cisco Smartnet, etc. In addition, you will most likely have service level agreements with providers of outsourced services like Cloud Services, Data Center Colocation Services, etc. You need to understand early on what level of services these SLAs commit to providing as well as the consequences for non-compliance. Equipment vendors will provide guarantees for such items as Time to Respond, Time to Repair/Resolution, time to provide replacement parts, etc. A Data Center colocation site will provide guarantees around such items as power and cooling availability, temperature range, humidity range, etc.

Services FROM YOU to your customers – I'll make the case that this group of SLAs is more important for you to fully understand and to focus on meeting or exceeding. The SLA to your users is the definition of what services and service levels they can expect from you. At one level this is defined to manage the expectations of your user community. The SLA provides a bar that can deflect undue criticism. The SLA also is used to define to your technical staff what the minimum acceptable performance is for the things that they do.

If your IT Organization has not created SLAs to define the service levels that the business should expect, you should. In some cases, the organization is not currently capable of delivering consistent service that will meet an SLA. In situations where I have found that in the past, I begin by defining the target service levels as Service-Level GOALS or Objectives. This may seem like simple semantics however the choice of words is carefully considered. If you defined something as a Service Level Agreement, it is considered an absolute commitment to the organization that you are capable of meeting that service-level and have every intention to do so. It might have negative consequences if you miss any specific commitment levels (such as financial impact to the individuals – bonuses or possibly the loss of your job). If you define these measures as Service Level Objectives, you are stating that the organization might not be capable of meeting these goals consistently. That is a huge distinction.

IT Processes

IT Process definitions are essential to providing a well-managed and predictable service. The challenge here is that, by and large, I find that organizations have not gone through the effort of formally defining the primary IT processes that occur in their environment. Many of those that have defined the processes do not enforce them with any rigor. Finally, fewer still measure the results of the processes to find out how they are performing and making changes where appropriate.

A Process Needs To Be Embraced ***And*** Enforced

I spent some time on an assignment at a very major US Bank. One of my goals was to understand why there were recurring power failure issues at one of their outsourced data centers. This bank proudly would proclaim that it is an ITIL shop. Their processes were well defined. OK, now let's test that claim.

When I asked to see copies of the root-cause analysis reports being produced by their "problem management" team, as expected I found that the entire process was lip service. Where any root cause analysis reviews were even being done, they were started weeks after the event. The people that were present and part of both the initial failure and the remediation to bring the systems back online were not the ones that produced the reports.

The root cause sections were basically a litany of anything and everything that could possibly have contributed to the failure. One "power failure" report read "The failure could have been caused by someone leaning against the power button on the server. It also could have been caused by a failure of the PDU in the cabinet or a failure of the circuit breaker feeding that PDU in the distribution panel. Finally, it could have been caused by a failure in a remote PDU feeding the distribution panel."

Everyone would agree that it **COULD** have been caused by any of those things – but the actual cause of the failure was never found. It was clearly obvious to me that the people that were producing these Root-Cause-Analyses were never trained in how to do them. It was also clear that nobody was actually ever reading these reports, and the people that were producing them knew that. As long as that "Green" indicator for problem management on the monthly dashboard could be lit, everyone was happy – but nothing ever got fixed.

IT Processes are a huge subject to take on. Defining these processes can be as large an effort as embracing a formal process methodology, such as ITIL, or as simple as taking a few of the most common ones and defining a process that works for your team. You need to approach the subject of process definition in a way that is appropriately scaled for your group or company.

If you and your organization are new to IT Process definition, I recommend starting slow. You should begin with those processes that have the biggest impact on improving services and build from there. I would recommend starting with Incident Management and Change Management – not necessarily at the full ITIL level of comprehensiveness. I would follow up these processes with a Disaster Recovery process.

Incident Management is defined to include both Service Interruptions and Service Requests. (Note: In the latest version of ITIL, Service Requests are moved into a new process called "Request Fulfillment")

Change Management is a larger – usually cross-functional – process that is designed to review proposed changes to the environment, ensure that any and all stakeholders are aware of the change and agree to its deployment, and that the proper plans are in place to address all technical dependencies and back changes out in the event of a post-deployment issue.

ITIL Processes

If you plan to take on the challenge of making your department a process-driven organization in a big way, then you will likely want to consider embracing one of the formal process methodologies. In the IT Infrastructure world, your best choice will be ITIL.

Here is a formal definition of ITIL:

"ITIL, formerly an acronym for Information Technology Infrastructure Library, is a set of practices for IT service management (ITSM) that focuses on aligning IT services with the needs of business. In its current form (known as ITIL 2011 edition), ITIL is published as a series of five core volumes, each of which covers a different ITSM lifecycle stage. Although ITIL underpins

ISO/IEC 20000 (previously BS 15000), the International Service Management Standard for IT service management, there are some differences between the ISO 20000 standard and the ITIL framework.

ITIL describes processes, procedures, tasks, and checklists which are not organization-specific but can be applied by an organization for establishing integration with the organization's strategy, delivering value, and maintaining a minimum level of competency. It allows the organization to establish a baseline from which it can plan, implement, and measure. It is used to demonstrate compliance and to measure improvement."

Some of the other processes you will want to consider within your IT Infrastructure Organization include

- Request Fulfillment
- Access Management
- Problem Management

Problem Management / Root Cause Analysis

Later in this book, we will discuss IT Metrics in some detail. I consider the collection, analysis, and publication of IT Metrics to be one of the single most important initiatives you can undertake in an infrastructure organization. You will hear lots of reasons why later.

Right now we will just mention them in the context of Problem Management and Root-Cause Analysis. Root Cause Analysis is defined as:

Root-Cause-Analysis is a process for identifying "root causes" of problems or events and an approach for responding to them. Root Cause Analysis is based on the idea that effective management requires more than merely "putting out fires" for problems that develop, but finding a way to prevent them.

The obvious goal of Problem Management is to uncover the underlying problem that is causing Service Interruptions within your environment. Once the root cause of a service interruption is known, you can either address the problem with a fix on all impacted pieces of technology (which may be every workstation for instance), or you can include the workaround to an issue in a Knowledge Base to be used by your technical staff.

You are not going to perform a root-cause analysis for every issue you have worked through in your organization, but there are two circumstances where this is necessary.

1. For Severity 1 events – We obviously do not want Severity 1 events to happen. Ever! Unfortunately, they do happen. When they happen, you need to communicate three things to the business (a) What Happened; (b) what your team did to fix it; (c) What you are doing to make sure it never happens again. In order to provide item (c), you need to understand the Root-Cause of the failure.
2. For Repetitive Issues – There will be issues that will occur over and over again. A piece of software that crashes, a problem with a certain type of printer. This list can be very long. One advantage of a Metrics initiative is that it will collect data that you can analyze looking for patterns. Once you see that a certain problem is occurring over and over again you can focus on finding what is actually causing that issue and taking it off the table for good. You would be surprised to see how this sort of process can bring your number of Help Desk calls down.

Problem Management reviews start by creating a Problem Management Report form. This is a document that captures all of the known facts of the failure. It should be completed immediately after a service interruption has been fixed by the people that directly worked on the issue. It is the information that is contained on this form that provides the basis of the Problem Diagnosis and Resolution.

Problem Management must be scaled to the size of your organization. Very large organizations sometimes have entire groups devoted to pursuing the underlying causes of repetitive issues. A small business may task specific individuals with performing a Root-Cause-Analysis of a repetitive problem occurring in their specific space. You must define a Problem Management Report that is appropriate for your organization. There are plenty of templates out on the internet to get you started. Understand that, especially in a company of any significant size, a formal Problem Management Function will require resources to focus on the investigations; however, whatever the size of your company and the resources you devote to Problem Management, the impact of improved availability and performance will make devoting these resources worthwhile.

Incident Management

The goal of Incident Management is to restore any service interruptions as quickly as possible. In the older versions of ITIL, The Incident Management process included user requests for new items like software, etc. In the latest version of ITIL, Requests are broken down into a different process (although still handled by the same people.)

While Incident Management is a process that hits the entire organization, the folks most involved are the Help Desk and End User Support (Desktop Support) teams.

The Help Desk

As the focal point in the organization for user related issues, the Help Desk has a disproportionate impact on user perception of IT. Frankly, I have never seen any company where the IT Help Desk gets enthusiastic positive reviews. The best assessments I have seen include such statements as "they do pretty good considering the overall lack of resources they have" or the delightful "well, they certainly aren't as bad as they *USED* to be!" Why are Help Desks almost universally held in such low esteem?

My Most Challenging Turnaround

When I first joined MasterCard International to lead corporate technology there was essentially no Help Desk in place. User requests were phoned directly into the techs themselves and it wasn't going well. How could it? If the technicians were around at all (not away from their desk doing user support or network work) they would wait for a caller to try someone else – they essentially refused to answer the phone (yes, I did make changes to the staffing). I tried an experiment and called the desk, leaving a voice mail. After 3 days of not getting a response (no response to a call from their boss), I asked if anyone had heard my voice mail. They didn't. Now admittedly, this was the worst I have ever seen.

I quickly engaged a few temps to just answer the phone and log the calls (manually in a spreadsheet). This helped a bit, but clearly wasn't the solution – it was just designed to slow the bleeding.

My path to fixing the Help Desk took several years and included:

- Sourcing qualified and committed End User Support staff

- Installing the tools to track and manage user tickets
- Installing a telephone environment that can track the number of phone calls, hold times and abandoned calls
- Developing processes to classify the severity of an issue or event and deploy the correct skills to address it. Also defined escalation procedures and trigger points for escalation
- Identify the Help Desk expert for the different types of technologies being supported
- Developing monthly Help Desk Metrics that were used both as a communications tool to Senior Management and to drive improvements to how the Help Desk was managed. (much more on this later)
- Communicating with users during the resolution process and afterward. Every call was followed by a user satisfaction survey.

At this point, the Help Desk was running pretty good, but good wasn't good enough – we wanted GREAT! So we engaged an outside consulting firm to help us move up to the level where our users were actually our fans. This process was part presentation, part watching videos and part focus group, where the focus group consisted of the End User Support organization, and also my complete set of direct reports and me.

To say this was interesting is an understatement. The Help Desk team had a huge number of great and relevant recommendations. The most memorable one to me had to do with the process of authorizing the Non-Standard Standard software (remember, that's the group we will support, but it is not pre-installed on every machine). I was part of the approval process, but frankly "added no value", since I had not rejected anyone's request that had been approved by their management. THEY redefined the process at that meeting, streamlining it and resulting in a noticeable improvement in customer satisfaction. (yep, I was the problem here). I was voted off the process.

The message here is to make sure you have skilled people on the Help Desk that want to work on the Help Desk and will take pride in creating a first class group. Make sure you have the tools in place to manage the calls, analyze what the call issues are and how well you are responding to them and communicate with the users. Over communication is better than under-communicating. Finally, listen to your people and reach out to them for their opinions.

Attempting First Contact Resolution of Issues

A Service Interruption incident must be solved within the agreed solution period, as we will discuss later in the Incident Triage section. The aim is the fast recovery of the IT Service, where necessary with the aid of a Workaround. The best case goal is for the solution to be achieved during the first attempt by 1st Level Support – the Help Desk. As you will see in the section on Metrics, this "First Contact Closure" is SO important that it must be tracked through your metrics program. If after exhausting the possible solutions to a problem the service interruption is not fixed, the Incident is transferred to a suitable group within 2nd Level Support. (End User Support, Network, Systems, etc.)

Triage of Issues and Incident Prioritization

All issues are not created equal. If an EMAIL or application server is down, that's way more important than the person that is waiting for Photoshop to be installed on his or her machine. User support calls are always triaged into a set of well-defined call severity levels. The higher the severity, the greater the response.

Typical Severity Level Classifications are:

- Severity 1-Critical/Emergency - Critical Impact/System Down
- Severity 2-High - Significant Impact
- Severity 3-Medium - Minor impact and priority
- Severity 4- Scheduled or Low priority
- Severity 5 – Very Low / Project Work

The Incident Prioritization Guideline describes the rules for assigning priorities to Incidents, including the definition of what constitutes a Major Incident. Since Incident Management escalation rules are usually based on priorities, assigning the correct priority to an Incident is essential for triggering appropriate Incident escalations.

An Incident's priority is usually determined by assessing its impact and urgency, where

- *Urgency* is a measure how quickly a resolution of the Incident is required
- *Impact* is measure of the extent of the Incident and of the potential damage caused by the Incident before it can be resolved

Incident Urgency (Categories of Urgency)

This section establishes categories of urgency. The definitions must suit the type of organization, so the following table is only an example. To determine the Incident's urgency, choose the highest relevant category:

Incident Urgency	
Category	**Description**
High	- The damage caused by the Incident increases rapidly.
- Work that cannot be completed by staff is highly time sensitive.
- A minor Incident can be prevented from becoming a major Incident by acting immediately
- Several users with VIP status are affected.
Medium	- The damage caused by the Incident increases considerably over time.
- A single user with VIP status is affected.
Low	- The damage caused by the Incident only marginally increases over time.
- Work that cannot be completed by staff is not time sensitive

Incident Impact (Categories of Impact)

This section establishes *categories of impact*. The definitions must suit the type of organization, so the following table is only an example. To determine the *Incident's impact*, choose the highest relevant category

Incident Impact	
Category	**Description**
High	<ul><li>A large number of staff is affected and/or not able to do their job.</li><li>The financial impact of the Incident is (for example) likely to exceed $10,000.</li><li>The damage to the reputation of the business is likely to be high.</li><li>Someone has been injured.</li></ul>
Medium	<ul><li>A moderate number of staff is affected and/or not able to do their job properly.</li><li>A moderate number of customers are affected and/or inconvenienced in some way.</li><li>The financial impact of the Incident is (for example) likely to exceed $1,000 but will not be more than $10,000.</li><li>The damage to the reputation of the business is likely to be moderate.</li></ul>
Low	<ul><li>A minimal number of staff is affected and/or able to deliver an acceptable service but this requires extra effort.</li><li>A minimal number of customers are affected and/or inconvenienced but not in a significant way.</li><li>The financial impact of the Incident is (for example) likely to be less than $1,000.</li><li>The damage to the reputation of the business is likely to be minimal</li></ul>

Incident Priority Classes

Incident Priority is derived from urgency and impact.

Incident Priority Matrix

If classes are defined to rate urgency and impact (see above), an *Urgency-Impact Matrix* (also referred to as *Incident Priority Matrix*) can be used to define priority classes, identified in this example by colors and priority codes:

		Impact/Urgency Priority Code Matrix		
		Impact		
		High	Medium	Low
Urgency	High	1	2	3
	Medium	2	3	4
	Low	3	4	5

Incident Priority Definitions			
Priority Code	Description	Target Response Time	Target Resolution Time
1	Critical	Immediate	1 Hour
2	High	10 Minutes	4 Hours
3	Medium	1 Hour	8 Hours
4	Low	4 Hours	24 Hours
5	Very Low	1 Day	1 Week

Incident Response Time & Escalation By Priority

Priority Level	Description	Response Time	Communication w/ Customer	Escalation Trigger Point	Escalated to
Priority 1	Critical Emergency	Immediate	Every 4 hours	1 Hour	Head of Technical Organization Head of Infrastructure Senior IT Management
Priority 2	High	10 min.	Daily	End of Day	Head of Technical Organization
Priority 3	Medium	1 hour	Every 3 days	After 3 Days	Head of Technical Organization
Priority 4	Scheduled or Low	4 hours	Weekly	End of Week	Head of Technical Organization
Priority 5	Very Low / Project	1 days	Bi-monthly	Weekly	Head of Technical Organization

Severity Definitions

Support Requests that are made to the Help Desk are prioritized based on the nature, severity and time of the request. The following descriptions provide some guidance on how you should develop a Support Request Prioritization

Severity 1 - Critical [Emergency] – This Severity Level is assigned to a problem, or issue, impacting a significant number of users and/or any mission critical IT issue affecting a single customer.

Examples: (but not limited to)

- Critical network server is down.
- Any Senior Management Issue
- E-mail system is not functioning.
- Primary Internet connection is lost or slows enough to drop connections.
- Unable to access shared data resulting in a work stoppage.

Severity 2 - High – Noncritical but significant issue affecting a single user; or an issue that is degrading the performance and reliability of supported IT Services; however, the services are still operational. Support issues that could escalate to Severity 1 if not addressed promptly.

Examples: (but not limited to):

- Setting up new user accounts which have been properly submitted.
- Single user's system is down and unable to use other workstations to remain productive.
- Printing issues for multiple users.
- Locked or restricted user accounts.

Severity 3 - *Normal*– Routine support requests that impact a single user or non-critical software or hardware error.

Examples: (but not limited to):

- Single user's workstation is down, but the user may be able to use other workstations to remain productive.
- Printing issues for a single user.
- User productivity affected but not completely halted.
- Frequently used software corrupted and needing re-installation.
- Software and hardware installation, upgrades, and other similar requests.

Severity 4 - *Low*– A Priority resulting from a minor service issue or general inquiry from the customer that does not affect the customer's ability to utilize the technology.

Examples: (but not limited to):

- Intermittent problems with workstation, but user still able to remain productive.
- Non-critical tutorial questions.
- User productivity may be slightly affected, but never completely halted.
- User requesting assistance with copying or moving of non-critical files.
- Technical consultations for pending purchases.

Severity 5 – *Project Work* – Project work is by definition work tasks that will take some time to complete. This can be as simple as upgrading the operating system in a department or as complex as building the technology for a new facility. More complex Project Work should be subject to the complete Project Management process

Circumstances That Warrant the Incident to be Treated as a Major Incident

Major Incidents call for the establishment of a Major Incident Team and are managed through a special process designed to apply the required resources and focus.

Indicators

The above prioritization scheme notwithstanding, it is often appropriate to define additional, readily understandable indicators for identifying Major Incidents (see also the comments below on identifying Major Incidents). Examples of such indicators are:

1. Certain (groups of) business-critical services, applications or infrastructure components are unavailable and the estimated time for recovery is unknown or exceedingly long (specify services, applications or infrastructure components)

2. Certain (groups of) Vital Business Functions (business-critical processes) are affected and the estimated time for restoring these processes to full operating status is unknown or exceedingly long (specify business-critical processes)

Identifying Major Incidents

It is not easy to give clear guidelines on how to identify major incidents although the 1st Level Support often develops a "sixth sense" for these. It is also probably better to err on the side of caution in this respect.

A Major incident tends to be characterized by its impact, especially on customers. Consider some examples:

- A high-speed network communications link fails and part of or all data communication to and from outside the organization is cut off.
- A website grinds to a halt because of unexpected heavy demand prior to a deadline (for example to reserve tickets or make a legal submission) resulting in large numbers of customers failing to meet that deadline.
- A key business database is found to be corrupted.
- More than one business server is infected by a worm.

- The private and confidential information of a significant number of individuals is accidentally disclosed in a public forum.

Note also that all disasters are *Major Incidents* and often smaller incidents that are compounded by errors or inaction can become major incidents.

Key Characteristics of Major Incidents

Some of the key characteristics that make these Major Incidents are:

- The ability of significant numbers of customers and/or key customers to use services or systems is or will be affected.
- The cost to customers and/or IT is or will be substantial, both in terms of direct and indirect costs (including consequential loss).
- The reputation of IT and the company is likely to be damaged.

AND

- The amount of effort and/or time required to manage and resolve the incident is likely to be large and it is very likely that agreed service levels (target resolution times) will be breached.

A Major Incident is also categorized as a critical or high priority incident.

Communications and Escalation for Unresolved Issues

Each of these severity levels has an escalation trigger point defined. The trigger point is the time from when the issue is first discovered (user help desk call, network or system alerts, etc.) to when a more senior manager must be notified that the issue is not resolved.

Escalations are necessary because the particular resource that is working on the issue may have a skill gap that they are afraid to expose by asking for help. Also, the solution may require another department be brought into the effort to fix the issue. The more senior person to whom a call is escalated to can also become a buffer between the technical staff working on the problem and the impacted users, who may be calling every 5 or 10 minutes. Whatever the reason, if you can't get a problem addressed quickly, escalate to a more senior staff member.

As an example, if a Severity 1 issue is not fully resolved within 1 hour, the issue must be escalated to the Senior Manager in that particular technology tower (such as the head of networks for a network issue or head of systems for a server issue). In addition, for a Severity 1 issue, the Head of

Infrastructure and the IT Organizational Head (CIO, CTO) must be informed.

The escalation must include the pertinent information (1) What went wrong; (2) Where are we in the recovery process; (3) What is the projected Time or Repair. If you know enough about the cause of the failure, you should include what changes need to be made to ensure this does not happen again.

In addition to escalation, there is a requirement for ongoing communication with the user. Users need to hear from someone with a status update on their issue from time to time. Obviously, the more critical the issue is, the more often that the communication should happen.

Make sure the Head of IT knows!

I do want to emphasize the need to ensure the most senior IT management is aware of this Severity 1 problem. Never ever put that most senior person in the position of walking into a meeting with his/her peers or management and learn about the outage there. Your senior manager will feel blindsided and I can absolutely assure you, you will be the target of whatever "frustration" ensues.

Contracts & Finance – IT Cost Control & Reduction

Once you have a solid inventory of devices, you can then link contract finance data to the asset data. This provides visibility at the asset level to your Maintenance, Warranty, Lease, Support and License agreements. It also allows for cost analysis at a more granular level. At the operational level, more proactive management is introduced to control IT spend such as re-harvesting, re-purposing, and inventory/purchase controls. This layer allows you to control IT spend, optimize purchasing strategies, as well as laying the foundation for Software Compliance Management. This component of the IT Asset Management process is what distinguishes it from a simple inventory system. When Contracts and Finance information is added to the database, you are positioned to manage the assets from initial purchase through decommissioning and disposal.

Software Compliance

Within your Asset Management Process, the Software Compliance layer enables the organization to respond to an audit, control the licensing position, and avoid uncontrolled costs. This layer also enables Software License Management which includes the full capability around purchasing and deployment strategies to actually reduce the overall spend on expensive IT software.

It's not uncommon to find that some amount of the software that has been deployed across the business is unlicensed. This could be as simple as the End User Support team unknowingly building out additional systems beyond the current license agreements, or adding specialty software to user computers without tracking the number of licenses. This behavior can be deadly if you are subjected to a software license compliance audit – which could result from a frustrated employee or ex-employee "turning you in" to the vendor.

The complexity and costs to respond to an unexpected audit not only decreases your negotiating strength with your vendors, but places risk around unforeseen fees to "true up" the license numbers. *As a bit of advice here, this can be one of your organizations greater areas of Risk*. You should complete an annual review of software compliance across your business and "true-up any deficiencies in valid license numbers.

Finally, by allowing system administrators to quickly isolate vulnerabilities, such as illegal/unauthorized software, outdated software, games and unauthorized/malicious downloads, your ITAM system makes it easier to see where potential risks may exist, so they can be prevented before major problems arise

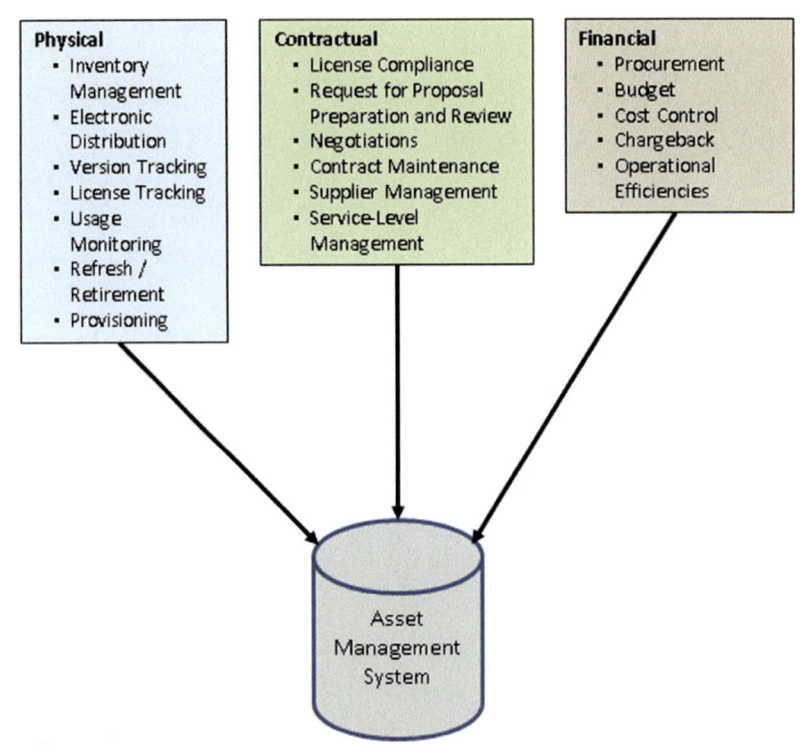

Physical
- Inventory Management
- Electronic Distribution
- Version Tracking
- License Tracking
- Usage Monitoring
- Refresh / Retirement
- Provisioning

Contractual
- License Compliance
- Request for Proposal Preparation and Review
- Negotiations
- Contract Maintenance
- Supplier Management
- Service-Level Management

Financial
- Procurement
- Budget
- Cost Control
- Chargeback
- Operational Efficiencies

Asset Management System

The Three Components of IT Asset Management

How Effective Is Your Company's Asset Management Process?

As mentioned, the quality of the IT Asset Management efforts at different companies is all over the map. There are firms that are doing little to no real IT Asset Management and there are also larger firms that have an entire organization dedicated to the task. Gartner, Inc. created a Maturity Model that defines the various states of IT Asset Management. Once you have located your company's current state of control, you can use this table to decide how far up the Maturity Model you need to take your process. From there you will develop a Roadmap that gets you there.

\multicolumn{3}{c}{**IT Asset Management Maturity Phases**}
Step	**Attributes**	**Goals**
1. Chaotic Uncontrolled environment 30% of enterprises	- No processes, dedicated people or tools - No assigned accountability or accounting for change - Unpredictable services, support, and costs - Purchasing is ad hoc - Unused hardware and software are not controlled - Success depends on quality of people, not processes - Sub-optimization of efforts occurs	- "Just want to know what we own, where it is, and who is using it" - One-time activity rather than systematic process -
2. Reactive Limited accountability 45% of enterprises	- Focus is on asset counting - Employs physical inventory and some auto-discovery recorded on spreadsheets or in a database - Accountability lies with IS organization but there is ineffective change accounting - Hardware and software viewed separately, not as single complex asset	- Perform annual physical inventory and periodic spot audits - Report on asset counts, but cannot produce solid detail data to identify and resolve problems -

IT Asset Management Maturity Phases

Steps	Attributes	Goals
3. Proactive Lifecycle focus 20% of enterprises	• There is an IT Asset Program and manager with a dedicated staff that reports to IS and finance organizations. • ITAM with auto-discovery tools is integrated with service desk • Use of cross-functional teams for major asset management projects • Life cycle management process goes from requisition to deployment, to retirement • Inventory system linked to financial and contractual data	• Clearly defined processes with accountability that detail the practical application of people, processes, and tools that support the ITAM Program • Effective change and configuration management processes • ITAM projects use repeatable processes that are well defined, adhered to, reviewed, and re-engineered when necessary. • ITAM operations manual with asset taxonomy produced and maintained
4. Service Oriented Service level management 5% of enterprises	• Metrics are available to measure program value • Services are delivered according to SLA-based plans • TCO processes in place • Automated requisition is integrated with purchasing and ERP systems • Just in time inventory practices used	• Create SLAs for asset management and use them as a basis for planning • Conduct periodic reviews of service delivery quality • Institute an enterprise technology refresh plan for replacement and retirement of equipment

IT Asset Management Maturity Phases		
Steps	**Attributes**	**Goals**
5. Value Creation Cost recovery < 1% of enterprises	• There is a cost recovery process • Repository, auto-discovery, and asset usage tools all in place • Seamless integration with strategic systems like HR, accounting, ERP, purchasing, network and systems management, IT service desk, problem and change management tools, and business continuity process • Decision support and analytic tools available for mining asset information	• Continuous process improvement with improving metrics • ITAM data used for problem prevention • ITAM is a core business process and business enabler • Measurement of efficiency (employee productivity) and effectiveness (customer satisfaction) of business processes across all IT assets in the enterprise.

What is Your End-State Goal for IT Asset Management?

When determining your ITAM Service end-state goal, consider that some of your requirements may not require a full, robust ITAM implementation. The target must be weighed against the cost of service versus the value it delivers. Building a roadmap to this end state obviously requires that you have a good understanding of where you are today.

To assess your ITAM current state, consider all the dimensions that enable the ITAM building blocks; namely Organization, Process, and Tools. Also consider the landscape across the Asset Classes (Data Center equipment, Network, Desktops, etc.); there are different tools and processes that come into play for each major Asset Class and there may be a significant difference in your current state capabilities for each Asset Class as well.

Planning Your Roadmap

Once you understand the current starting point and targets, create an ITAM roadmap around immediate, short term and long range goals. There are certain aspects of deploying an IT Asset Management solution that must be considered.

Understanding that true Asset Management will require purchasing and contractual information, the solution will cross organizational boundaries. Just within IT, this will impact Help Desk/End User Support, Network, and Application Development. Outside IT the staff in Procurement, Finance, and Contracts (Legal) will benefit from the environment. In order to get the maximum benefit from the system, you will need to understand the current processes in all of these departments and assemble a solution that works for everybody.

Designing a consolidated system that manages both equipment and software inventory and financial, legal and procurement data has additional benefits. One clear benefit is that all activities will now be focused on one single data repository. When this is not true, each of the environments tends to keep its own version of the inventory, leading to obvious differences in data sets.

Here are some additional "Best practices" Items:

- **Good Inventory Practices Start With An Accurate Baseline** - Establish your baseline at the very beginning of the project. An accurate inventory of installed hardware and software forms the foundation of a solid ITAM program. This baseline identifies in ITAM which assets need to be redeployed, reused or retired. Doing a physical baseline is a first necessary step to make sure you have all connected and non-connected IT assets in your repository. Perform an automated inventory first, which you will validate during the physical Inventory. In this fashion, you only need to manually add the items that were not captured during the automated sweep.

- **Go Deep and Then Go Wide** - A winning strategy for companies is the start of an inventory practice around one asset class, such as servers. This way, you can put processes in place to capture and reconcile the detail you need and test the processes through regularly scheduled updates to ensure they are thorough and yield the right results. Once successful, the same processes can be implemented for PCs, network equipment, and detailed software inventory.

- **Have a Process Owner** - Inventory management needs a single process owner who can consider the needs and requirements from all stakeholders and assure accountability throughout the entire process.
- **Ensure Stakeholder Alignment** - Going beyond stakeholders in IT operations, IT Asset Management has stakeholders in contracts, procurement, finance, and compliance. Because each department is involved in discrete parts of the IT Asset Management lifecycle, defining cross-departmental processes upfront helps meet multiple goals.
- **Establish IT Asset Management project milestones** - Implementing IT asset management requires careful coordination between IT and process owners. Best practices call for setting project milestones for process definition, software implementation, integrations, training, testing, and rollout.
- **Set specific operational and financial goals** - Most IT Organizations initiate IT Asset Management projects to gain specific, measurable results in three areas: cost control, risk mitigation and service level improvement. You must set specific operational and financial goals to show incremental progress against each of these. Defining, collecting and communicating a comprehensive set of metrics around IT budget impact assessments, service quality levels and decreased risk of compliance irregularities attributable to the IT Asset Management process will demonstrate the impact.
- **Standardize on hardware configurations and software license titles** –One of the most important themes throughout this book, instituting standardized configurations means selecting fewer hardware configurations and software titles, which enables significant volume purchase leverage and also reduces the burden on the service desk and End User Support.
- **Conduct internal audits** - Regularly review asset management practices to ensure cross-functional processes are supported by automation as much as possible. Document these processes so that you can show proactive resource control in the face of an audit.

Inventory Reconciliation

Another benefit of the automated IT Asset Management system is the asset reconciliation function that most commercial products include. Most simply put, the inventory that is captured in today's sweep is compared to what is in the database. Differences (extra items or missing items) are noted. You now have the opportunity to investigate why there are differences. The most likely causes will be changes to the environment that did not go through the Change Management process, such as software installed on a desktop machine. Whatever the cause, you will have the opportunity to fix the asset inventory and perhaps plug a hole in one of your other processes that caused the discrepancy.

Lifecycle Management

IT Asset Management extends inventory and configuration management by layering in processes that manage each asset throughout its complete lifecycle. For each asset in your environment, there is a beginning (procurement), a middle (moves, adds, changes) and an end (retirement).

Managing the asset lifecycle requires a full appreciation of each of the processes associated with the stages of the lifecycle. These processes can be automated through an integrated system that leverages inventory and configuration management systems.

Summarizing and putting it all together, here are some of the processes that can be automated using a capable Asset Management System:

- **Request Management** - Request Management provides a standardized order and approval process gives users the ability to order equipment and software, using an automated workflow system that embodies the management controls defined for the process.
- **Stock/Inventory Management** - Stock and inventory management provides a centralized ability to check stock across multiple physical locations. This helps reduce the cost of unnecessary purchases by locating existing assets.
- **Asset Reporting and Alerting** – This function provides the ability to generate asset inventory reports, and receive alerts on asset warranty and lease expiration
- **Online Procurement** - Integrated with Request and Stock management, online procurement allows requests that cannot be

- fulfilled through existing inventory to be included in bulk purchase orders.
- **IMACs** - Installs, Moves, Adds and Changes comprise the bulk of day-to-day work in an IT operations organization. Standardizing and automating these processes provide tremendous efficiencies. Recognizing the costs, productivity levels and cycle times associated with various IMAC types can help establish baselines for workload distribution and can also be used for chargeback systems.
- **Software Asset Management** - Software license contracting and utilization is a complex subject. A large percentage of companies do not manage this very effectively. In order to ensure compliance, many IT organizations purchase extra licenses in the event they missed some installs.
- **Contract Management** - Lease and maintenance contract management present considerable opportunities to reduce risk, save money and increase efficiencies. Automating the cycle of lease returns results in reduced fines and the ability to actually locate and return assets on time and in the requisite physical state. With maintenance contracts, systems can ensure that contracts cover only those assets that are actually in production.
- **Financial Management** - Key elements of IT asset financial management include cost center budgeting, service and product pricing, and chargebacks.

IT Asset Management Tools

There are a huge number of available tools that can support part or all of an IT Asset Management program. The hardest part of the selection will be to choose a tool that is the right size for your organization and which can integrate with other software components in your environments. I have seen several efforts where a "do-everything" tool was selected at a cost of millions of dollars but was so complex that it never reached production status – never had any real data or real users. The lesson here is that it is better to get something running and producing value, even if it only supports a piece of your long-term goal. Selecting a product that can be deployed in stages is a good strategy.

If you are running a tiny IT shop with less than 100 PCs, a few servers, and network gear, you're best advised to develop a minimalist type of Asset Management environment. You likely won't have an extensive set of tools to seek out and identify the equipment on the network and your central Database will likely be built in Excel.

As you move up the value chain there are two primary features that you need in an Asset Management Toolset:

- **Auto-Discovery** – The tool must be capable of identifying equipment connected to the network and give an inventory or each piece. Yes, you can do this manually, however the effort required to get someone to every device in the company and log such items as device name, type, make, model, serial number, what software is installed on it, patch levels, etc., and THEN enter all of that into a database will make auto-discovery a dream come true.

- **Integration with Help Desk Ticketing System** – If the Asset Management tool is not already part of the Help Desk Ticketing System, it should flawlessly integrate with it. Your technicians need to be able to look into the user's device setup and history to properly support any calls.

Chapter 11

Risk Management – Understanding What Can Impact or Derail Something You Are Responsible For

With the exception of larger companies, where Risk Management is often an official functional unit within the organization, I have found few, if any, companies that actually manage Risks within the IT organization. This is too bad because taking a proactive approach to Risk Management is possibly the most significant step you can take to improving the availability of the systems as well as the success rate of projects your organization is undertaking.

Exactly what is meant by "Risk Management"?

A "Risk" is defined as "a possible event that can cause harm or loss, or affect the ability to achieve objectives". While there are always many risks and uncertainties, the key challenge is to identify those that will contribute the most uncertainties to the desired outcomes. Risk Management is the systematic process of identifying, analyzing, and responding to risks in our projects and operations.

A Risk has both a cause and if it occurs, consequences which could threaten the success of your activity. The Risk Management Process Consists of six basic components:

- Risk Management Planning
- Risk Identification and Tracking
- Qualitative Risk Analysis
- Quantitative Risk Analysis
- Risk Response Planning (Risk Mitigation)
- Risk Monitoring and Control

In a formal Risk Management environment, the standard way of compiling and tracking Risks is in a database called the "Risk Register". This is relatively simplistic in terms of implementation – it can be as simple as a spreadsheet or a SharePoint Database. More will be said about the Risk Register later.

Before we go too far, let's define some terms that we will be using when we discuss Risk Management:

Incident – An Incident is defined as "Any event which is not part of the standard operation of a service and which causes, or may cause, an interruption to, or a reduction in, the quality of the service". The key differentiation between Incidents and Risks is Incidents are events that have already occurred.

Issue – Issues are problems that have already occurred – Risks are potential problems that have a potential to occur but may not. An Issue, therefore, is a realized Risk. Issue Management can be minimized by effective Risk Management.

Risk – A Risk is defined as "a possible event that can cause harm or loss, or affect the ability to achieve objectives". Risks are potential problems that have the potential to occur but may not.

Risk Register – The Central Repository of Risk Data for your organization or an individual project. This is most effectively implemented as a list in SharePoint and set up in Spreadsheet format. Each Risk occupies one record in the list.

As with a number of items in this book, the depth of the Risk Management Process you implement in your organization will depend on the size and scope of the activities you perform. Whatever the scale of what you are doing, you must include some form of Risk Process in your activities.

Again, what is meant by a Risk? Let's give some real world examples (meaning they actually have happened) for an IT Infrastructure organization. We will use our example of building a new Headquarters Facility for your company.

Here is the setup:

You are responsible for engineering, implementing and integrating all of the technology in this new building. That will consist of a new Server Room where the servers and the core of your network will reside, IDF closets on each floor, a new Trading Floor, where there will be a high density of users, each having a substantial amount of equipment and all of the Audio/Video systems in the building. You must additionally connect this new facility to both your Primary and Disaster Recovery data centers. The relocation of the staff has been broken into three separate move events each separated by only 2 weeks.

What could possibly go wrong??

Let's examine the carnage that will result in this project one step at a timely based on the planned sequence of deliveries:

Delivery of a Functioning Server Room – This is usually the first thing you need to get started. It will be the location where any external circuits are terminated. It is where the Network Core, WAN edge equipment, and local processing resources are located. You are dependent on the facilities group to deliver this room. They have promised it will be delivered on April 1st (yes, I did pick that date because it's a joke that it will come in on time). Here is your first risk:

Risk: The facility group will miss its delivery date for the server room

Impact: The communications circuits are scheduled to be terminated and activated two days after the room turnover date. The room will not be ready for their arrival, so you will need to reschedule the carrier to return at a future date. The carrier cannot come back for two weeks if the termination and activation are rescheduled.

Mitigation Plan: What will you do? You need to come up with a plan on how you will address this situation if it happens. You need to come up with

n when you first start the project, NOT when the Risk turns into an

Also note that in this first example, the Risk was based on a Dependency on something outside of your control.

This is a great hint – Look at the dependencies on your Project Schedule. They will most always become Risks you need to plan for!

Delivery of External Circuits – The next step in a typical project like this is to have the external circuits brought into your building and terminated in your server room. We will assume here that the server room has been turned over to you. What sort of Risks might you encounter here?

Risk	Impact
Cannot get permit to install conduit to manhole	Delay in provisioning circuit
No Point of Entry Sleeves Available	Delay in provisioning Circuit Increased cost of providing building entry
Difficulties installing riser from Point of Entry to Server Room Floor	Delay in provisioning circuit Increased Cost of Provisioning Riser
Circuit delivery delayed by Carrier	Delay in provisioning circuit

Note that in all of these cases there was a delay in delivery of the circuit. This means that any of the subsequent tasks that are dependent on the circuit delivery will be impacted

Beyond these two milestone events, the following are some additional Risks you should plan for in the scenario we described:

- Network Equipment Delivery Delayed
- IDF Closets not turned over to IT two weeks before a move date for that floor (or as scheduled)

- Structured cabling to desks not completed one week before move-in date
- People space not turned over to IT one week before move-in to allow time to place equipment
- Trading Floors are not turned over to IT two weeks before move date
- A/V Systems not installed and tested one week before move-in date
- Equipment damaged or lost during relocation
- Applications not properly tested from new site before relocation (IP subnet dependency issues, etc.)
- Insufficient budget for technicians to relocated equipment (budget risk)
- Freight Elevators break down during relocation weekend
- Insufficient time for decommissioning of vacated space before turnover back to Landlord

I'm sure you can see by now that this isn't really hard.

Risk Management Process

While Risks can be identified in many ways, they are most likely to be self-identified through a project planning process or similar activity on the operations side, as well as through status and project reviews.

It is important to make Risk Management part of everybody's job. When one of your staff members identifies a risk, they can either log it themselves or communicate it to someone with the responsibility for collecting and managing risks.

What Information is required when registering a risk?

- Definition of the Risk
- Scope of the Risk
- Impacted Region or Location
- Impacted organization
- Impact of the Risk
- Probability of Occurrence

- Mitigating Controls and their effectiveness
- Residual Severity (Inherent Severity – Control Effectiveness)
- Urgency in Remediating the Risk

New Risks should be reviewed by the Project Manager for a specific project related risk or the technical department manager for an operational risk.

The Risk Lifecycle

There are five stages of the Risk Lifecycle

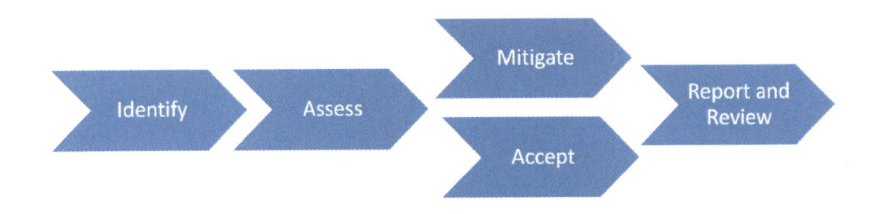

Identify → Assess → Mitigate / Accept → Report and Review

The Five Stages of A Risk Lifecycle

Risk Identification

Risks are identified via multiple sources including audits, project planning, project reviews and operational incidents. The Risk definition should capture the event (such as "Server Room not turned over on time), and not the cause, the failure of a control or the effect of the risk. The Risk should map into one of the Risk Categories that is defined.

Risk Categories

Risks are categorized into groups that define what aspect of a project or the business will be impacted if the risk is realized into an issue. The following are the typical categories that Risks in an Infrastructure environment will be mapped into:

Summary of Risk Categories	
Category	Potential Risks
Business Risks	<ul><li>Decision Risk (Timing)</li><li>Requirements Scope Creep</li><li>Changing Market Pressures</li><li>Reputational Risks</li><li>Loss of Life or Property</li><li>Litigation</li></ul>
Schedule Risks	<ul><li>Unrealistic Schedule</li><li>Inadequate Schedule Estimates</li><li>Excessive Time to Market</li><li>Exiting of Existing Facilities</li></ul>

Summary of Risk Categories (cont.)	
Category	**Potential Risks**
Operational Risks	- Not Meeting All required Functionality - Not Meeting MTTF/MTTR - Inadequate Operational Monitoring - Failure of BCP Under Disaster Recovery Support for A-B Synchronization - Utility and Backup System Failures - Security Failures
Financial Risks	- Cost Overruns - Lease Terms / Exit Strategy - Valuation of Existing Assets

Summary of Risk Categories (cont.)	
Category	Potential Risks
Resource Risks	<ul><li>Inadequate Staffing</li><li>Inadequately Trained Staff</li><li>Inadequate Staff Productivity</li><li>Inadequate Tools</li></ul>
Vendor Risks	<ul><li>Cost Overrun</li><li>Inadequate Cost Estimates</li><li>Financial Viability</li><li>Decision Risks</li></ul>
Design Risks	<ul><li>Vendor/Client Disagreements</li><li>Inadequate Cost Estimates</li><li>Financial Viability</li><li>Decision Risks</li></ul>
Technology Risks	<ul><li>Changes in Technology</li><li>Unproven Designs</li></ul>

Risk Assessment

Risks are assessed (or analyzed) to evaluate the potential scope of the risk, the likelihood of occurrence and the potential impact

- The first step is to assess the Risk Impact, using the information in the Risk Impact section, which describes the Risk Business and Project Impact Level Descriptions
- The Second Step is to determine the Likelihood of Occurrence for the risk
- The third step is to generate a Risk Summary Status using the Impact and Likelihood data
    - Critical Risks require immediate attention and escalation to Senior Management, as there is a risk of loss that is perceived to be both likely and significant in terms of impact to the business.
    - High Risks require review and escalation to determine the appropriate course of action, as incident or accumulation of incidents are perceived to be sufficiently probable or sufficiently serious that some negative impact on the business is anticipated without remediation.
    - Moderate risks should be monitored and mitigation or remediation strategies considered, but an incident or accumulation of incidents are considered possible (not probable) or generally are expected to have only a limited impact on the business
    - Low risks are considered minimal such that, under existing controls, an incident or accumulation of incidents is not expected to be so frequent or significant so as to have an impact on the business.

Determining the Impact Level

Determining the impact of a risk depends on two factors (1) The type of risk with associated potential impacts to the business or project and (2) The impact level- which can range from minimal to no impact up to critical impact that must be addressed immediately. The following tables define the impact level criteria for the various categories of Risks:

Risk Type	Risk Description
Business	Business Risks may include Requirements Scope Creep, Reputational Risk, Loss of Life or Property, potential Litigation Risks and Changing Market Pressures
Financial	A Risk that can materially impact the project budget, the long-term operational costs of IT or alternately cause a significant business loss
Scope	A Risk that can have a significant impact on the project Scope or business operations, such as preventing the production startup of a facility, or potentially preventing exiting from a current facility prior to lease expiration
Schedule	A Risk that can have a significant impact on the project schedule or business operations, such as preventing the production startup of a facility, or potentially prevent exiting from a current facility prior to lease expiration

Risk Type	Risk Description
Vendor	Vendor Risks can include the ability to deliver products or services, financial viability, key employee risks, etc.
Design	A Design related issue or risk that can prevent the production startup of the facility, nullifies some basic design considerations or assumptions driving the justification of the project or prevents exiting a current facility according to the planned schedule. This type of risk can include Vendor/Client disagreements and Decision Risks.
Migration	A Migration related issue or Risk that has the potential to impact achieving the goals of the project, including financial, technology, schedule, etc.
Operational	An Operational related issue or Risk that has the potential to impact achieving the goals of the project, including financial, technology, schedule, etc.
Resources	A Resource related issue or Risk that has the potential to impact achieving the goals of the project, including financial, technology, schedule, etc. This type of risk can include inadequate staffing, inadequately trained staff, lower than planned productivity or lack of appropriate tools.

Impact Level	Impact Description
1	Considered minimal such that, under existing controls, an incident or accumulation of incidents is not expected to be so frequent or significant so as to have an impact on the business
2	Considered possible (not Probable) or generally are expected to have only a limited impact on the business. Should be Monitored and mitigation ore remediation strategies defined
3	Requires review and escalation to determine the appropriate course of action. It is perceived to be sufficiently serious that some negative impact on the business is anticipated without remediation.
4	A Risk that can prevent the production startup of the facility or materially impact the business and requires immediate Senior Management attention

The Risk Summary Status Matrix

As we discussed, the Summary Status of a Risk is defined as a combination of the Impact of the risk and the Likelihood that it will occur. The combination of these elements is mapped into the following matrix, where the Summary Status, or Severity, is defined.

		Impact			
		1 = Low	2 = Moderate	3 = High	4 = Critical
Likelihood	4 = Sure to Happen	A Risk which is sure to happen that can impact one or more aspects of the program, but which can be mitigated relatively easily	A Risk which is sure to happen, that may cause us to miss or temporarily miss one of the overall goals of the program	A Risk which is sure to happen that can cause significant miss of the project goals, or seriously impact the business	A Risk which is sure to happen that can materially impact the project or the business and requires immediate senior management attention
	3 = Likely	A Risk which is Likely to happen that can impact one or more aspects of the program, but which can be mitigated relatively easily	A Risk which is likely to happen, that may cause us to miss or temporarily miss one of the overall goals of the program	A Risk which is likely to happen that can cause significant miss of the project goals, or seriously impact the business	A Risk which is likely to happen that can materially impact the project or the business and requires immediate senior management attention
	2 = Possible	A Risk which is possible that can impact one or more aspects of the program, but which can be mitigated relatively easily	A Risk which is possible, that may cause us to miss or temporarily miss one of the overall goals of the program	A Risk which is possible that can cause significant miss of the project goals, or seriously impact the business	A Risk which is possible that can materially impact the project or the business and requires immediate senior management attention
	1 = Unlikely	A Risk which is identified but unlikely to happen that can impact one or more aspects of the program, but which can be mitigated relatively easily	A Risk which is identified but unlikely to happen, that may cause us to miss or temporarily miss one of the overall goals of the program	A Risk which is identified but unlikely to happen that can cause significant miss of the project goals, or seriously impact the business	A Risk which is identified but unlikely to happen that can materially impact the project or the business and requires immediate senior management attention

Red Blocks = Critical Risks

Orange Blocks = High Risks

Yellow Blocks = Moderate Risks

White Blocks = Low Risks

Risk Mitigation

If it is possible to put action plans in place to mitigate a risk, it should be done. The mitigation plan should be summarized in the Risk Register (in the field remarkably called "The Mitigation Plan")

When developing a mitigation plan, the following should be considered:

- The timing of the risk and the necessary mitigation activities. How quickly must the team respond to the risk to address it with the mitigation plans?
- Whether there will be any residual risks still to contend with after the Mitigation Plan is put into place. If there is, what is the severity of the residual risk?

Residual Risk Severity

Often, the Risk Mitigation Plan will not result in a zero impact outcome. The Risk Mitigation Plan will address some (hopefully most) but not all of the consequences of the Risk. What is left behind is called the "Residual Risk Severity". Residual Risk Severity is calculated by taking the strength and effectiveness of the mitigating controls into consideration when assessing Risk Impact and Risk Likelihood (Risk Impact Analysis). The controls (Risk Mitigation Plan) are defined as processes and procedures which are put in place to effectively manage or mitigate Risk. If these controls do not completely mitigate the impact, the remaining impact is the Residual Risk Severity.

Mitigation / Remediation Activity

- Where action plans have been identified, prioritized and agreed with relevant parties, these action plans will be stored in the Risk Register with progress monitored and reported in standard mechanisms.
- When action plans can be identified to remediate the risk, a value proposition should be created to help secure funding for the remediation effort.

Risk Acceptance

If a risk cannot be mitigated, or if the severity of a risk is not in line with the cost of mitigation, that risk must be "Accepted" by the management of the organization. Basically, this means that either there is nothing we can do to mitigate the Risk or we don't want to spend the money required to control it. In essence, we are going to take our chances this will not occur. In these cases, the Risks are documented centrally in the Risk Register and presented to management, governance committees and impacted business areas for acceptance.

The risk severity, impact, and type will typically determine the signoffs required for risk acceptance

- Technology Policy Exceptions, Critical and High Technology Operational Risks and Technology Supplier Risks are reviewed by Senior IT Management
- Moderate and Low Operational Risks that have impact on their associated Business Units are signed off by senior Technology group management
- Budgetary Impacts need the appropriate IT and Senior Management to be informed of the situation and get their concurrence.

Information Security Risks

Information Security Risks cannot be taken lightly. Depending on the size of your company and the organizational structure of the Information Security function your course of action when an Information Security Risk is discovered will vary.

In order to accept an Information Security Risk, there must be a serious evaluation of the Risk by senior Information Security personnel. If you don't have such people in house, you should engage the appropriate consulting resources to evaluate the risk.

One of two courses of action must be taken:

- After the risk has been completely evaluated, a plan must be defined to remediate the risk within a reasonable amount of time. The divisional CIO MUST support the plan, its funding, and the Risk during the specified period.

OR

- The divisional CIO must explicitly request a permanent acceptance of the risk if he/she is unwilling to fund the remediation AND any impacted business unit must also accept the Risk. Both the CIO and Business Unit approvals must be received in writing.

Risk Documentation

The Risk Register is the single repository for Risks. The Risks should all have remediation plans, which will also be managed within the risk register. Tracking of the risk progress will occur within this environment.

When you are developing the entry of a Risk for the Risk Register, the following information should be collected:

- Workstream and Workstream lead manager details
- Risk Description – a statement of fact about the risk
- Risk Category
- Business or Project Impact
- Impact and Likelihood
- Risk Mitigating Controls or Actions
- Costs should be provided for any proposed mitigating activities, with associated benefits specified
- Rational for Acceptance of the Risk, if it will be accepted as opposed to mitigated
- Cost, time, technical limitations or restrictions
- Stakeholder details

Tracking Risk In The Risk Register

Risk Categories
- Business Risks
- Financial Risks
- Schedule Risks
- Resource Risks
- Site Selection
- Design Risks
- Vendor Risks
- Operational Risks
- Technology Risks

Risk Register Components
1. Name and Description
2. Date Created
3. Current Status
4. Detailed Risk Description
5. Estimated Probability of Occurrence
6. Estimated Impact / Consequences
7. Risk level
8. Planned Mitigation Actions

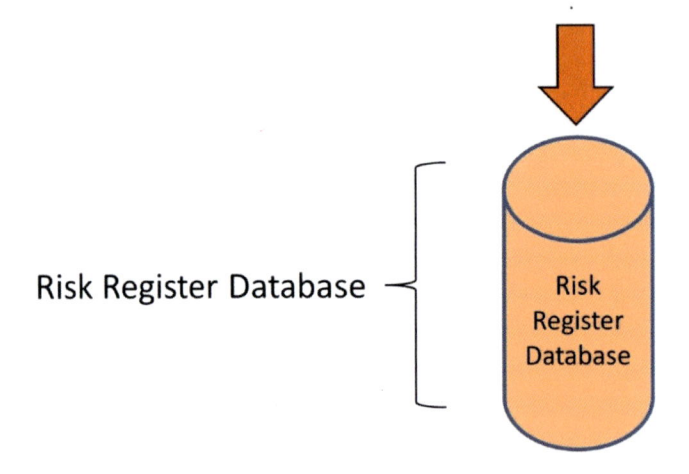

Risk Register Database

Risk Reporting and Review

Risk reviews and status reporting will depend on the timing of the project and the risks. Critical, High, and Moderate risks should be reviewed often, either bi-weekly or monthly. Low risks can be reviewed monthly, quarterly or after a significant operating environment change.

Risk Status – one of the fields within the Risk Register is Risk Status. This defines the state of the risk and can be either:

- Being Assessed – A risk has been reported and is being tracked, however, no mitigation plan has been developed and the risk has not been accepted. This is the initial stage of the Risk.
- Open – Actions are underway to mitigate the risk. Action Plans will be formally tracked in the Risk Register for risk mitigation activity.
- Closed – the risk is no longer in existence. Risk Acceptance is mandatory when the risk being closed has an associated Residual Severity.
    - A Risk item can be closed without "Acceptance" only when the Residual Severity is zero or minimal
    - Residual Impact and Residual Frequency are mandatory fields when closing risks
- Accepted – the Risk is open with no actions underway. These risks may remain open for a significant period of time.

Risk Reporting Process

Communications of IT Risks to management and other stakeholders should occur on a scheduled basis

- Critical, High, and Moderate accepted risks are reported on a weekly basis as part of the management dashboard
- Accepted risks are recorded centrally and reviewed by management, if appropriate, as follows:
    - Critical Risks should be reviewed monthly when there is no active remediation effort in flight
    - Critical, High, and Moderate risks should be reviewed monthly and when the operating environment changes occur that could result in impact or frequency

- - Low risks should be reviewed quarterly and when operating environment changes occur that could result in impact or frequency changes
- Critical, High and Moderate risks are included in monthly company Risk reports

The following charts provide typical Risk Reporting slides that can be included in weekly management reports.

The classic four quadrant Executive Summary on the next page defines a matrix that includes listings of each type of Risk, the quantity of that Risk, as well as accomplishments (mitigation accomplishments) status of critical Risks and Actions (mitigation activities) planned for the next reporting cycle.

Headquarters Relocation — Executive Summary High-Level Risks

March 2016

	This Period		Likelihood				Impact			Sum Probability
	New	Closed	Total	Critical	High	Medium	Low	Critical	High	Medium	Low	X Impact Items
Business				0	1	0	1	1	0	1	0	
Financial				1	0	3	4	1	2	3	2	
Scope				0	0	0	0	1	0	0	0	
Schedule				2	5	4	3	3	6	4	1	
Vendor				0	0	0	0	0	0	0	0	
Design				0	1	0	0	0	1	0	0	
Migration				1	0	0	0	0	0	0	0	
Operational				0	0	1	0	1	0	1	1	
Resource				0	0	2	1	0	1	2	0	
Technology				0	0	0	0	0	0	0	0	
Total				4	7	10	10	5	12	10	4	

Critical Risks and Issues

1. **Risk 1**- xxxxxxxxxxxxxxxxxxxxxxxxxxxxxxxxxxxx alkjdlaksdjlkjslkjsaljsldjlsjdlsjljsalksjdlksjljs
2. **Risk 2** – yyyyyyyyyyyyyyyyyyyyyyyyyyyyyyyyy lakdkad;ksalksa;dlka;slkd;laksd;lkassd;lks;kd
3. **Risk 3** – zzzzzzzzzzzzzzzzzzzzzzzzzzzzz akjd;ka;sdk;ksadljeouwrjerjfrpewfoncnen

Accomplishments Last Cycle

1. **Accomplishment 1**- xxxxxxxxxxxxxxxxxxxxxxxxx alkjdlaksdjlkjslkjsaljsldjlsjdlsjljsalksjdlksjljs
2. **Accomplishment 2** – yyyyyyyyyyyyyyyyyyyyyyy lakdkad;ksalksa;dlka;slkd;laksd;lkassd;lks;kd
3. **Accomplishment 3** – zzzzzzzzzzzzzzzzzzzzzzzzz akjd;ka;sdk;ksadljeouwrjerjfrpewfoncnen

Actions Planned Next Cycle

1. **Action 1** - xxxxxxxxxxxxxxxxxxxxxxxxxxxxxxxxxxxx alkjdlaksdjlkjslkjsaljsldjlsjdlsjljsalksjdlksjljs
2. **Action 2** – yyyyyyyyyyyyyyyyyyyyyyyyyyyyyyyyy lakdkad;ksalksa;dlka;slkd;laksd;lkassd;lks;kd
3. **Action 3** – zzzzzzzzzzzzzzzzzzzzzzzzzzzzzzzzz akjd;ka;sdk;ksadljeouwrjerjfrpewfoncnen

This second Risk reporting chart provides a more focused view of Project Risks and drills further down into the specific profile of each specific Risk, including a summary of the business impact and mitigation plan for each.

The second table on this page articulates decisions that are open or in-process and the impact of not making those decisions. There will be one of this page for each major project you are reporting on.

Project Risks / Required Decisions — March 2, 2016

Top 10 Risks

Risk Description	Logged Date	Severity	Risk Type	Horizon	Business Impact	Owner	Mitigation Plan
Construction of the Server Room delayed	11/25	4	Schedule	3-6 M	Potential delay of Relocation	Facilities	Move IT into unfinished space
Stable power in the Server Room and IDFs	11/25	4	Schedule	3-6 M	Inability to keep site running	Facilities	Provide Local UPS
32nd floor technology on 31	11/25	4	Schedule	3-6 M	Inability to support traders	Facilities/IT	Keep 31
Video/Audio Conferencing for early moves	12/1	2	Business	3-6 M	Insufficient Video Conf. capabilities	Facilities/IT	Purchase additional systems

| Describe The Risk / Title | Date First Added | Critical High Moderate Low | Design Financial Schedule Vendor | 0-3 Months 3-6 Months 6-12 Months Over 1 Year | Describe what happens if this risk becomes an issue (actually happens) to the project or the business | Architects Construction IT Real Estate | What are we doing to make sure this doesn't happen or what if it does happen |

Required Decisions

Decision Description	Logged Date	Severity	Decider (Name)	Required By (Date)	Project or Business Impact	Owner of Impact
Wireless Video Distribution in CRs	11/18	Low	Rich B.	ASAP	Desire to have improved Video Dist is Delayed	Sean W
IP TV Technology Decision	12/1	Low	Rich B.	ASAP	Requirement to support TV on Trading Floor At Risk	Sean W

| Describe The Risk / Title | Date First Added | Critical High Moderate Low | Who needs to make this Decision? | Date where no decision becomes a problem | Describe what happens if this decision is not made or is delayed | Who is waiting for this decision to be made | What are we doing to make sure this doesn't happen or what if it does happen |

150

This final chart was developed to describe how the impact of a Risk will change over time. In the early stages of a Risk the impact was moderate, however, if the Risk was not addressed, the impact becomes high or even critical over time. The message here (and to the recipients of this report) is to address the Risk as early as possible.

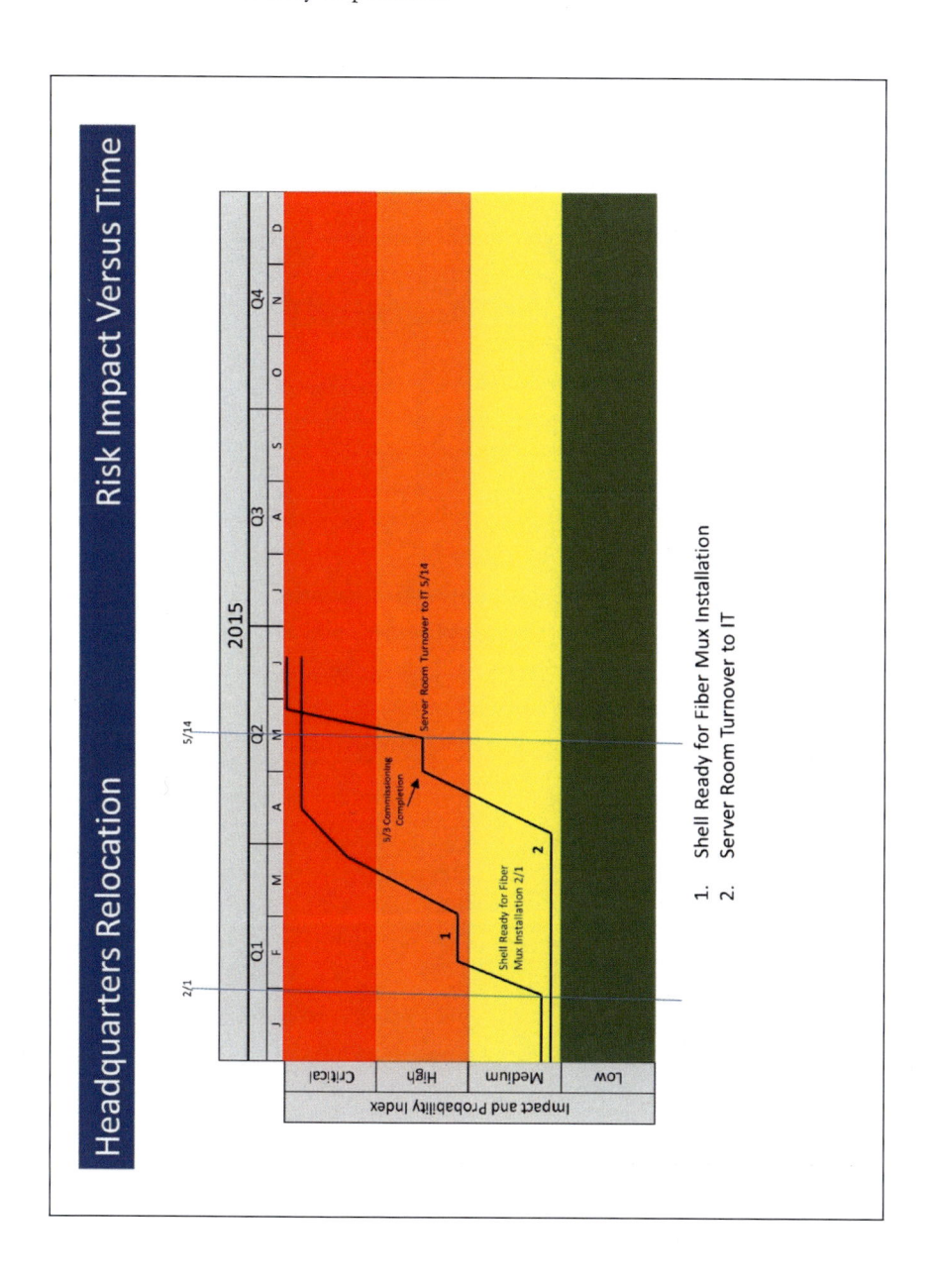

Chapter 12

Project Management

As an IT manager, you will oversee a number of individual initiatives or projects. In some cases, these will be exclusively or almost exclusively an IT initiative, such as rolling out a refresh to a desktop image or upgrading PCs in mass. In other instances, IT will be a component of a much larger initiative, such as building and equipping a new headquarters or another facility.

If you're running an Infrastructure of any size, you will assign a member of your team, or possibly you will bring in a resource with the specific skills, to lead a project initiative. That person will be your Project Manager.

What Should Your Project Manager Be Like?

This role will be exceptionally critical to your success so choose carefully. What characteristics should you focus on?

- Your Project manager must be exceptionally organized, passionate about the project and goal-oriented.
- Project Managers are by definition change agents that are to a large extent driven by the challenge of reshaping the business in such a way to seriously improve results. You should look for someone whose

nature is to identify how the business and technology can be improved.

- Managing a project is a high-pressure and high-stress role, so be sure the person you select can demonstrably work well under pressure. You just cannot afford to have someone in that role that cracks under pressure and reverts to a blame everybody management philosophy.

- Projects often suffer from changes to scope and schedule from the very top of the company. You need to select someone that can be agile and effective during these redefinition events. In addition, they should be capable of articulating the impact of the change to the project minimally in terms of cost and schedule.

- Much of the work that a Project Manager is responsible for involves interaction with the project team members (and the managers of the organizations that those resources come from), vendors, project stakeholders, the project sponsors and the eventual users. To be successful, your Project Manager must have a well-cultivated set of people skills.

- Your successful Project Manager must have developed the ability to unwind a complex project into a series of independent activities or workstreams and then into tasks and sub-tasks that constitute those larger pieces of work. He/She must understand how to monitor and control those individual tasks to ensure success at a higher level and most importantly understand when it is necessary to adapt their techniques for different types of projects.

- A person that manages a number of projects that are all associated or related in some fashion is referred to as the Program Manager. A portfolio manager is responsible for selection, prioritization, and alignment of projects and programs with an organization's strategy.

Project Management Responsibilities	
Project Phase	**Activity**
Project Initiation	Strategic Influencing
	Business Partnering
	Planning and Defining Scope
	Developing and Getting Signoff for the Project Charter
Planning	Final approval of the design specification.
	Activity Planning and Sequencing
	Developing and maintaining a detailed project plan.
	Time Estimating
	Cost Estimating
	Developing Task Lists and Schedules
	Developing a Budget
	Developing A Communications Strategy and Plan
	Initial Risk Analysis
Organizing	Determine the organizational structure of the project team
	Identify roles and positions
	Resource Planning
	Identify services to be provided by external companies
	Recruiting project staff and consultants.
	Identifying and Managing Dependencies
Leading	Overall Team Leadership
	Resolving cross-functional issues at the project level.
	Managing project deliverables in line with the project plan.
	Managing Risks and Issues
	Monitoring and Reporting Progress
	Managing project evaluation and dissemination activities.
	Managing consultancy input within the defined budget.
	Working with Vendors

| Project Management Responsibilities ||
Project Phase	Activity
Controlling	Controlling Quality
	Working closely with users to ensure the project meets business needs.
	Definition and management of the User Acceptance Testing program.
	Managing project scope and change control and escalating issues where necessary.
	Monitoring project progress and performance.
	Providing status reports to the project sponsor.
	Liaises with, and updates progress to the project board/senior management.
	Identifying user training needs and devising and managing user training programs.
	Managing project training within the defined budget.

Project Initiation (getting it correct up front)

The eventual fate of a project is very often determined by how well the project is defined and scoped in the earliest phase of activities. If not done right, this can come down to "what I said – what you heard" types of situations. The best way to avoid misunderstandings and the chaos they bring is to always have a written definition of the project, its goals, expectations, limitations, required timeframes, software and hardware components (if any) and so on. This document should be agreed to by both the appropriate manager in IT and the Project Sponsor. That agreement should be in writing, ideally as a signature on the last page of the project specification (or charter, as we will soon discuss).

You will find you are at greater risk when significant portions of the project are outside of your direct control. This makes the definition of roles and responsibilities on a project even more important. Where your work is dependent on something that someone else is responsible for, you must define that dependency as well as the date that that dependency impacts what you are doing. Recognize that YOU will be at risk if the project goes off the rails – even if you are not the cause.

Here is a great example:

A business user, such as Finance, wants to move to a new financial application. You, as the infrastructure manager, are responsible for delivering the entire environment to them, server, storage, network, application installation, and any client-side pieces. Unfortunately, the project was poorly defined on day 1. The net results are changes to the requirements, schedule delays and increased costs both on the capital equipment side and also for extensions to consulting engagements. User trials are delayed and when they eventually happen it becomes clear that the environment would not deliver the required functionality in its current form and configuration. The project is canceled; however, a huge amount of money has been spent. The business attributes this result to the failure of IT (that would be you) to deliver the environment on schedule in a form that met the goals of the project.

Ouch! How did this happen? Was it really YOUR fault? How can you address this?

I cannot emphasize enough the need to have a paper trail for virtually everything you do. In the example above the failure will immediately slip into the "blame IT" storyline, one that every IT manager knows well.

The mistakes that occurred on this project include:

- Not defining exactly what was asked for by the business and what you would be providing and getting documented agreement from both sides
- Accepting the functional change requests from the business without communicating back to them what the impact of those changes would be to the schedule and cost of the project
- Another likely error was not engaging the software vendor tightly into the design and implementation process. If that had been done they most likely would have picked up any disconnect between the requirements (and the changes to the requirements) and the environment being deployed.
- Not engaging the user base for this application early in the process to ensure that what is being built is aligned with what they need.

Frankly, every IT manager will get burned during their career with a bad project that sticks to him or her. What you need to do is to ensure that you communicate extensively with the other project team members and the stakeholders to minimize the chances of a project going bad AND make certain that you have a comprehensive paper trail of everything you said and everything you did. If you can point to the reporting you did to the world and the warnings you gave about risks turning into unmitigated issues, you will at least come out of it as a competent individual.

Warning Will Robinson!!!

I have an important warning for you here! Take this seriously for sure!!! You will undoubtedly cross paths with other managers on your project teams that will insist:

"We don't need to bury each other in paper, let's handle things face to face, talking to each other. More talking and fewer EMAILs. That's the best way to develop a strong team working relationship."

Hear the alarm bells go off, hear them loud, watch for warning flares because this guy is setting you up to take whatever fall there may be coming. Never, ever, ever believe someone that tells you this and always interpret his or her words as proof positive that the person is a political game player. At this point, document everything, including every discussion you have with him or her in a meeting, in the hallway or on a street corner, because you're gonna need it. Also, consider copying the next level up in management on at least the more important communications. Finally, think through everything you say to this person; they will surely attempt to twist your every word to his or her advantage.

For projects that span organizations there are a few pieces of collateral material that are essential to create:

- Project Charter
- Communications Plan
- Project Schedule
- Project Budget
- Weekly Reporting Dashboard

The Project Charter

Possibly the most important document for larger cross-functional projects is the **Project Charter**. This document defines:

- What the Project is
- Why the Project is being done
- Who is (what groups are) participating in the Project
- Some Project Parameters (size, scope, number of users, locations served, etc.)
- What the major milestones are
- What the budget is for the Project

The Project Charter is signed-off on by the leads of the major participating organizations. In the example above it would be Finance and IT. In addition, the IT manager in the example above should have communicated the consequences of any changes, such as the change to the requirements. A simple note that informed all of the stakeholders that all future milestones would be pushed day for day, by whatever delays are incurred in the finalization of the requirements, and that there would be cost consequences, would have at a minimum, provided some protection from being wrongly accused.

The Project Justification

The simplest way to describe the Project Justification is that it is the project's business case. This actually can be considered part of the Project Charter. The justification typically has a few parts to it:

- The business reason for completing this project
- The cost of the project
- The project schedule (or major milestone dates)
- The benefits of the project – both financial and functional
- The impact on the company if this project is not done

Although there are companies that don't go through this chartering and justification process, it is valuable to complete in all but the smallest projects.

The process itself helps clarify your thinking about what you are trying to achieve and whether it is really worth the effort.

The Business Reason for a Project – The Project Justification

Justifying projects in IT is a bit different than in some other business groups. Projects can be spawned from a number of different sources for many different reasons:

- A major Infrastructure environment, such as Cisco network gear or a large centralized storage system may have reached the end of manufacturer support, requiring an upgrade
- Increased user load may require systems to be scaled up or replaced
- A request may come from a Business Unit to upgrade or replace a major application system
- A company-wide upgrade of a standardized platform (such as Windows) or application (such as Office) may be required or desired

I think you get the picture. When you are building this project justification you will naturally be forced to utilize best estimates for much of the information. Cost and schedule are good examples. From a cost standpoint, you may (and hopefully, do) have solid quotations for the big purchases (in our Cisco gear upgrade, as an example, you should have a solid quote from Cisco or a Cisco Integrator). On the other hand, you may have preliminary estimates on the schedule, resource requirements, the cost of other parts of the project, etc. That's OK at this point. When creating the project justification, I am always conservative in my estimates. From a schedule standpoint, I would use the longest estimates. From a cost standpoint, I would use the highest cost. If you feel uncomfortable doing that, you can give a range that represents the most optimistic to the most conservative.

The benefit to the organization is usually a bit tricky. I have seen lots of justifications where the benefit is defined as "this will save 15 minutes of time per employee per day". OK, that's great, but what does that mean to the company? These people aren't going to get paid for 15 minutes less time and it's unlikely that this will result in a reduction in headcount, so this becomes a big "so what?"

Well, if that same 15 minutes of less time means that a customer gets an answer 15 minutes sooner, resulting in a projection of closing a predictable increase in deals, OR, that a customer service agent can support 10% more call volume, now you have something that management can get excited about.

Going back to our Cisco upgrade example, if the reason that you need to upgrade the Cisco environment is because support for the current environment is no longer available, your justification would be the end of security fixes and updates, exposing the company to a data breach, or potential for extended periods of downtime, resulting from outages that the manufacturer won't support.

Justifications always work best when they are framed in dollars.

- "The business estimates this workflow automation will increase deal closure by 10% which will result in between $10 million and $20 million dollars of additional revenue per quarter."
- "This project will reduce our business error rate by 15%, which currently represents losses of $5 million per year"
- "Without this upgrade, our systems will be exposed to an external data breach. Our research has shown that data breaches for similar size companies in our industry typically cost in excess of $20 million to fix, and would result in our needing to upgrade the equipment anyway."

The final part of the justification is the impact to the company if the project is not done. The data breach example pretty much has the benefit and impact in that one statement, however, for some of the others, you may need to look to the broader industry for the answer.

- For the deal closure example – "We have seen that our direct competition (companies A & B) are currently ahead of us in automating their workflow and will capture some of our market share if this is not done"
- For the business error rate example – "We've charted our error rates and they have been growing by 10% per year, due to increased reliance on this business function. If we don't complete this project, we will reach $10 million dollars in losses annually within X-years."

The justification can be framed around a number of different business benefits. Here are some of the categories you should consider when developing yours:

- Strategic Match – The project aligns with the business strategic goals

- Competitive Advantage - The investment will provide a strategic advantage to the company. You also can define how significant it is in measurable terms

- Management Information – The project gives management more visibility into the organization and control over it. Again, this must be framed in resulting dollars, market share increases, avoidance of losses, etc.

- Strategic Architecture – How well does it align with the IT standards, policies and enterprise architecture? Your IT upgrades will fall into this general class – likely driven by policies for ensuring the network security is ensured through timely application of updates and patches.

High Level Project Risk Assessment

A component of the Project Charter will be the results of a high-level risk assessment. At the very beginning of the project, this can obviously only touch on macro-level items. Here are the types of questions you should answer:

- How capable is the organization to carry out the project?
- Scope Risk – Is there a risk that the project is not sufficiently well-defined and that all of the costs and resulting benefits have been assessed?
- Technology Risk – Is the company prepared technically to utilize the resulting technology from this project? Is the technology being deployed sufficiently mature that it will operate as advertised? Will the new technology properly integrate with the current systems?
- Vendor Risk – Is the vendor financial stable? Does the vendor have a significant share of the market for this product? Can the vendor identify sufficient reference accounts and deployments to provide the confidence they can successfully implement the technology in your company? Does the vendor have a history of meeting delivery and implementation schedules?
- Schedule Risk – Is enough known about the requirements and various components and workstreams of the project implementation to provide a high-level of confidence in the schedule that has been referenced in the Project Charter? Do any of the risks that have been identified have the potential to derail the schedule?

I don't like giving either time or cost estimates until I have had the opportunity to fully assess the complexity of the project. Here are some reasons why:

- I won't know the answer to time, cost and risk questions until I'm in a position to develop a work breakdown structure that goes at least three layers deep.

- I'd rather not provide a SWAG (scientific wild-ass guess) because of the rule of corporate numbers, which states that any number uttered within the distance of anyone else's hearing is immediately chiseled into a slab of granite, there to be enshrined forever as an absolute commitment.

- I also need to know whether my estimate should include or exclude an allowance for contingencies.

Project Planning

We've talked through the concept of a Project Charter, what it is, why it is needed and how you will go about creating one. Let's assume at this point you created a Project Charter and have been SO incredibly successful with it that the project is now approved and you are moving forward.

I spent a good amount of time looking at the literature out there online that focuses on project planning and frankly came away shaking my head. Like so many subjects we are covering in this book, if you strip away the information on project planning available online that are really nothing more than a thinly veiled sales pitches for a particular tool, there are only a few basic articles on project planning whose content is copied over and over again.

So what do we mean by Project Planning here? This is the real meat and potatoes segment of a project where you structure everything that will be done. The components you need to focus on are:

- *Schedule* – This part I will best describe as a compilation of tasks and milestones that you will arrange in the proper time sequence, along with connected dependencies.
- *Resource Plan* – This defines the resources that you will be using on your project and the percentage of their time that they will spend

devoted to this project specifically. The goal here is to ensure (1) that you have the necessary resources identified and (2) that you do not commit the resources to more than 100% of their available time.

- *Budget* – We talked about this previously. This defines the actual funding you will receive for the project. It's your job to either meet this budget or come in under budget
- *Risk Assessment* – A review of the Risks that can derail your project and how you plan to address them. There is an entire section on Risk assessment and management in this book.
- *Project Communications Plan* – This defines how you will be communicating to the world about your project.

These four components will provide you with the tools you need to manage a project successfully. Notice I wasn't prescriptive (yet) about how any of these items will be created and managed. That's because there are just so many tools available to address these areas. As an example, if you're in a small company running a small to medium size project then you may manage everything start to finish using a combination of Microsoft Project, Excel and Word. On the other hand, if you work in a giant bank, you may be using Enterprise Class Project Management tools that are designed to integrate the status of all projects into management reports. I will not be spending any time on the latter, as you would most likely receive specialized training at your place of employment.

I also want to point out that, although I recommend that you have all four of these pieces in place for your projects, that's not a requirement. For very small projects, or projects completely bound within your group, a Project Communication Plan may be overkill.

The Project Schedule

The project schedule is basically a compilation of tasks and milestones that get you from the start of the project to completion. You should try to make this initial version as comprehensive as possible. To produce this schedule you will need to collect information from every group that is participating. As an example, if you are planning to build a new office and move the staff, you will need information from facilities, the network team, the systems team, and end user support at a minimum.

In each case, you will need to have a list of each group's activities or tasks to complete the effort, as well as the duration of each task, the resources needed to complete it, any costs associated with the task (exclusive of internal resources), any dependencies and any risks.

Taking our example of a new office buildout and migration, the network component of that schedule might look something like the diagram, shown on the next page, in a simplified form:

In this example, the block diamonds are the Milestones, The blue lines are the task durations and the green arrow depicts that the Integration and testing phase of the project is dependent on the completion of Provisioning Services on the Circuits.

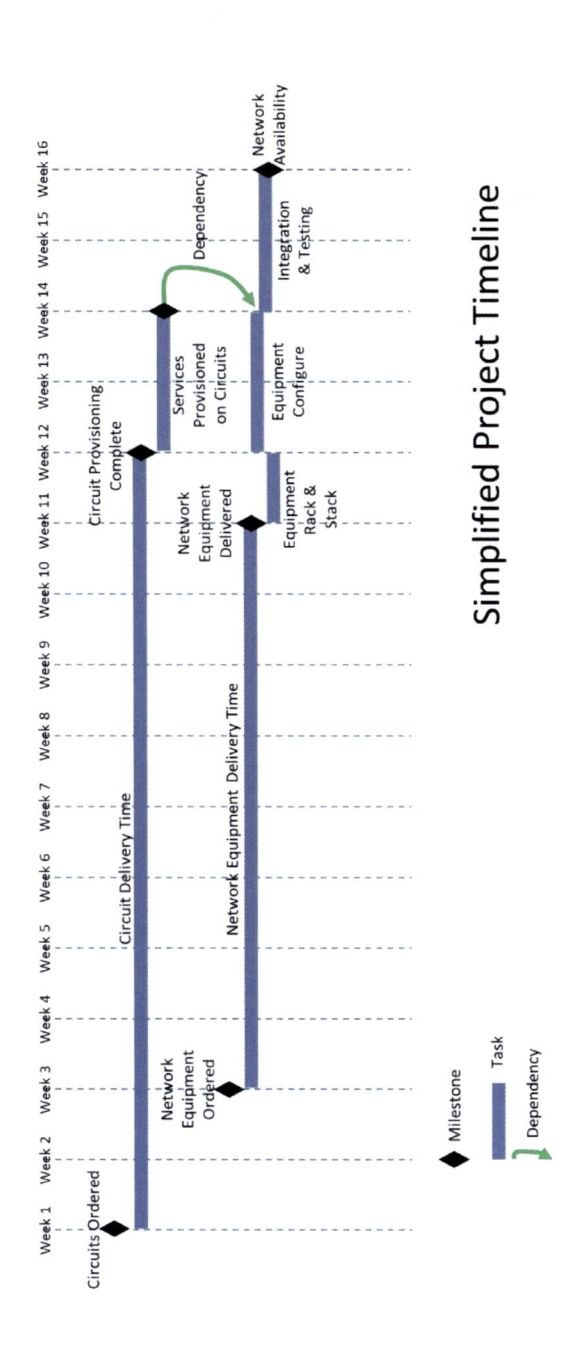

Chapter 13

Creating and Managing the Project Schedule

Once the task, dependency and resource information is collected you will be in the position to create your schedule. There are many tools you can use to create and manage the schedule, however, the most common will undoubtedly be Microsoft Project and Excel.

Microsoft Project is the most effective tool for developing your project schedule. Using Microsoft Project you can create tasks, subtasks, milestones, and resources. You can assign resources to tasks and analyze the overall resource allotment to ensure that resources are not overcommitted. You can assign dependencies between tasks – task "B" cannot be started until task "A" is complete. As the completion dates of tasks change, any dependent tasks that are impacted will change in time too.

Microsoft Project will display your schedule in the form of a Gantt chart if desired. Using this tool allows you to calculate and display the critical path of the project.

While Microsoft Project is a spectacular tool for setting up your project schedule, it's a bear to use on a daily basis when managing tasks day to day.

In order to more simply manage tasks on a day-to-day basis, many project managers export the task list into Excel and manage them in a more simplistic environment.

The exact form of spreadsheets used to manage project tasks vary wildly. Some project managers utilize very simple sheets that just compile tasks and projected end dates. Other project managers utilize much more complex spreadsheets that calculate upcoming task completions, tasks behind schedule, etc.

Project Execution

The Project Execution phase of the project lifecycle is where you will actually execute the plans that were developed for the project. In the standard Project Management Institute lifecycle, this phase is referred to as Project Execution and Control.

When entering this phase of the project, all of the up-front planning has been completed. The project definition, schedule, budget, and resources are all in place. The project team and specifically the Project Manager's focus now shifts from planning the project efforts to participating in, observing, and analyzing the work being done.

The actual work that is happening to complete the project is being done within your technology organizations and often by additional outside groups. Whether you are reading this from the perspective of the Head of Infrastructure or as the Project Manager of one or more projects, your role is more focused on the control aspects of the project.

Your activities will include:

- Time Management
- Cost Management
- Quality Management
- Change Management
- Risk Management
- Issue Management
- Procurement Management
- Acceptance Management
- Communications Management

Put most simply, during this Project Execution phase your job as a senior IT Infrastructure leader is to ensure that the project goals are attained on time (as per the project schedule) and on budget (or better yet, under budget).

Project communications are of paramount importance during the Project Execution Phase. This is accomplished within the team through ongoing recurring status meetings (no less than weekly meetings) and through formal project status reporting to senior management.

Project Status Reporting

The Weekly Dashboard

I have long since developed a PowerPoint document which I use to report on Project Status on all but the smallest of projects. I call this document the weekly dashboard. It is a synthesis of the best reporting characteristics I have encountered over the years. The weekly dashboard consists of several sections that are assembled together into a document that is built-to-purpose (so to speak) for each project I work on.

The majority of the pages in each of the dashboards I produce utilize the same underlying template. That template includes the following components or sections on the page:

Program Description – This section is the initial description of what a specific page in the dashboard is about and how it relates to the overall Project.

Key Deliverables – This section tracks progress against various task-related items. Progress is tracked on a 10 cell graphical bar. I color each block in the bar (using the PowerPoint fill) green when we have reached that point in the task – in other words, if the task is 40% complete, I fill in the first four boxes. When I reach completion of the task (100%), I change the background color to Blue. Those are my color choices; you choose the fill colors that are best for you.

Required Decisions – This block on a Dashboard page lists the outstanding decisions for that particular workstream. These entries are consolidated on the Risk / Decision page of the Dashboard (to be described shortly)

Key Accomplishments This Period – Pretty straightforward, what has been accomplished since the last Dashboard report was issued?

Key tasks Next 30 Days – In this section, you define those tasks and milestones that the plan says will be completed within the next 30 days. If there are any challenges to achieving those goals, you can also mention that here too.

Status – At the top of the slide in the Header line is an indicator of the overall status of the workstream. It consists of the word Status with a colored arrow to the right. That colored arrow is designed to provide that top-level status indication of the workstream, using the standard Red/Amber/Green (RAG) indicators. Where:

- Red = workstream status is bad or negative
- Yellow = Workstream is trending negatively from good to bad and needs additional attention
- Green = Workstream is on track, meeting all goals

The template for the Workstream Dashboard is shown on the next page.

Workstream Name Status ⬆ January 26, 2016

Program Description
Workstream description and how it relates to the overall project

Key Issues / Risks

Description	Logged Date	Remediation
Risk 1		Here's how to fix it

Dependencies
- Dependency 1
- Dependency 2

Key Milestones

Key Deliverables	Due Date	Complete
Task 1		0%
Task 2		0%
Task 3		0%
Task 4		0%
Task 5		0%
Task 6		0%
Task 7		0%
Task 8		0%
Task 9		0%
Task 10		0%
Task 11		0%
Task 12		0%

Key Accomplishments This Period
- Accomplishment 1
- Accomplishment 2

Key Tasks Next 30 Days
- Key task 1
- Key task 2

Required Decisions
- None

Critical Path Awareness
- Item 1

Assembling Your Weekly Dashboard

As mentioned earlier, the actual weekly dashboard document is assembled from a series of individual PowerPoint Slides. My Dashboards typically consist of the following:

- Dashboard Summary Status Front Page
- Risk and Decision Page
- Project Budget Reporting Page
- Project Timeline Page
- Workstream Pages (as required)
    o Network
    o Market Data
    o Storage
    o Systems
    o End User Support
    o Office Buildout

Dashboard Summary Status Front Page

This is a top level status page directed at most senior management. It is heavily based on go/no-go (or good/bad) indicators and heavy use of color to define status (OOOooooo, color!). The goal is for a senior manager to be able to quickly identify those areas that need to be discussed or reviewed in greater detail.

DR Data Center Migration Program

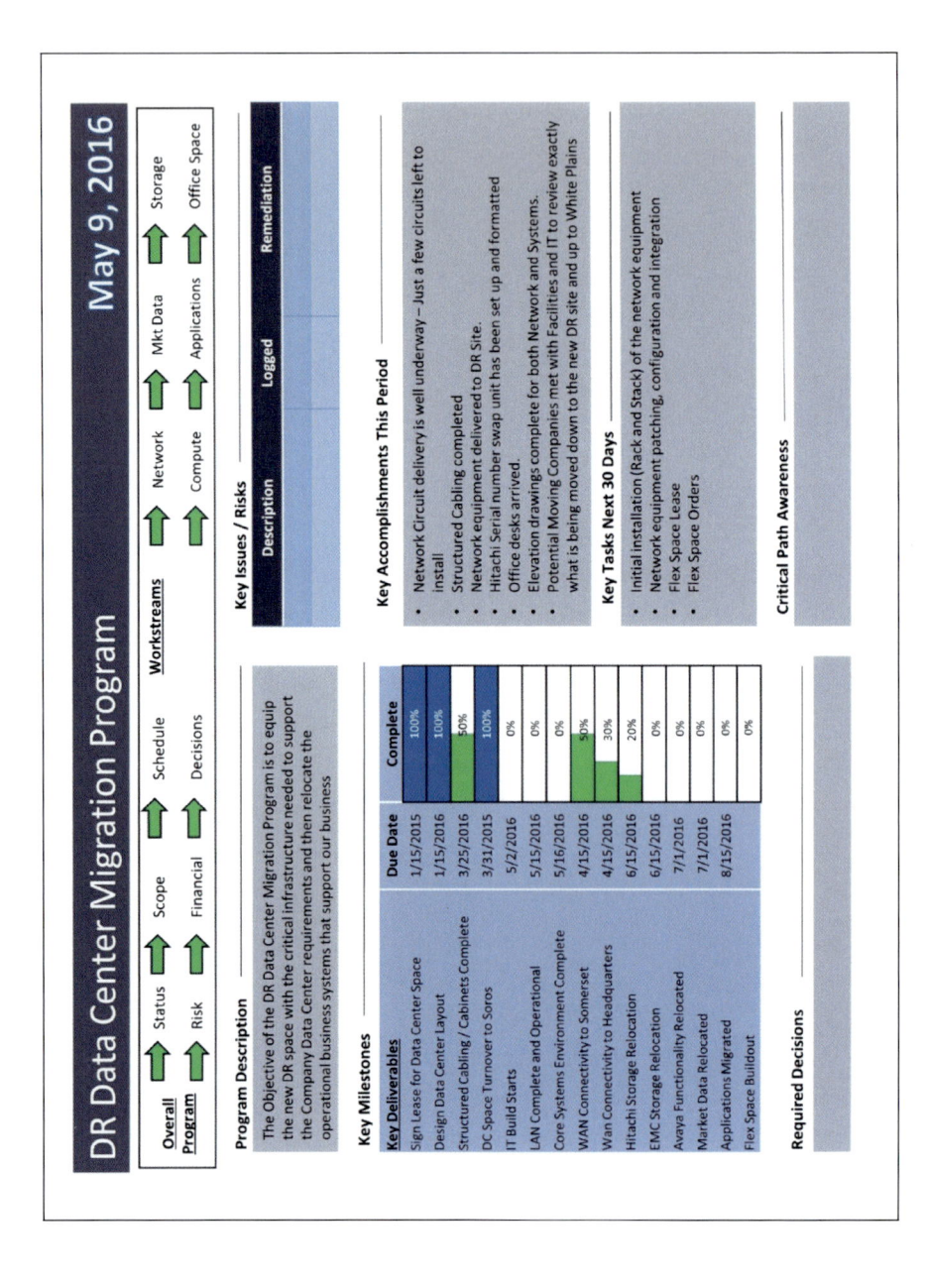

May 9, 2016

Overall	Status	Scope	Schedule	Workstreams	Network	Mkt Data	Storage
Program	Risk	Financial	Decisions		Compute	Applications	Office Space

Program Description

The Objective of the DR Data Center Migration Program is to equip the new DR space with the critical infrastructure needed to support the Company Data Center requirements and then relocate the operational business systems that support our business

Key Milestones

Key Deliverables	Due Date	Complete
Sign Lease for Data Center Space	1/15/2015	100%
Design Data Center Layout	1/15/2016	100%
Structured Cabling / Cabinets Complete	3/25/2016	50%
DC Space Turnover to Soros	3/31/2015	100%
IT Build Starts	5/2/2016	0%
LAN Complete and Operational	5/15/2016	0%
Core Systems Environment Complete	5/16/2016	0%
WAN Connectivity to Somerset	4/15/2016	50%
Wan Connectivity to Headquarters	4/15/2016	30%
Hitachi Storage Relocation	6/15/2016	20%
EMC Storage Relocation	6/15/2016	0%
Avaya Functionality Relocated	7/1/2016	0%
Market Data Relocated	7/1/2016	0%
Applications Migrated	8/15/2016	0%
Flex Space Buildout		0%

Key Issues / Risks

Description	Logged	Remediation

Key Accomplishments This Period

- Network Circuit delivery is well underway – Just a few circuits left to install
- Structured Cabling completed
- Network equipment delivered to DR Site.
- Hitachi Serial number swap unit has been set up and formatted
- Office desks arrived.
- Elevation drawings complete for both Network and Systems.
- Potential Moving Companies met with Facilities and IT to review exactly what is being moved down to the new DR site and up to White Plains

Key Tasks Next 30 Days

- Initial installation (Rack and Stack) of the network equipment
- Network equipment patching, configuration and integration
- Flex Space Lease
- Flex Space Orders

Critical Path Awareness

Required Decisions

Risks and Decisions Status Page

This is always Page 2. It identifies the Risks that have been identified, who owns them, what mitigation plan has been defined, the impact of the Risk if it turns into an issue (an issue is a Risk that has become real – it happened) and the likelihood the Risk will become an issue.

The second table on this page articulates discussions that are open or in process and the impact of not making those decisions.

There will be one of this page for each major project you are reporting on.

Project Risks / Required Decisions — May 13, 2015

Top Risks

Risk Description	Logged Date	Severity	Risk Type	Horizon	Business Impact	Owner	Mitigation Plan
Video/Audio Conferencing for early moves	12/1	2	Business	3-6 M	Insufficient Video Conf. capabilities	Facilities/IT	Purchase additional systems
Shared Printer Communications Plan	2/12	4	Business	1-3 M	Staff Productivity Impact/ Staff Pushback	Facilities	Communications of the Shared Printer Plan is Essential ASAP
Document Management System	3/11	3	Schedule	1-3 M	Development of business metadata needed for migration of documents is slow	IT/Facilities	Need to drill down into this one
Describe The Risk / Title	Date First Added	4=Critical High Moderate 1=Low	Design Financial Schedule Vendor	0-3 Months 3-6 Months 6-12 Months Over 1 Year	Describe what happens if this risk becomes an issue (actually happens) to the project or business	Architects Construction IT Real Estate	What are we doing to make sure this doesn't happen or what if it does happen

Required Decisions

Decision Description	Logged Date	Severity	Decider (Name)	Required By (Date)	Project or Business Impact	Owner of Impact
Printer Technology and Secure Printing	2/5/2015	Medium	Rich C.	ASAP	Potential User Concern over Shared Printer Security	Benny T
New Monitors on all desks	2/5/2015	Medium	Rich C.	ASAP	Potential higher costs as old monitors fail – Higher electrical costs	Benny T
PC Relocation company	4/21/2015	Low	Rich B.	5/15	Potential need to just add to staff	Benny T
Describe The Risk / Title	Date First Added	Critical High Moderate Low	Who needs to make this Decision?	Date where no decision becomes a problem	Describe what happens if this decision is not made or is delayed	Who is waiting for this decision to be made

Project Budget Status Page

On the Project Budget status page, I produce a snapshot of where we stand against the budget that we defined for the project. I want to make an important distinction from what you could get from Finance here. My report defines what we have spent or committed to spend, as opposed to what has been invoiced and paid, which is what the finance department would have. This is hugely important in a project because you will not find any other place where you can get a listing of what you have already spent and what is left to spend going forward.

Since I publish this every week and there is NOT always a change to what we have spent against budget every week, I have that marker in the top of the slide that in this example's case says "Not Updated". This means there has been no update since last week

Also, you should know that the information that is presented is an embedded Microsoft Excel Spreadsheet. I manage budget tracking in Excel and then embed the final version into this sheet. I actually keep track of the expenses in this sheet and make use of lots of roll-ups to only show the summary lines. That is convenient when you are trying to reconcile your numbers with Finance and need to see where they posted payments.

Project Budget — Updated — May 9, 2016

Services

	Extended Costs	Tax Rate	Total Costs (inc Tax)	Spent	Remaining
Overlapping Space	104,073	0.08875	113,309	-	113,309
Network Consulting	85,740	0.08875	93,349	93,349	-
Server Consulting	28,800	0.08875	31,356	31,356	-
Hitachi Consulting for Storage Move	-	-	-	10,841	(10,841)
Technology Group (Netscalar Support)	-	-	-	1,380	(1,380)
Ciena (support for reconfiguring the multiplexers)	-	-	-	41,325	(41,325)
Total Network Circuits	140,000		152,425	-	152,425
Total Equipment Relocation	92,000		92,000	-	92,000
Total Services	450,613		482,440	124,705	304,188

New Equipment

	Extended Costs		Total Costs (inc Tax)	Spent	Remaining
Total Systems Equipment	450,000		450,000	120,000	330,000
Total Network Equipment	1,077,552		1,077,552	1,519,364	(441,812)
Total New Equipment	1,527,552		1,527,552	1,639,364	(111,812)

Site Work

	Extended Costs		Total Costs (inc Tax)	Spent	Remaining
Supplies (cables, etc.)	100,000		100,000	63,590	36,410
User Space Furniture & Equipment	25,000		25,000	6,108	18,892
Structured Cabling for New Site	200,000		200,000	299,543	(99,543)
Cabinets & PDUs	190,000		190,000	193,970	(3,970)
Decommissioning Equinix	25,000		25,000	-	25,000
Total Site Work	540,000		540,000	563,211	(23,211)
Contingency (10%)			200,008		200,008
Total Relocation Costs	2,518,165		2,750,000	2,327,281	369,173

The Project Timeline Status Page

I use this page to present the overall timeline and indicate the status of the various milestones. Everything starts out in black. If a milestone was reached it is then colored Green. If it is at risk it is colored yellow and if it was missed, it is colored Red. I create this timeline using Visio. You can also create it in PowerPoint or some other graphics program.

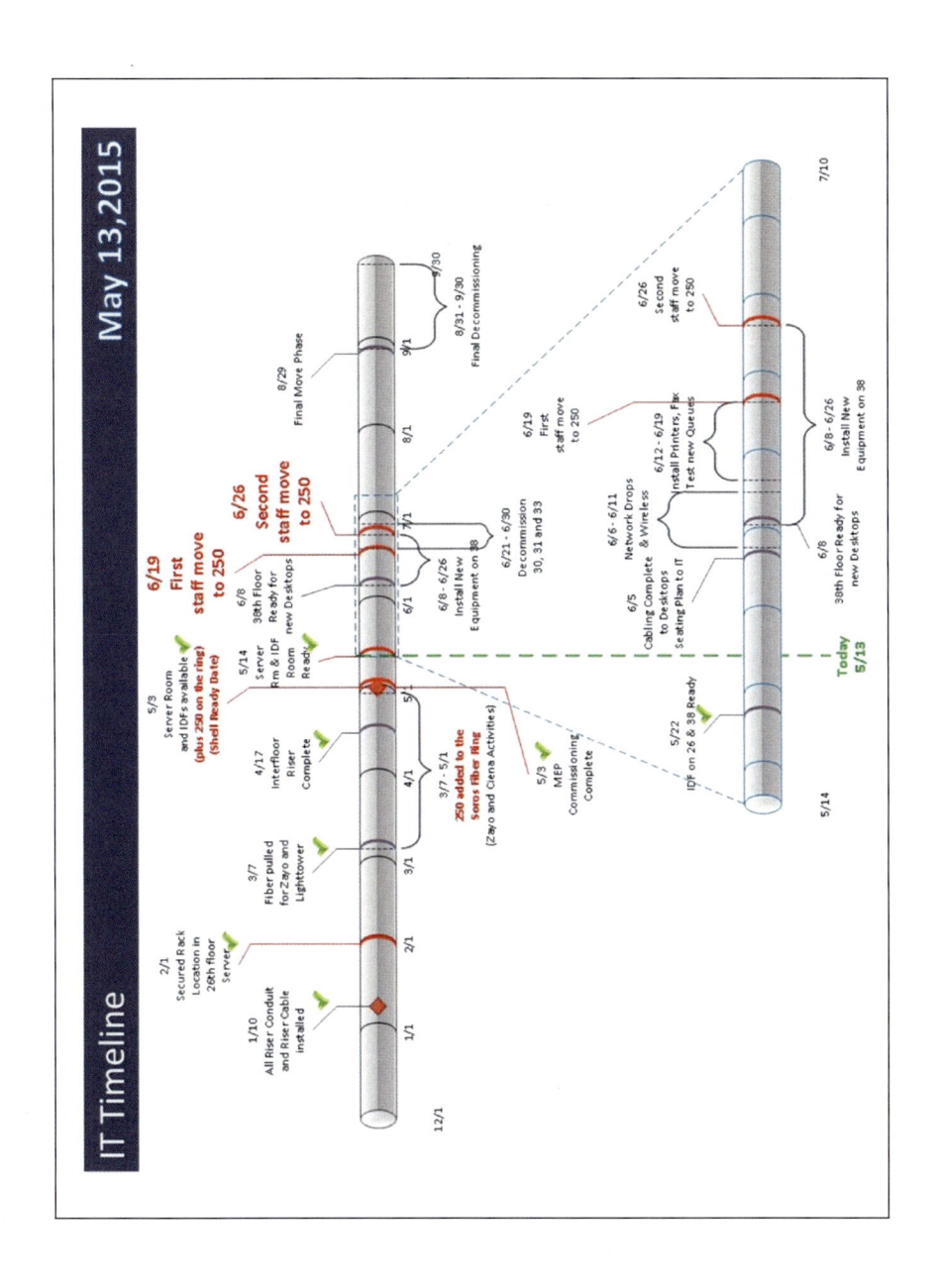

Workstream Dashboard Status Pages – The Template

Here again is the template for the Dashboard's workstream pages. This page template is modified to produce the pages for the individual departments and activities such as:

- Network
- Systems
- Storage
- End User Support
- Etc.

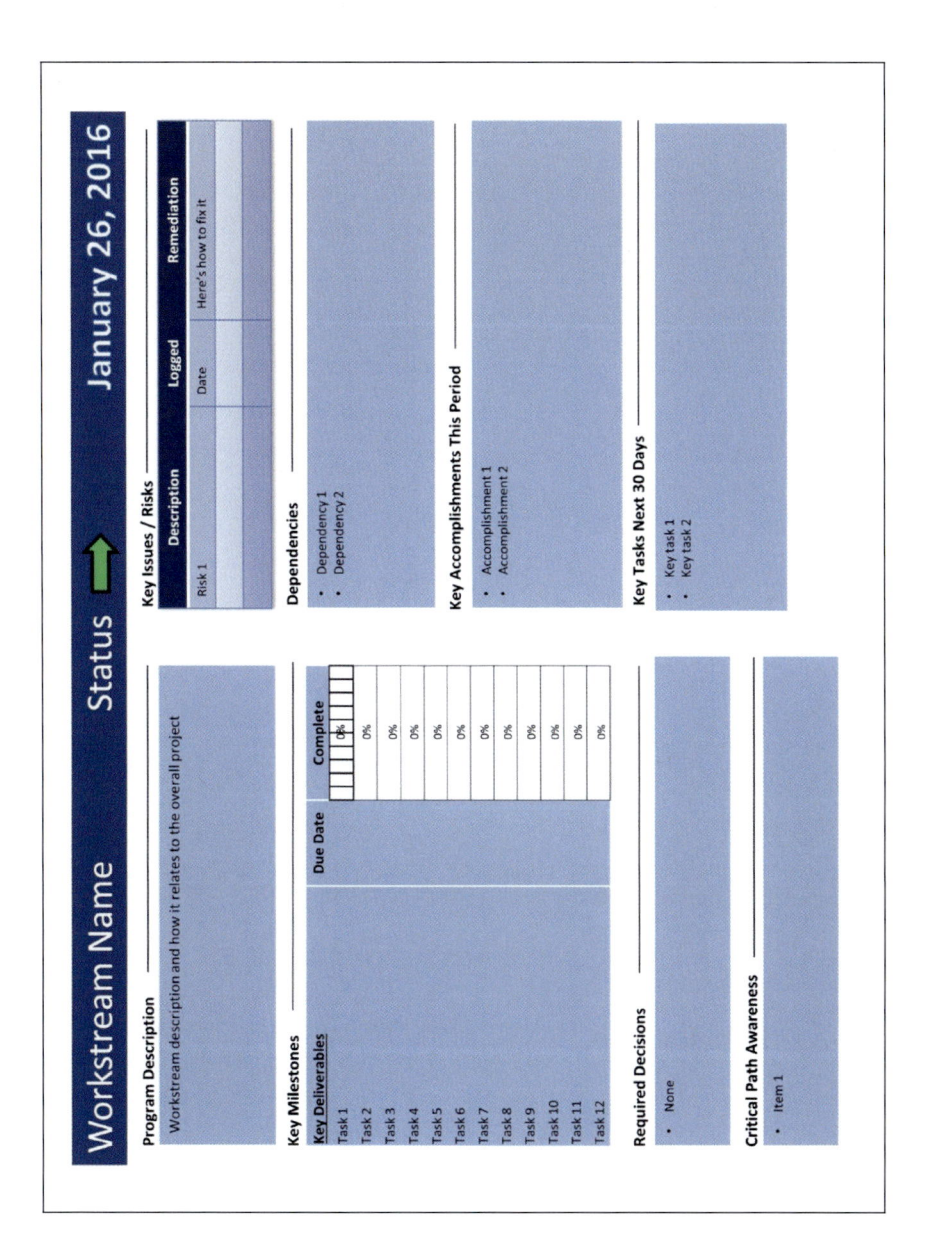

Workstream Name Status ⬆ January 26, 2016

Program Description
Workstream description and how it relates to the overall project

Key Issues / Risks

Description	Logged Date	Remediation
Risk 1		Here's how to fix it

Dependencies
- Dependency 1
- Dependency 2

Key Accomplishments This Period
- Accomplishment 1
- Accomplishment 2

Key Tasks Next 30 Days
- Key task 1
- Key task 2

Key Milestones

Key Deliverables

	Due Date	Complete
Task 1		0%
Task 2		0%
Task 3		0%
Task 4		0%
Task 5		0%
Task 6		0%
Task 7		0%
Task 8		0%
Task 9		0%
Task 10		0%
Task 11		0%
Task 12		0%

Required Decisions
- None

Critical Path Awareness
- Item 1

Some Workstream Page Examples

The following charts show some typical workstream pages from projects I have managed.

Machine Room Construction Status — May 9, 2016

Program Description

The Objective of the Machine Room Construction workstream is to define the design for the DR Data Center machine room and to build that data center room for the relocation of the systems and applications

Key Milestones

Key Deliverables	Due Date	Complete
Lease Signed	1/15/2016	100%
Cabinet changes defined	1/15/2016	100%
Cabinets Ordered	1/18/2016	100%
Electrical distribution defined	1/15/2016	100%
Room Layout Defined	1/15/2016	100%
Electrical Distribution Installation Complete	2/29/2016	100%
Cabinets Delivered	3/4/2016	100%
Cabinets Installed	3/11/2016	100%
Structured Cabling Installed	3/25/2016	70%
Physical Security Installed	3/25/2016	100%
Room Commissioning	3/31/2016	100%
Turnover to IT	3/31/2016	100%

Key Issues / Risks

Description	Logged	Remediation
Delay could impact schedule	1/4	Focus on Lease signing

Dependencies

Key Accomplishments This Period

- Structured Cabling installation started

Key Tasks Next 30 Days

- Complete Structured Cabling Installation
- Decide on Surveillance Contract

Required Decisions

Critical Path Awareness

Office Space Dashboard   Status ⬆   May 9, 2016

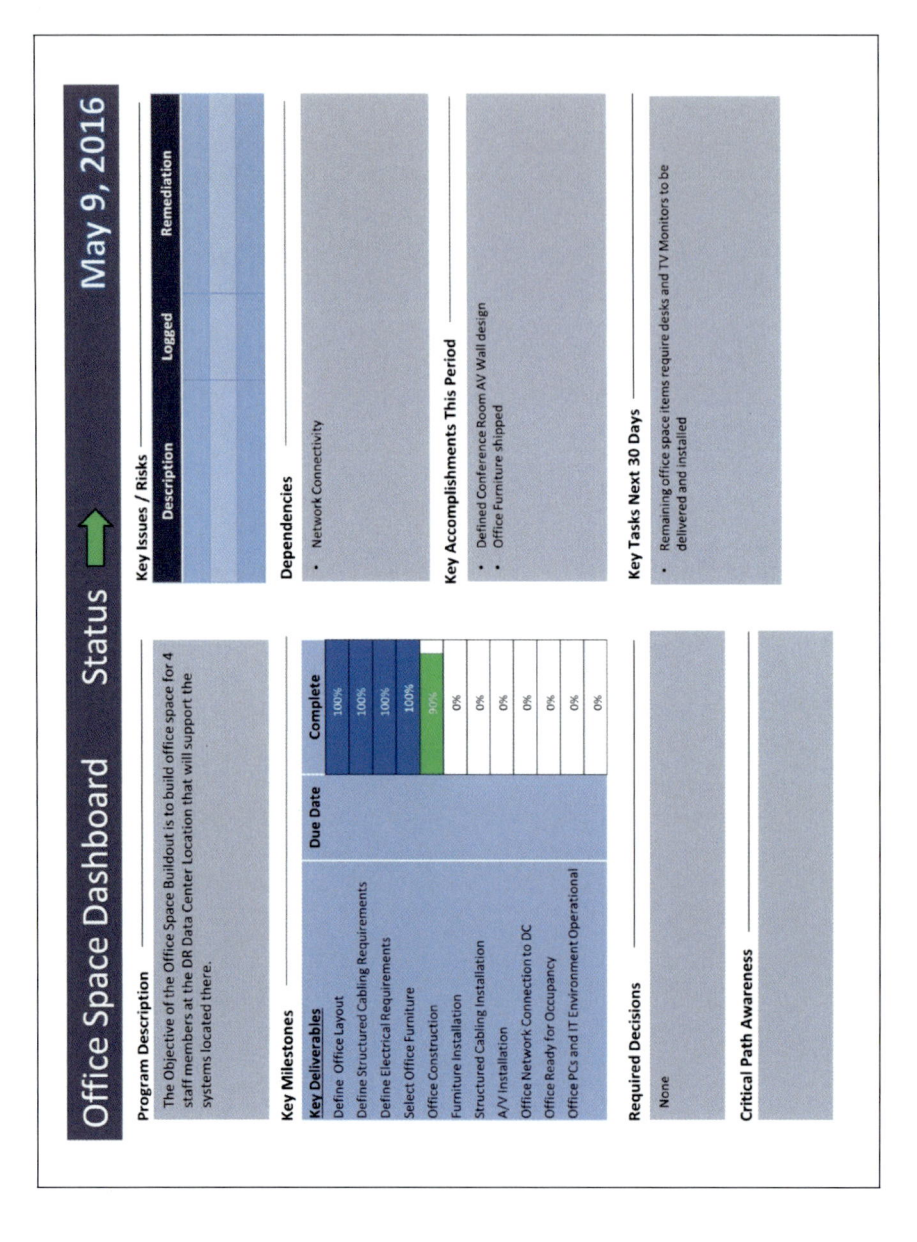

Program Description

The Objective of the Office Space Buildout is to build office space for 4 staff members at the DR Data Center Location that will support the systems located there.

Key Issues / Risks

Description	Logged	Remediation

Dependencies

- Network Connectivity

Key Milestones

Key Deliverables

	Due Date	Complete
Define Office Layout		100%
Define Structured Cabling Requirements		100%
Define Electrical Requirements		100%
Select Office Furniture		100%
Office Construction		90%
Furniture Installation		0%
Structured Cabling Installation		0%
A/V Installation		0%
Office Network Connection to DC		0%
Office Ready for Occupancy		0%
Office PCs and IT Environment Operational		0%

Key Accomplishments This Period

- Defined Conference Room AV Wall design
- Office Furniture shipped

Required Decisions

None

Key Tasks Next 30 Days

- Remaining office space items require desks and TV Monitors to be delivered and installed

Critical Path Awareness

Network Dashboard — Status ⬆ May 9, 2016

Program Description

The Objective of the Network Migration is to design and deploy a next-generation network environment both within the data center itself and among the various office locations

Key Milestones

Key Deliverables	Due Date	Complete
Network Equipment Ordered		100%
External Circuits Ordered		90%
Core & Initial Fiber Extenders Installed		0%
Full LAN Network Operational		0%
Protected Circuits Operational		0%
Unprotected Circuits Operational		0%
Interoffice (London/HK) Circuits Operational		0%
Avaya Environment Relocated		0%
DC Office LAN Installed / Tested		0%
SIP Trunking Tested		0%
Internet Relocated		0%
Ring Downs Relocated		0%

Required Decisions

Critical Path Awareness

Key Issues / Risks

Description	Logged	Remediation

Dependencies

Key Accomplishments This Period

- Circuit order committed installation dates being received
- Network Equipment being staged and configured at vendor in Teterboro – Planned ship date to DR Site is week of 5/2

Key Tasks Next 30 Days

- Complete network equipment configuration
- Complete circuit installations

Project Portfolio Management

Project Scoring & Prioritization for Maximum Results

The growing challenge for IT management and PMOs is contending with increasing project demands while keeping the selected initiatives aligned with overall business objectives. Maintenance projects need to be balanced with strategic initiatives and all while focusing on driving the business forward and delivering value.

As the number of projects within the IT department increase, it soon becomes apparent that you will be asked to undertake more projects than you will have either the time or the resources to complete. We've already discussed the need to say "no" to requests. You will be asked to start projects that clearly should not exist, either because the clearly have no inherent value or they violate some IT or Business Process or rule.

Saying no to the obvious ones will leave you will a group of projects that do make sense at some level, but that pile may just get too big for you to complete successfully. The obvious answer is to define a process (yes we need one more) that allows you to rank the various projects in terms of relative benefit to the company.

Your job in managing the IT Organization is to deliver the maximum possible value to the company for the investments that are made. Looking at that responsibility from a project perspective, you will be looking to apply the following types of criteria to project selection:

- Projects that directly *drive* the business goals and align with the overall business objectives should be the highest priority for your team.

- Eliminating the tendency to prioritize work requests based on politically-driven decision-making

- Freeing resources from low-payback / low-value work, thereby optimizing resources for high-priority strategic projects

When I have reviewed how companies prioritize their projects I have found a number of really bad ranking criteria:

- In some cases, I have found projects were prioritized and accepted based on the seniority of the requestor. A project that is requested by senior management should not automatically qualify for acceptance.

They should meet the same implementation criteria as a project from anyone else.
- Projects that are fully within the bounds of IT often get automatically green-lighted. Whatever the value of the IT project, it should be evaluated within the mix of all projects, in order to provide an assurance that IT has the broad view of business value and takes the needs of the customer base seriously.

Categorizing Potential Projects

While the potential for a strong financial payback would be great criteria for ranking potential projects, determining the correct financial benefit is very difficult. In addition, if that was the only or chief deciding factor, many projects that are mostly technical improvements (such as infrastructure upgrades) would not make the cut. These projects may be needed, however, to scale the company upward. A better solution is to utilize a criteria scale for making decisions such as Gartner, Inc.'s five-perspective methodology.

1. Strategic alignment – How well does the IT investment strategy align with the long-term goals of the business?
2. Business process impact – How much would the initiative force the company to change existing business processes?
3. Technical architecture – How scalable, resilient, and simple to integrate with existing technology are the databases, operating systems, applications, and networks that would be implemented?
4. Direct payback – What benefits does the initiative have in terms of cost savings, access to increased information, or other advantages?
5. Risk – How likely is it that the initiative will fail to meet expectations, and what are the costs involved

Building Project Scoring Models

In addition to determining criteria for categorizing projects, you will need to determine a methodology for scoring. There are several models to choose from:

1. Binary (No range and unweighted) - Under this model, a project either meets specific criteria or it does not. It will receive one point for each criterion met, and projects will be chosen based on the total number of points. In this model, all criteria are assumed to be of

equal importance. This isn't the best way to rank projects because it does not allow companies to determine to what extent criteria points are met.

2. Range and unweighted – In this methodology, the project is scored on a range (i.e., from one to five). This option provides a more detailed analysis of how projects fit with corporate goals.

3. Weighted scoring - In addition to scoring criteria within a range, this option provides a weighted score for each criterion to determine how important each consideration is to the organization overall. This scoring model provides a more comprehensive look at how well a project fits the company's priorities. When creating weighted scoring models, companies can break down the importance of the top priorities of the business to determine how much value to assign to each one, adding up to a total of 100 percent. More simplistically the weighting can also be in a range of say 1 to 5.

As a company refocuses its objectives over time, the weighting calculations may be modified to fit with the organization's current goals. In determining a ranking score for each criterion, businesses can build charts that clearly define each numerical value's role, from zero ("does not meet objectives") to the highest value (i.e., five or 10), which is reserved for projects that closely align with the company's goals.

Developing the Scoring System

The more literature you will read about project prioritization, the more different criteria you will see for evaluating projects. Here are a few that I have compiled:

- Organizational Benefits – Revenue, Cost, Profit, Company Image
- Risk – Risk of failure, Risk to the company of NOT doing the project, Elimination of some current Risk
- Competitive Advantage
- Customer Satisfaction
- Ease of Implementation
- Expertise – What types of expertise is needed? Do we have it in house?
- Innovation – Will this project result in significant innovation from either a company or industry perspective?

- Cross-cultural Communication – Impact of using offshore expertise,
- Virtual Teamwork – How geographically dispersed is the team?

Using a Matrix to Rank Projects

Once the scoring methodology has been determined, it is simple to build a project prioritization matrix that will clearly lay out the relative values of the projects to your company. This then becomes the main driver for project selection.

I tend to like using the Weighted Scoring method of prioritization. That is because I find few things are so black and white that a binary (no range) assessment of a criteria makes sense. Also, I find that some criteria are usually more important to me than others, hence the weighting.

All this said I put together a super fast spreadsheet to calculate the [value] scores for three fictitious projects. Here is what that looks like:

Criteria		Project 1	Project 2	Project 3
Competitive Advantage	Rating (1-5)	4	3	5
	Weight (1-5)	5	5	5
	Total Score	20	15	25
Customer Satisfaction	Rating (1-5)	5	4	3
	Weight (1-5)	5	5	5
	Total Score	25	20	15
Estimated Project Cost	Rating (1-5)	4	4	5
	Weight (1-5)	2	2	2
	Total Score	8	8	10
Potential Revenue	Rating (1-5)	3	3	3
	Weight (1-5)	3	3	3
	Total Score			
Ease of Implementing	Rating (1-5)	3	5	2
	Weight (1-5)	4	4	4
	Total Score	12	20	8
Total Score		**65**	**63**	**58**

Matrix for Prioritizing Projects

Another example Matrix using the Gartner Criteria:

Matrix for Prioritizing Projects				
Criteria		Project 1	Project 2	Project 3
Strategic Alignment	Rating (1-5)	4	3	5
	Weight (1-5)	5	5	5
	Total Score	20	15	25
Business Process Impact	Rating (1-5)	5	4	3
	Weight (1-5)	5	5	5
	Total Score	25	20	15
Technical Architecture	Rating (1-5)	4	4	5
	Weight (1-5)	2	2	2
	Total Score	8	8	10
Payback	Rating (1-5)	3	3	3
	Weight (1-5)	3	3	3
	Total Score			
Risk	Rating (1-5)	3	5	2
	Weight (1-5)	4	4	4
	Total Score	12	20	8
Total Score		**65**	**63**	**58**

Prioritize Projects Based on Plotted Scores

After you have determined a scoring methodology and taken the time to rate potential projects according to a set of criteria and their weighted values, you then can prioritize upcoming projects based on values such as the project's relevance to overall strategy, potential return on investment, and the amount of risk involved.

High-strategy, high-return, low-risk projects will generally be viewed as a high priority. As the scores in individual categories go down, you may find it more difficult to identify clear winners. In this situation, it may be helpful to use visual modeling tools.

Several visual modeling options include:

I. A bubble chart that illustrates strategy (x-axis), return (y-axis), and project size (bubble size) – See example below.
II. A bubble chart that illustrates strategy (x-axis), risk (y-axis), and return (bubble size)
III. An organized list sorted by overall score, from high to low

The Bottom Line on Project Prioritization and Selection

More progressive IT shops are using scoring methods to rank potential projects.

When a proposed project receives a score below a cut-off number, you should just reject that project, or shut it down if it is something in process. Remember, the goal is to spend your available budget dollars on those activities that will provide the most value to the organization.

It's crucial for company leaders to revisit the scoring values and criteria on a regular basis to ensure

Chapter 14

Operational Management

Daily Operational management consists primarily of a series of processes or activities that are designed to provide non-stop IT availability. As with any activity that drives the value to the business, the availability of the systems and the level of customer satisfaction, the processes need to be well defined and rigorously enforced.

In this book we will define a few more common processes that you should consider implementing in your organization:

Daily System Checks

There is usually a number of activities that take place overnight in an organization's IT department. These will range from systems back-up to patching servers and workstations to changes to network configurations, and so on. While these changes are usually well understood and hopefully tested before being deployed into production environments, the overnight processes sometimes will break something. It's important that each of the key system environments is checked for operation before the time the users start arriving each day to ensure nothing has been broken overnight, and if they have, the issue is corrected before the staff starts using the systems.

Each of the key functional areas must be checked.

Here are some typical Network Start of Day Tests

- All defined security and event logs should be reviewed for anomalies and unauthorized systems changes
- Check VoIP Communications Manager Systems are free of alarms.
- Check all VoIP Session Manager Servers are free of alarms; SIP links are up and replication for all Session Managers are synchronized.
- Check Web Filters are working as expected and all appliances health status is good. Test by attempting to browse a blocked website and a regular site.
- Check Primary and failover Voice Recording servers are operational. Check both primary and secondary servers for recent recordings.
- Check that no RSA tokens expiring in the next month and replication between servers are working.
- Review overnight EMAIL and Management System alerts and take action if necessary.
- Login to Turret Management systems and check for alerts
- Check that all Firewall gateway status is good.
- Check Fiber DWDM nodes are free of alarms.
- Ensure any and all anomaly events have been entered into Ticketing System for investigation and resolution

Systems Administration Checklist:

- Check that all scheduled and rescheduled backups completed successfully. Note remaining capacity of backup systems
- Schedule all failed backup jobs for review
- Ensure all shares are mounted and accessible
- Ensure Unix servers are up and operational
- Review file activity notifications for suspicious activity
- Check that all virus signatures are up to date
- Review overnight alerts and take actions as required
- Verify Message Archiving succeeded
- Review certificate expiration report for expiring certificates

- Review SAN weekly report for performance issues
- Review DHCP Report for any issues
- Review Disk Space Report for any utilization issues
- Check versions of all critical software

End User Support Checklist:

- Check that Emergency Hotline +1-212-555-1212 is functional
- Check that Outlook is functional and connectivity to Exchange is verified (Inc. Public Folder
- Send test e-mail to test account from the internet to test Postini
- Check that Enterprise Vault is functioning (search, retrieve, and restore)
- Verify company home page is up, Intranet is up, external links are functional and news ticker is scrolling
- Place internal and external telephone call to ensure phone environment is working
- Test that Voicemail is operational by retrieving messages
- Test BlackBerry is sending/receiving messages
- Test Print servers are working (send a test job to one PCL and PS printer)
- Test that Web Filter is operational
- Open shares on Server "A" and Server "B"
- Test that Bloomberg and Reuters (Market Data) are working
- Ping workstations in DR location to ensure they are operational
- Ensure company home page is up, and integrated search is functioning properly
- Verify IPTV channels are functioning
- Verify all conference room equipment is functional
- Ensure Citrix and OWA are functional by opening a session in each
- Test Audio Conference Bridge is operational on all dial-in numbers

Change Management

Change Management is another one of those processes that is essential for you to implement. Over the years I have seen a number of firms where Change Management did not exist. There were no rules about what could be changed, when you could and could not change something, who had to be notified, what sort of documentation was required and what sort of back-out plan needed to be in place. Literally, the only way to describe those IT environments was pure chaos, and that fact was well represented in the number of service interruptions that occurred.

In Change Management, all changes to the IT infrastructure and its components are authorized and documented, in order to ensure that service interruptions to the environment are kept to a minimum. The implementation steps are planned and communicated, in order to recognize potential impacts to the systems as early as possible.

A Change Management process has a person that is assigned the task of collecting and managing any changes that are proposed – the Change Manager. The Change Manager has this responsibility throughout the lifecycle of the change. In large companies, the Change Manager may be a full-time position. In smaller companies, the role may be assigned to one of the more senior managers.

In addition, there is a "Change Management Board" that is responsible for reviewing changes that have been requested by the various groups. This Change Management Board is made up of representatives of the various IT organizations.

The Change Manager and the Change Advisory Board bear the responsibility for reviewing all changes and providing the approval to move forward. Typically, a Change Management Meeting is held on a weekly basis where the person who is requesting the change, along with any significant stakeholders meet with the Change Management Board to review their change and answer questions.

The Change Management process usually looks like the following:

- Set the Rules – What changes need to go through the process and what changes do not. For those that do not, there should still be some process for handling these "standard changes"

- Register the Change – There is typically some form of Change Management Database (many are available for SharePoint and other platforms). The change is registered and documented. What is collected and documented will depend on your specific environment.
- Clearance of the Change by the Change Manager – The Change Manager accepts the change into the process. The request must conform to the general rules of the process, including setting a date that allows it to be properly considered by the Chang Management Board. If it is cleared it is then placed on the schedule for the next meeting
- Change Management Board Meeting – During the scheduled meeting the change is reviewed and the Change Management Board has the opportunity to review the change, ask questions and make a decision on whether to proceed.
- Schedule changes into Releases – Assuming the change is approved, the change will be assigned a date and time to be implemented.
- Change Implementation – The change actually gets implemented
- Post Implementation Review – The change is reviewed during the start of the next meeting to understand if it was successful and if not, why not.

What could possibly go wrong with this process? Well, you should know by now that lots of things can and will go wrong.

1. First, you will have those folks that just do not buy into this change management thing. You will ALWAYS hear from them about a change that has to go in tonight because (1) the company will implode if that doesn't happen (2) They just found out about this themselves and all life as we know it depends on this going in tonight (3) They can't wait for the process to work because their key guy is going on vacation starting this Friday for three weeks and there are 1 million five hundred and sixty-two items that will be happening between now and when he gets back that completely depend on this change. You know, of course, that in all cases that person is full of crap.
2. There will be the person that honestly is trying to go through the process but finds that there was some form of error in their submission package and they cannot wait for the next scheduled

       meeting. Unless this person ALWAYS does this, you should work with him/her to get it on the schedule.
3. Truly urgent changes can come up that should go through the process but cannot afford the time of a standard change cycle.

Clearly, you will need to define a special procedure for emergencies to deal with these urgent changes. Also, have a method in place to deal with the fallout when you have to reject either someone's fake emergency requests or changes that get rejected for good reason. If the Change Management Process falls into YOUR scope of responsibilities, you absolutely will be designated by the change requester as the person standing in the way of success. Document all rejected changes including the reasons for rejection. More on this in the Politics of IT section.

Chapter 15

Information Technology Metrics – A Critical Component of Your Toolbox

As the expression goes "You Can't Fix What You Don't Measure!" For Information Technology the number of activities that are constantly in process can only be understood by measuring activities, correlating them to understand trends and chart them over time to measure performance and improvement.

The Case for Developing an In-Depth Metrics Program

I have never seen an IT shop that didn't push back when a metrics program was started. The reaction is always the same – "We know what's going on and nobody is going to read this stuff anyway". It is a universal and completely predictable reaction. So universal that, YES, ***even I*** had that exact response the first time I was asked to start down this path.

I can tell you that I couldn't have been more wrong when I resisted implementing a metrics program. By starting simple and focusing efforts on those metrics that could have the biggest impact on operations, we were able to achieve a huge improvement in systems availability and the corresponding improvements in Customer Satisfaction.

I am going to present quite a bit of information and proposed metrics in this section. It can be a bit overwhelming if you're looking at this sort of program for the first time. The key to success is to think incrementally. Start with some basic metrics and build from there. You should start in two areas – Customer Satisfaction and Help-Desk / End User Support performance.

Benchmarking is important when developing a metrics program. Before you start any measurements, you should send a survey to all of the employees to understand their assessment of your team. Within this section of the book, I will present the ongoing customer satisfaction survey that my team used in one of my more substantial IT Transformation efforts. Variations of these questions will be fine as a component of your initial survey, but you need to go deeper. Ask questions about the entire suite of services your team provides, the equipment the staff is using, policies and procedures they must follow, etc.

Your biggest fear when you start to develop this survey is that you are going to be hammered by the staff's responses. If this is the first time they have ever been asked for their opinion, you are probably correct. Don't be afraid of this result, in fact, unless you've been running IT in this company for a long time, a bad first result is exactly what you need. THAT is the baseline against which all improvements will be measured. If customer satisfaction comes back at 95% satisfied (and you know you need to fix lots of things), it will be hard to quantify the improvement to your management. On the other hand, if satisfaction is around 20%, go out and start looking for the red and blue tights with a big "S" on the chest!

As your program moves on to additional areas of measurement you will need to take a benchmark reading of your team's results before any mitigation work begins. You will always need that baseline to compare against.

By the time you are finished developing your monthly reporting program you will find you are measuring virtually every area of services and technology you manage. There is good reason to take the program to this point:

- *You can't fix what you don't measure* – At the core of any metrics program is the goal of improving the performance of the systems and staff. The metrics you collect will absolutely lead you to those issues that most need your attention. They will also tell your management the story of how your management of your group is improving the results.

- *You need documentation when you or your organization is attacked* – You can be absolutely sure that you and your team will be attacked on an ongoing basis. You will see some of these types of attacks articulated in the "Politics of IT" section of this book. Sometimes the attacks are just based on a person's individual experience, which they then generalize as your group's overall performance. Sometimes the attacks are by a person that is using IT to explain their failures. Other times you are being attacked by someone that wants to take over some or all of your responsibility. In all of these cases, a good set of metrics that can unequivocally communicate the reality of your group's performance will be the tool you need to address the attack.

- *You need to chart and communicate improvements you have led your organization to achieve* – Metrics should be part of your communications plan to the organization as a whole. Everyone should know how hard your team is working and how much you all are achieving. This shuts down criticism and can be invaluable when bonus time comes around.

This book will present a very large number of IT Metrics that are focused on the Infrastructure itself and the services provided to support that infrastructure. Some of the knowledge a good metrics program will provide include:

- A measure of the utilization of the technical environments (networks/circuits, systems/servers, storage), a prediction of the how long the current environment can support increases in utilization and a prediction of how the environment will continue to scale in the future, allowing you to make more informed purchasing decisions.

- A measure of the amount of work, systems supported, or users supported by the current staff, allowing predictions for required growth in staffing when the company adds staff or when the number of systems being supported increase. This is most useful when building staffing strategies such as "one desktop technician for every 100 staff members"

- A quantitative analysis of the performance of individual members of the staff

- A quantitative measure of the satisfaction of the customer base and how that is trending over time.

- A deep understanding of the number and types of user calls or incidents that the organization is addressing. This allows you to identify recurring issues and focus your effort on truly understanding the root cause and addressing it permanently.

Customer Satisfaction Metrics

I always lead my Metrics reporting with Customer Satisfaction as the initial focus. At the most basic level, your organization's performance (and by definition your performance) will be judged by the overall satisfaction the organization has with your services. Customer Satisfaction is the one true measure of how your organization is performing, as perceived by those that matter the most.

In order to address the inevitable "everybody thinks the IT department's services are garbage" comments, you need a quantitative measure of what your users actually think. I can assure you that nothing feels better than being able to respond to criticism with "well in the last six months our customer satisfaction survey results were consistently above 96.8% very satisfied".

Customer Satisfaction is measured by using customer surveys to collect user feedback. Every call to the help desk and every ticket opened online resulted in a customer satisfaction survey being sent to the user. In order to maximize response, we limited the number of questions to five that focused on the key aspects of resolving a user issue, plus we included a section where the user could include any additional information they felt was relevant. The five questions were:

- The support person I dealt with was courteous and professional (Yes/No)
- The service provided by the Help Desk met my expectations (Yes/No)
- The service provided by the dispatched technician met my expectations (Yes/No)
- I was kept informed by the Global Technology staff throughout the service period (Yes/No)
- What is your overall impression of the quality of service delivered to you during this recent support experience? (Extremely Satisfied, Satisfied, Dissatisfied, Extremely Dissatisfied)

The results of the responses were collated by site and trended over time. We also looked at the results by technician to see if we had anyone that needed additional training or an attitude adjustment.

Any user that responded to the survey with an extremely dissatisfied response to the "Overall impression of the service delivered to you " question was called or visited by the Head of End User Support. We always would drill down into the reasons why people felt things had not gone well and communicated the results to the End User Support team in general and the technician that delivered the service in particular.

If the user that gave the "Extremely Dissatisfied" response included any detail in the survey response that was included in a section of the Metrics Dashboard.

The Dashboard Metrics pages for the Customer Satisfaction Sections are shown on the next page:

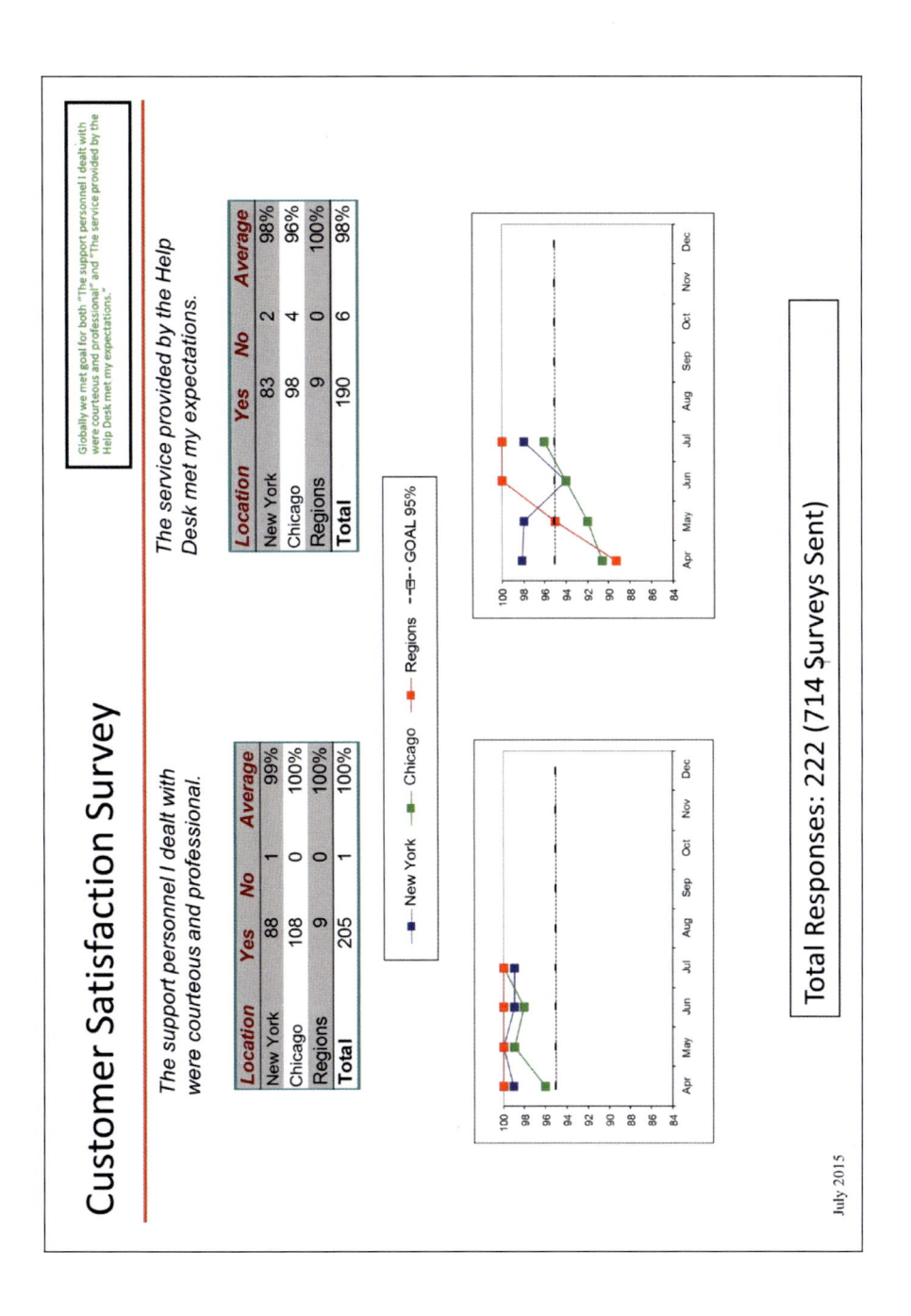

Customer Satisfaction Survey

Globally we met goal for both: "The support personnel I dealt with were courteous and professional" and "The service provided by the Help Desk met my expectations."

The support personnel I dealt with were courteous and professional.

Location	Yes	No	Average
New York	88	1	99%
Chicago	108	0	100%
Regions	9	0	100%
Total	205	1	100%

The service provided by the Help Desk met my expectations.

Location	Yes	No	Average
New York	83	2	98%
Chicago	98	4	96%
Regions	9	0	100%
Total	190	6	98%

— New York — Chicago — Regions --□-- GOAL 95%

Total Responses: 222 (714 Surveys Sent)

July 2015

Note that the responses are broken down by location, with the Regional Offices, which by and large are smaller offices, collected into a single category.

A Second page was devoted to the second group of two questions. The analysis methods and presentation was the same as for the first group.

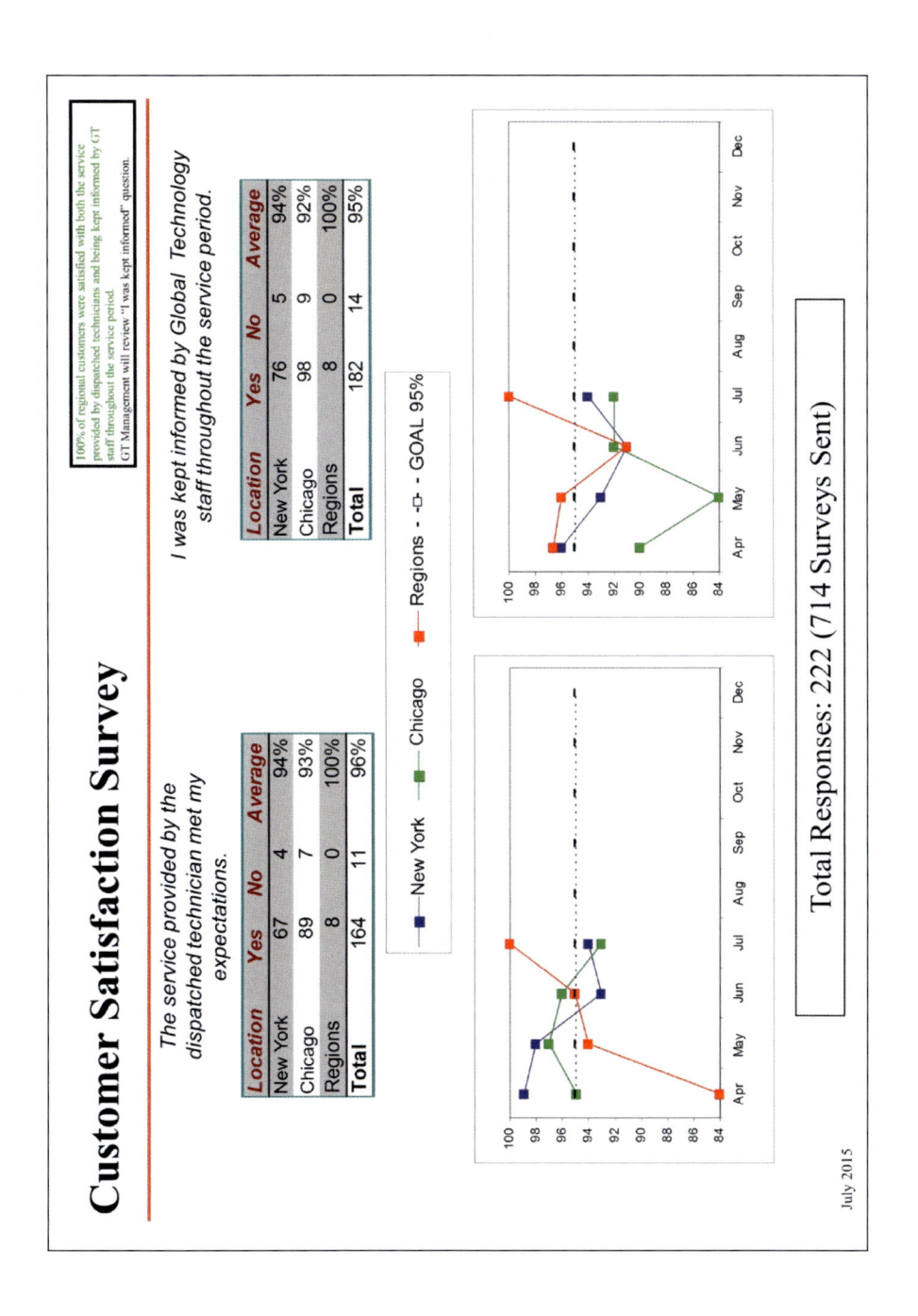

Customer Satisfaction Survey

100% of regional customers were satisfied with both the service provided by dispatched technicians and being kept informed by GT staff throughout the service period.
GT Management will review "I was kept informed" question.

The service provided by the dispatched technician met my expectations.

Location	Yes	No	Average
New York	67	4	94%
Chicago	89	7	93%
Regions	8	0	100%
Total	164	11	96%

I was kept informed by Global Technology staff throughout the service period.

Location	Yes	No	Average
New York	76	5	94%
Chicago	98	9	92%
Regions	8	0	100%
Total	182	14	95%

Total Responses: 222 (714 Surveys Sent)

July 2015

Finally, the last question that drilled down into the overall quality of the service delivered is analyzed in more depth than the previous questions, primarily due to the greater importance of this result.

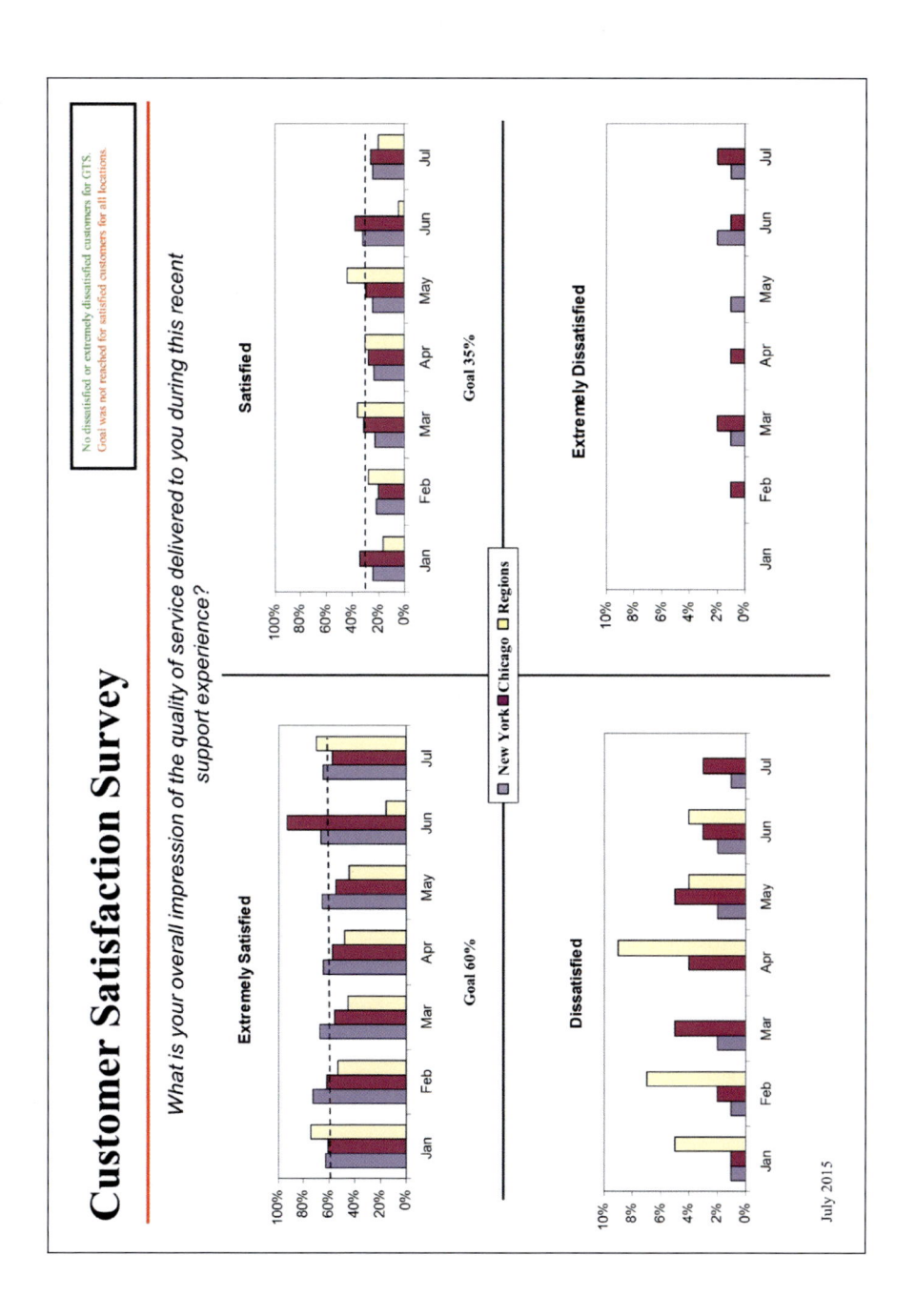

Customer Satisfaction Survey

What is your overall impression of the quality of service delivered to you during this recent support experience?

No dissatisfied or extremely dissatisfied customers for GTS.
Goal was not reached for satisfied customers for all locations.

Extremely Satisfied

Goal 60%

Satisfied

Goal 35%

■ New York ■ Chicago □ Regions

Dissatisfied

Extremely Dissatisfied

July 2015

It is also important to track the response rate to your surveys. You will never get 100% returns, however, if the response rate is too low, you may need to do some additional communications to the user community to explain the importance of the survey, why they are important and how their responses are being used.

We also found that in those situations where we had some work to do mitigating issues in an environment that the response rate for the surveys first peaked and then started to drop off – the users were getting tired of filling out the surveys, no matter how short they were. In those situations, we backed off and would only send one survey every two weeks to a single user.

Here is a chart we used to track the user response rate.

Customer Satisfaction Survey

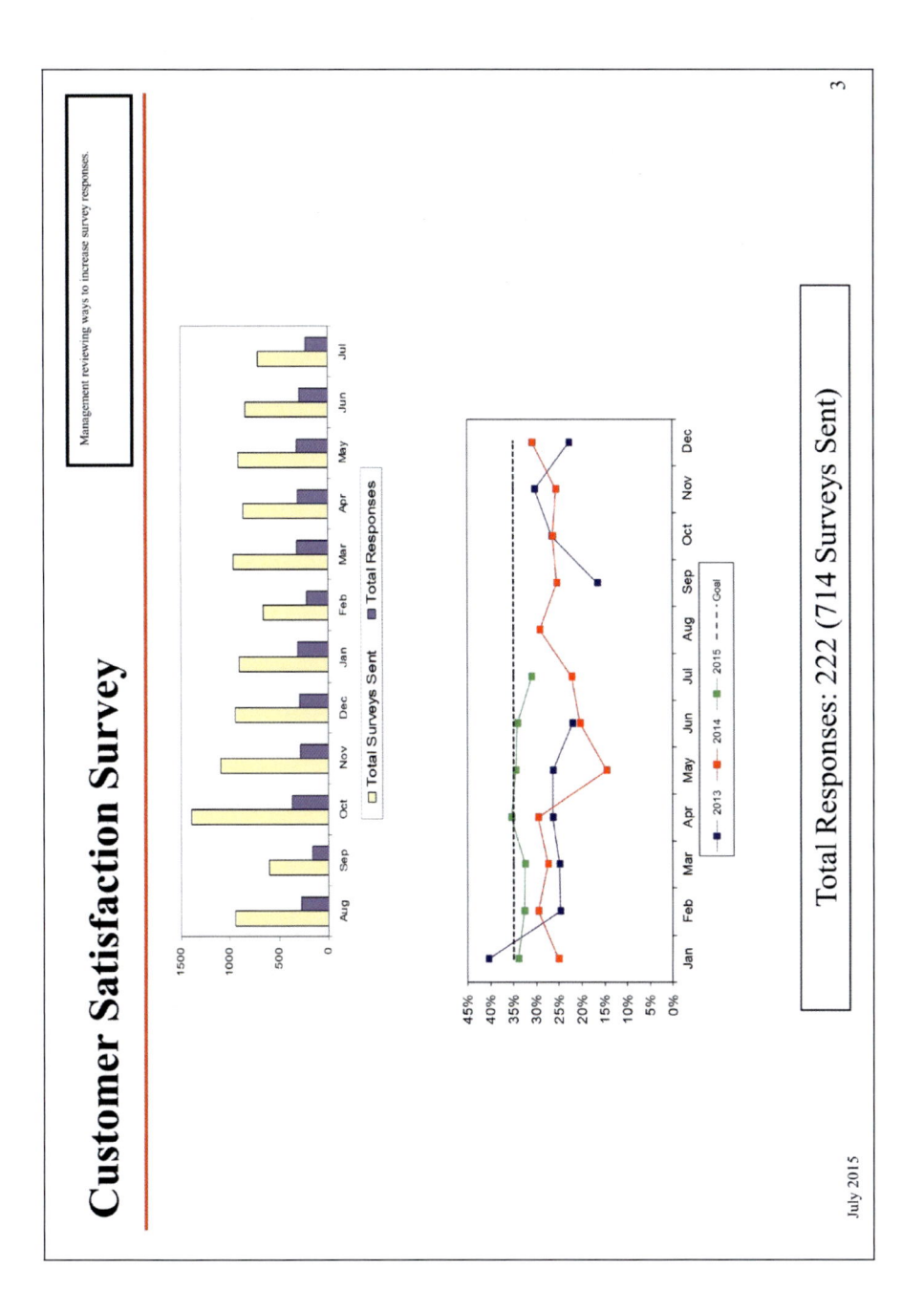

Management reviewing ways to increase survey responses.

Total Responses: 222 (714 Surveys Sent)

July 2015

Metrics for Analyzing What Is Driving Support Calls

The next most important component of your Metrics program will be to use the information you collected during the incident reporting and resolution process to gain insight into what is happening in your environment.

For our sample set of metrics pages we start with a summary page such as the following one:

Calls Closed by Category – Global Tech

No Uncategorized tickets this month.

Category	GTS	NYC	CHG	Total	
BREAK-FIX	7%	44%	49%	100%	% of Break-Fix
Hardware	42	230	255	527	34%
Software	29	174	202	405	
Notes	22	129	163	314	
Network	9	125	112	246	
SERVICE	7%	44%	49%	100%	% of Service
Software	34	236	314	584	66%
Install	44	229	224	497	
Notes	25	219	208	452	
Hardware	20	181	172	373	
Network	13	122	149	284	
Request for Information	17	108	135	260	
EA Transfer	23	83	106	212	
Application How-To	11	50	48	109	
Coordinated Services	0	42	60	102	

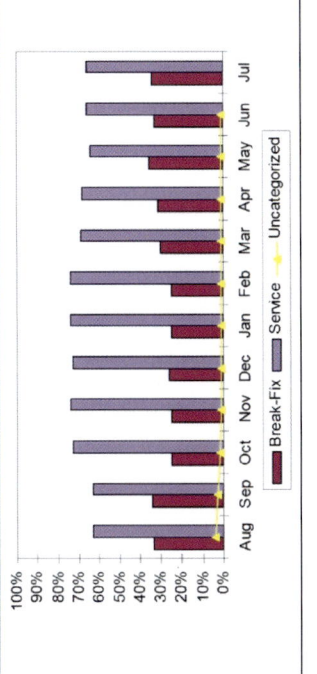

July 2015

You will see that the types of calls are broken down by location and then into two broad categories of Break/Fix and Service.

- Break/Fix amounts to repairs of something that is down. This could be at the workstation, server or network levels and usually requires a reasonably fast response
- Service amounts to anything else. It can be as simple as a call from a user that needs to know how to do something in Excel. It could also be new orders for additional equipment, a new staff member setup request, the installation of a new software package on a machine, etc.

If you find that the vast majority of activities are in the Break/fix category, you definitely need to drill down and find out what is happening!

Break Fix Drill Down

The next chart in our sample package drills down into the Break Fix Category. Note that this no longer is broken down by site. The Level 2 Categorizations are now further broken down into a Level 3 – the underlying items that are consuming the staff's time. This gives you a good window to identify recurring issues and address them permanently.

As an example of that below, If you looked at the Hardware category you will see that Printer (145 calls), laptop (132 calls) and Peripherals (127 calls) are the big consumers of tech time. At this point, you should pull the call records for each of those categories and see if there is a common theme. Printers may just be cartridge replacements, or it could point to an out of date driver that the techs are updating on a one-off basis when they get a call about it. It sure would be easier to push an update to all of the machines if that's what you find. Problem solved – next month watch that category drop to the bottom of the list. This exact methodology has worked for me a number of times and has resulted in significant reductions in call volume and significant increases in customer satisfaction.

Top Break-Fix Calls by Category

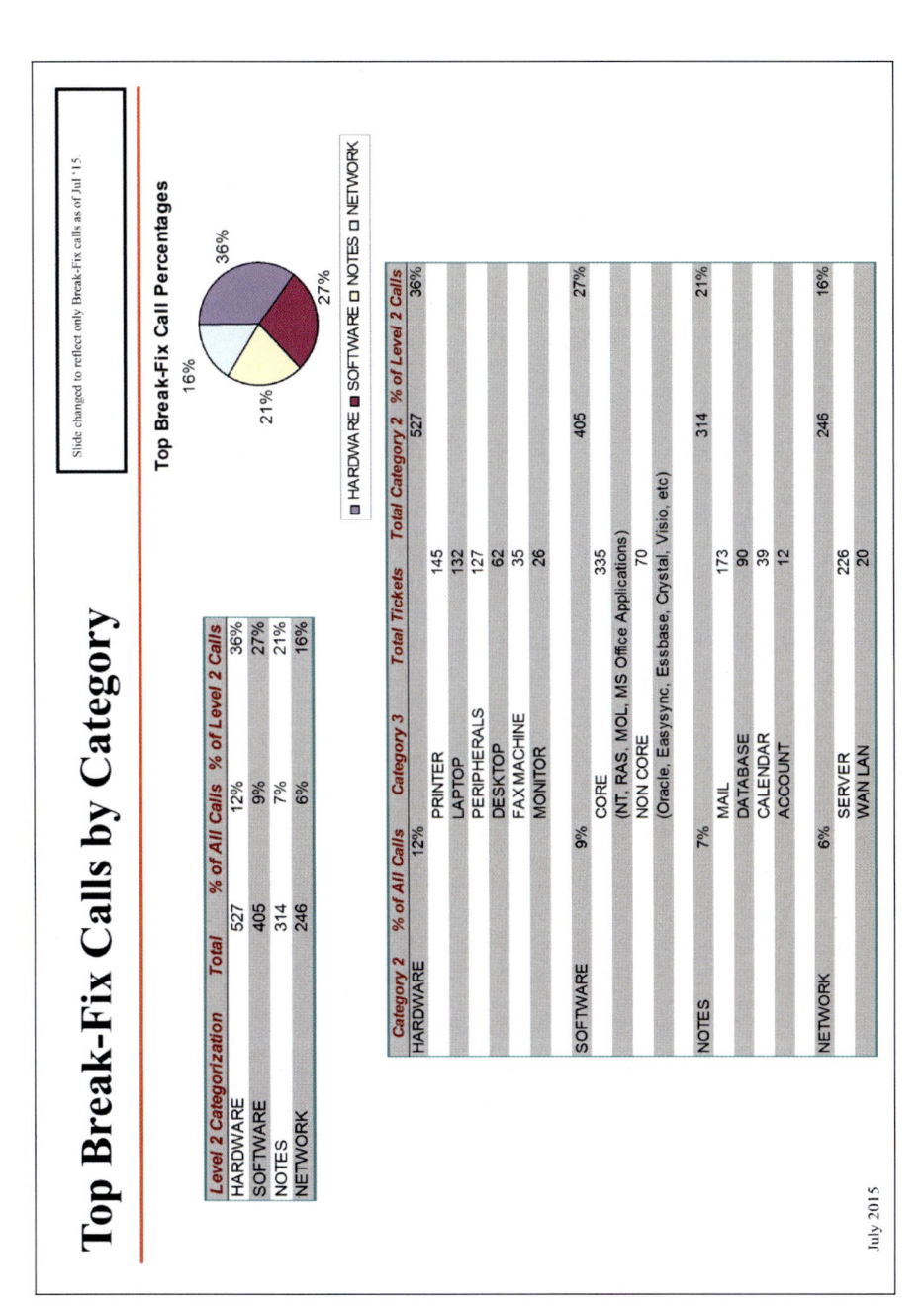

Slide changed to reflect only Break-Fix calls as of Jul '15.

Top Break-Fix Call Percentages

- HARDWARE: 36%
- SOFTWARE: 27%
- NOTES: 21%
- NETWORK: 16%

Level 2 Categorization	Total	% of All Calls	% of Level 2 Calls
HARDWARE	527	12%	36%
SOFTWARE	405	9%	27%
NOTES	314	7%	21%
NETWORK	246	6%	16%

Category 2	% of All Calls	Category 3	Total Tickets	Total Category 2	% of Level 2 Calls
HARDWARE	12%			527	36%
		PRINTER	145		
		LAPTOP	132		
		PERIPHERALS	127		
		DESKTOP	62		
		FAX MACHINE	35		
		MONITOR	26		
SOFTWARE	9%			405	27%
		CORE (NT, RAS, MOL, MS Office Applications)	335		
		NON CORE (Oracle, Easysync, Essbase, Crystal, Visio, etc)	70		
NOTES	7%			314	21%
		MAIL	173		
		DATABASE	90		
		CALENDAR	39		
		ACCOUNT	12		
NETWORK	6%			246	16%
		SERVER	226		
		WAN LAN	20		

July 2015

Call Trending

In order to see how any mitigation or transformation work is going, it's useful to graph the trend of issue and ticket volume over time. To do this we look at how the overall number of calls is trending, but also how the severity of the calls is trending. The obvious goal is to ensure that both the quantity and severity of the issues and service requests go down over time.

In this first chart, the total number of calls by location is trended over time.

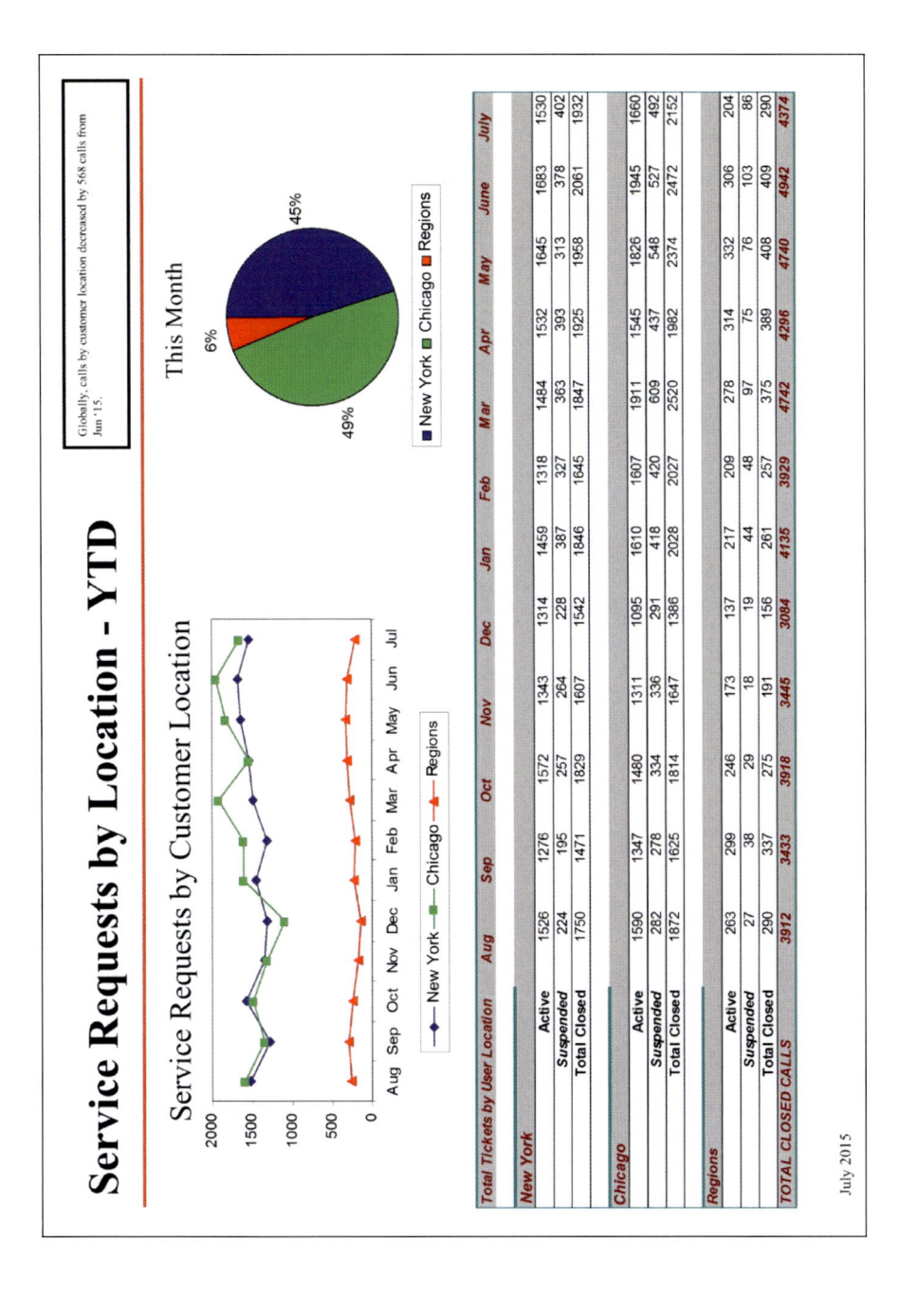

Service Requests by Location - YTD

Globally, calls by customer location decreased by 568 calls from Jun '15.

Service Requests by Customer Location

This Month

- New York: 45%
- Chicago: 49%
- Regions: 6%

Total Tickets by User Location	Aug	Sep	Oct	Nov	Dec	Jan	Feb	Mar	Apr	May	June	July
New York												
Active	1526	1276	1572	1343	1314	1459	1318	1484	1532	1645	1683	1530
Suspended	224	195	257	264	228	387	327	363	393	313	378	402
Total Closed	1750	1471	1829	1607	1542	1846	1645	1847	1925	1958	2061	1932
Chicago												
Active	1590	1347	1480	1311	1095	1610	1607	1911	1545	1826	1945	1660
Suspended	282	278	334	336	291	418	420	609	437	548	527	492
Total Closed	1872	1625	1814	1647	1386	2028	2027	2520	1982	2374	2472	2152
Regions												
Active	263	299	246	173	137	217	209	278	314	332	306	204
Suspended	27	38	29	18	19	44	48	97	75	76	103	86
Total Closed	290	337	275	191	156	261	257	375	389	408	409	290
TOTAL CLOSED CALLS	3912	3433	3918	3445	3084	4135	3929	4742	4296	4740	4942	4374

July 2015

This second trending chart focuses on the number of calls by Severity and the performance against the service level goals that have been set up for that severity. The dotted line on each chart represents the resolution time goal.

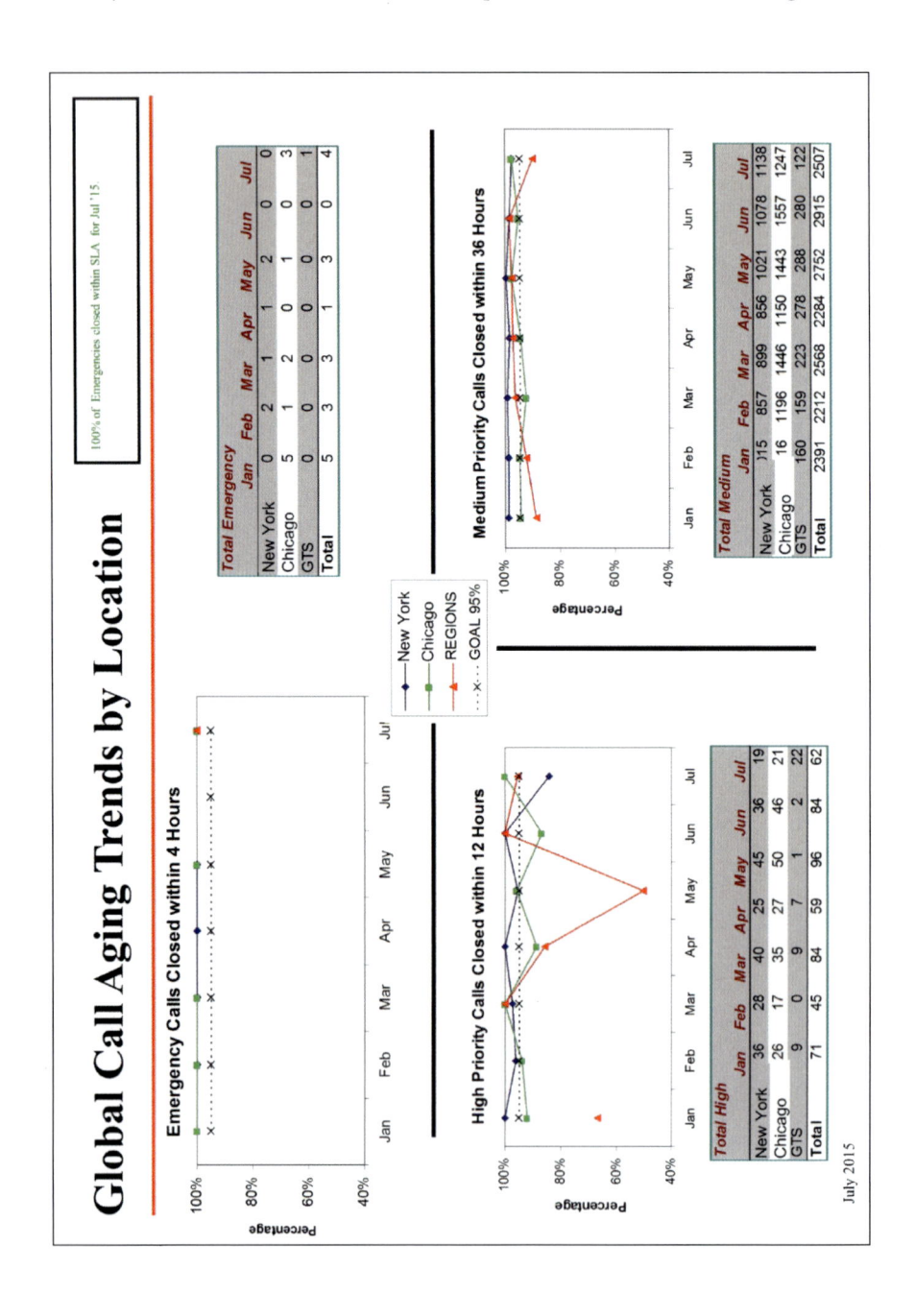

Global Call Aging Trends by Location

Emergency Calls Closed within 4 Hours

Total Emergency

	Jan	Feb	Mar	Apr	May	Jun	Jul
New York	0	2	1	1	2	0	3
Chicago	5	1	2	0	1	0	1
GTS	0	0	0	0	0	0	0
Total	5	3	3	1	3	0	4

100% of Emergencies closed within SLA for Jul '15

High Priority Calls Closed within 12 Hours

Total High

	Jan	Feb	Mar	Apr	May	Jun	Jul
New York	36	28	40	25	45	36	19
Chicago	26	17	35	27	50	46	21
GTS	9	0	9	7	1	2	22
Total	71	45	84	59	96	84	62

Medium Priority Calls Closed within 36 Hours

Total Medium

	Jan	Feb	Mar	Apr	May	Jun	Jul
New York	915	857	899	1150	1021	1078	1138
Chicago	16	1196	1446	278	1443	1557	1247
GTS	160	159	223	278	288	280	122
Total	2391	2212	2568	2284	2752	2915	2507

— New York
— Chicago
— REGIONS
···×··· GOAL 95%

July 2015

214

Finally, taking the location out of the analysis, this chart maps the call resolution time across the business over time. Each of the key severity levels is represented by a different colored line.

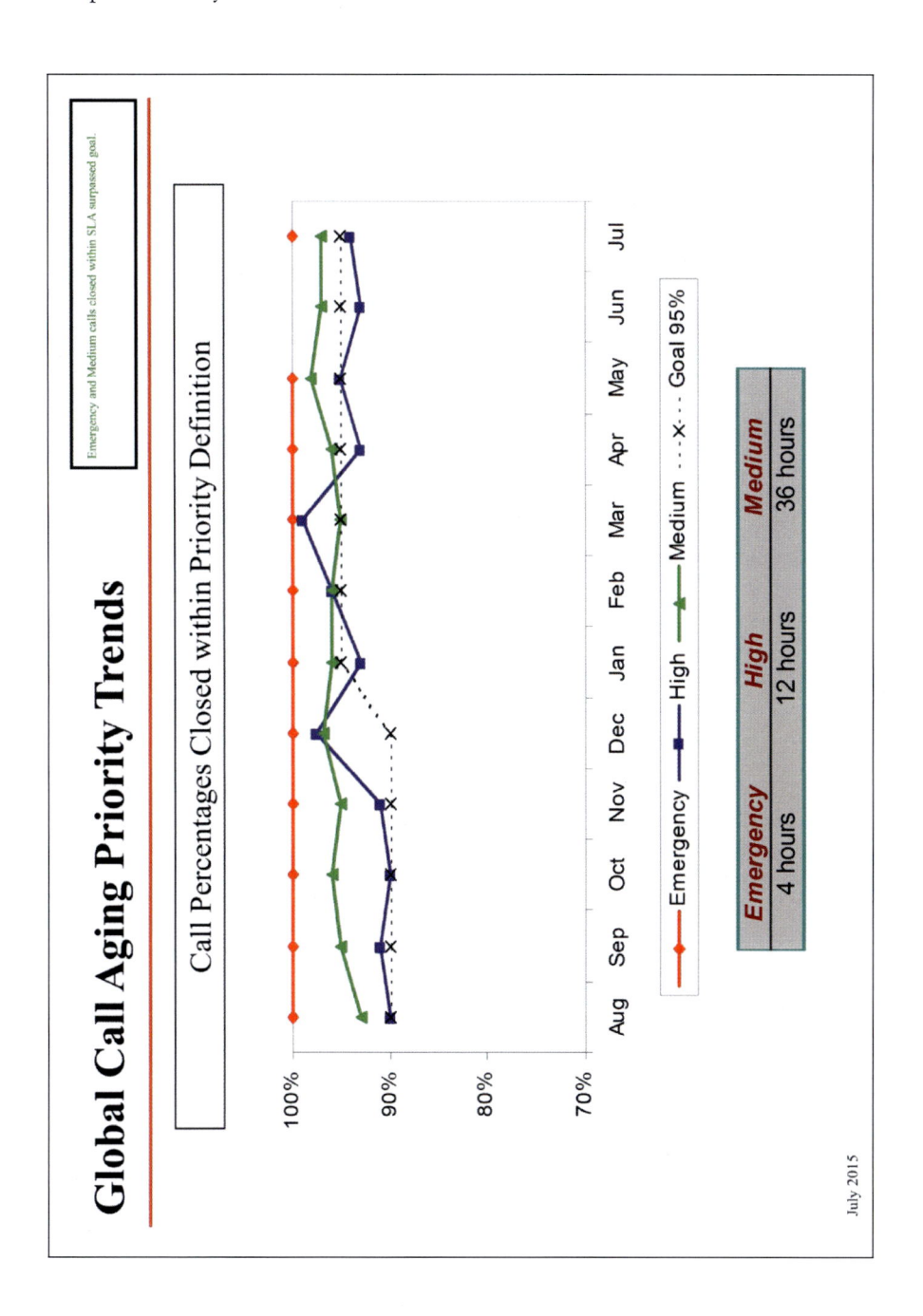

Global Call Aging Priority Trends

Call Percentages Closed within Priority Definition

Emergency and Medium calls closed within SLA surpassed goal.

Emergency	High	Medium
4 hours	12 hours	36 hours

July 2015

Call Aging Metrics

Under the general heading of "Call Aging" I typically would have charts that cover the organization both broadly (all incidents and trouble ticket calls) and also drilling down by location and technical area. So, in the realm of one of my larger Infrastructure roles, my Call Aging Metrics included charts that covered the following

- Global – All calls for all sites and all types of incidents
- Staffed Locations – Focuses on all calls for sites that had onsite IT support.
- Remote Locations – Focuses on sites that did not have any onsite IT group.
- Help Desk –Focuses on calls & incidents that are 100% completed at the Help-Desk.
- Messaging Services –Focuses on Messaging Services related incidents and service requests
- Technical Services by Location – Three charts focused on major sites (New York, Chicago, And Regional Offices collectively)
- Network Services by Major Site - Three charts focused on major sites (New York, Chicago, And Regional Offices collectively)

A single example of the chart's construction is shown below. It consists of four quadrants, one each to the top three severities and the last one being devoted to the aging of "all calls".

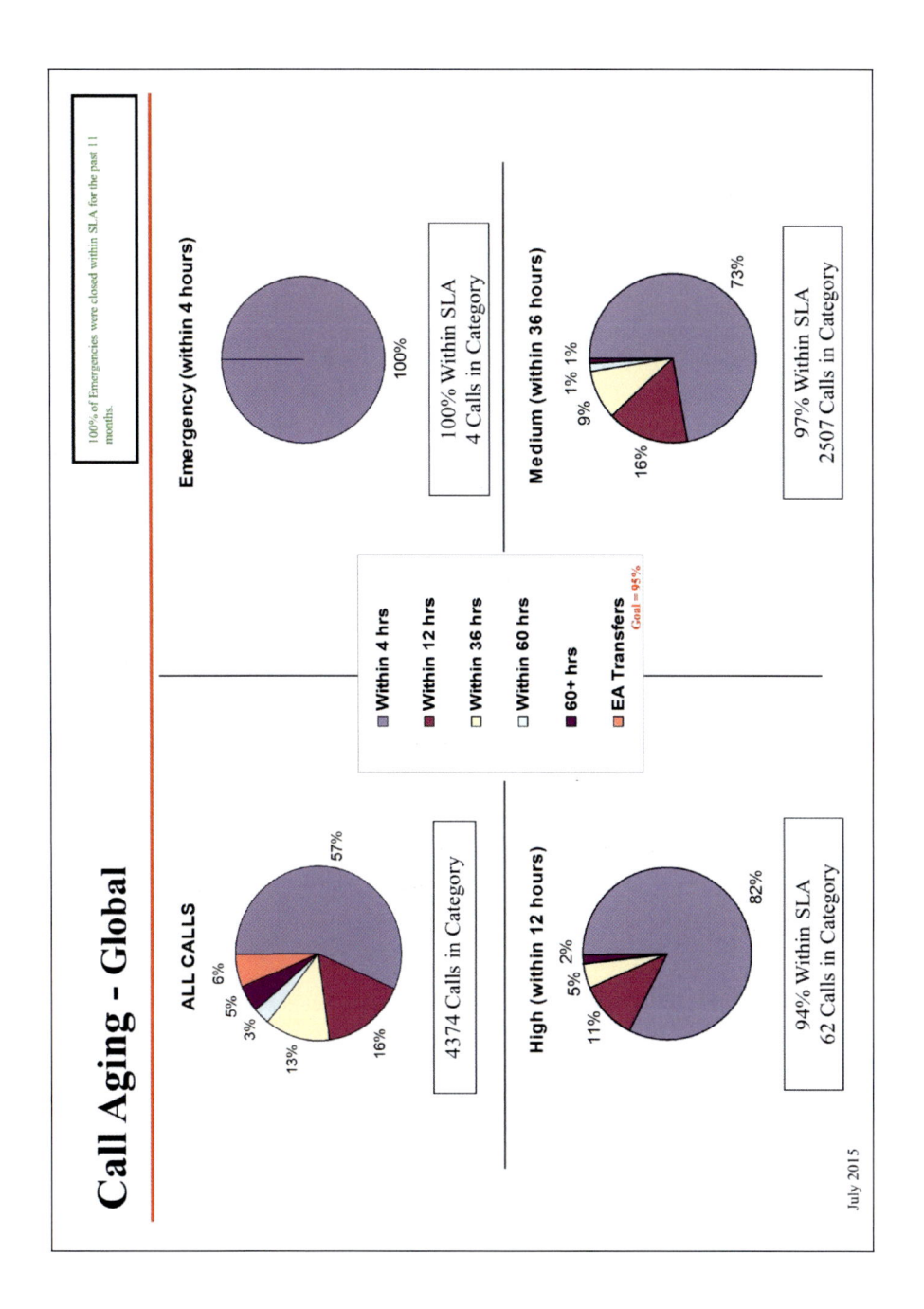

Call Aging - Global

100% of Emergencies were closed within SLA for the past 11 months.

Emergency (within 4 hours)
- 100%

100% Within SLA
4 Calls in Category

Medium (within 36 hours)
- 73%
- 16%
- 9%
- 1%
- 1%

97% Within SLA
2507 Calls in Category

Legend:
- Within 4 hrs
- Within 12 hrs
- Within 36 hrs
- Within 60 hrs
- 60+ hrs
- EA Transfers

Goal = 95%

ALL CALLS
- 57%
- 16%
- 13%
- 3%
- 5%
- 6%

4374 Calls in Category

High (within 12 hours)
- 82%
- 11%
- 5%
- 2%

94% Within SLA
62 Calls in Category

July 2015

The "Key" to the various colors in each pie chart is shown in the center box, along with the designated closure goal of 95% adherence to any SLA for that Severity level. Each quadrant also contains an information box explaining how many total calls in that severity were generated during the reporting period (in this case one month) and the percent of those calls that were resolved within the SLA commitment.

Automatic Call Distribution Metrics

As the size of the organization gets larger, the support staff naturally grows. You will eventually reach a point where you will have peaks and valleys of calls to the Help Desk that need to be understood and managed. At this point, you may be large enough to justify the investment in an Automatic Call Distribution (ACD) System.

An ACD provides a large number of benefits. Most simply, it will distribute calls in whatever fashion it is configured to do so. Most importantly, it will provide Metrics on what is happening – how many calls came in overall; how many calls by hour of the day; How many calls were serviced; Average and peak call wait time (Time to answer calls), Call Duration and Abandoned calls.

Help Desk ACD - Statistics

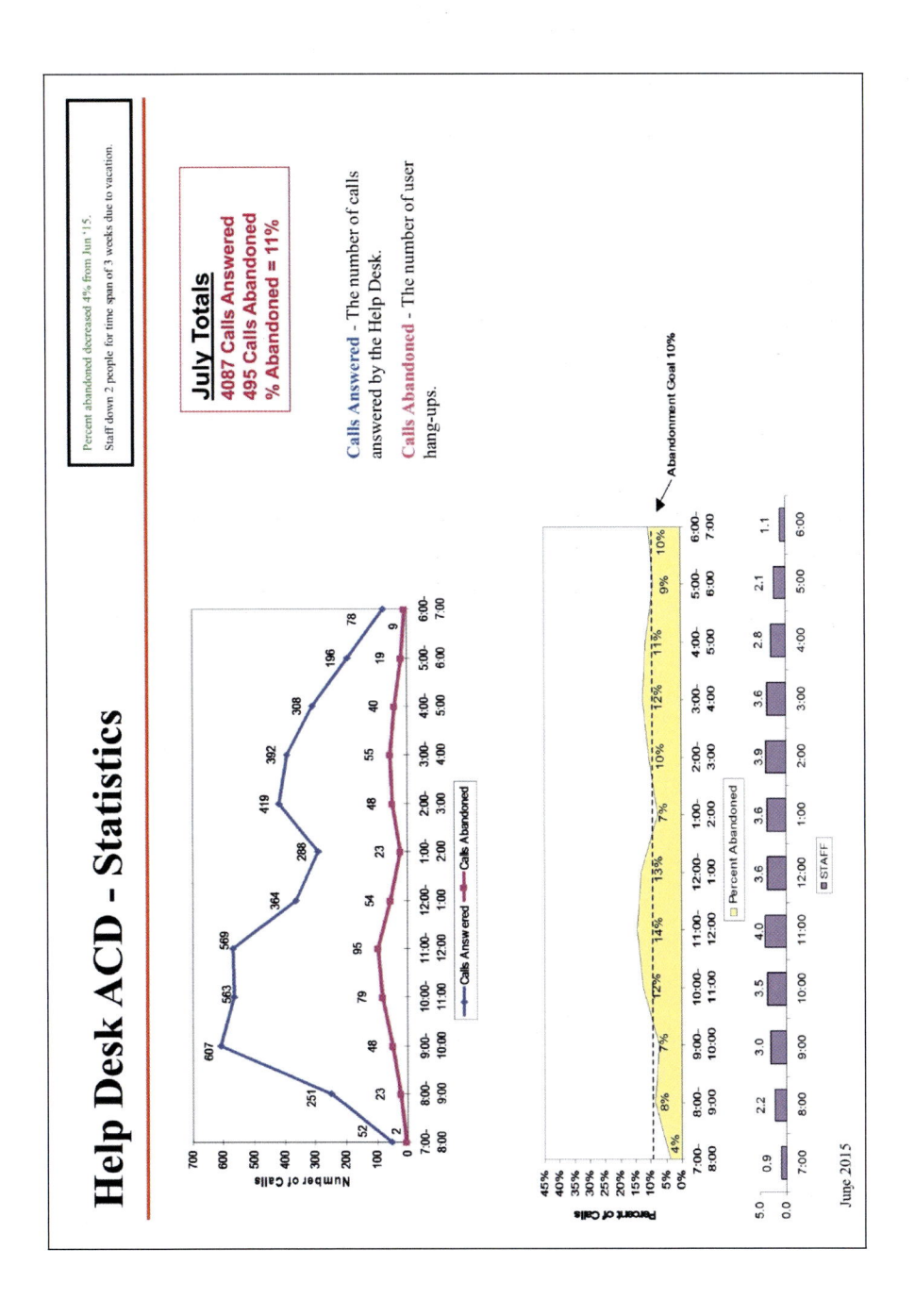

Percent abandoned decreased 4% from Jun '15.
Staff down 2 people for time span of 3 weeks due to vacation.

July Totals
4087 Calls Answered
495 Calls Abandoned
% Abandoned = 11%

Calls Answered - The number of calls answered by the Help Desk.

Calls Abandoned - The number of user hang-ups.

June 2015

Note in the chart on the next page, that some key characteristics of the call are displayed on an hourly basis for the month. Each hour interval is the average of the calls for that hour across the month. In addition, the chart also provides a graph of the average staffing during each hourly interval across the month. This gives you the ability to understand peak times and the associated staffing in place. If the call wait times and abandoned calls increase dramatically during peak times, you can adjust the amount of staff assigned during those hours.

ACD Response Time

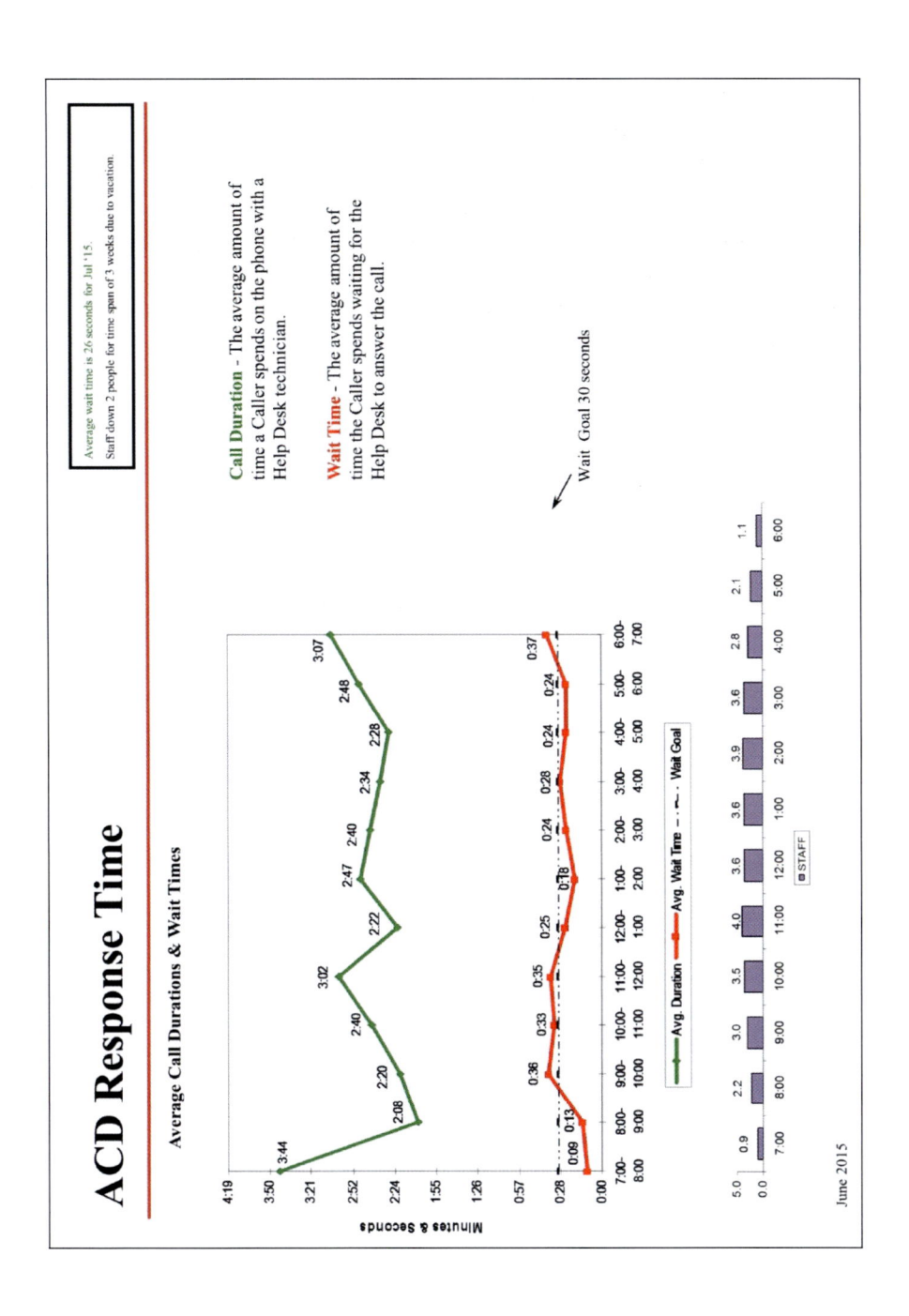

Average wait time is 26 seconds for Jul '15.
Staff down 2 people for time span of 3 weeks due to vacation.

Call Duration - The average amount of time a Caller spends on the phone with a Help Desk technician.

Wait Time - The average amount of time the Caller spends waiting for the Help Desk to answer the call.

Wait Goal 30 seconds

Average Call Durations & Wait Times

June 2015

In the chart on the next page, call volume, answered calls, abandoned calls, abandonment rate and average wait time are plotted year to year to show overall growth in help desk volume. This is essential to demonstrate any performance improvements and also to demonstrate that the growth will require additional staffing.

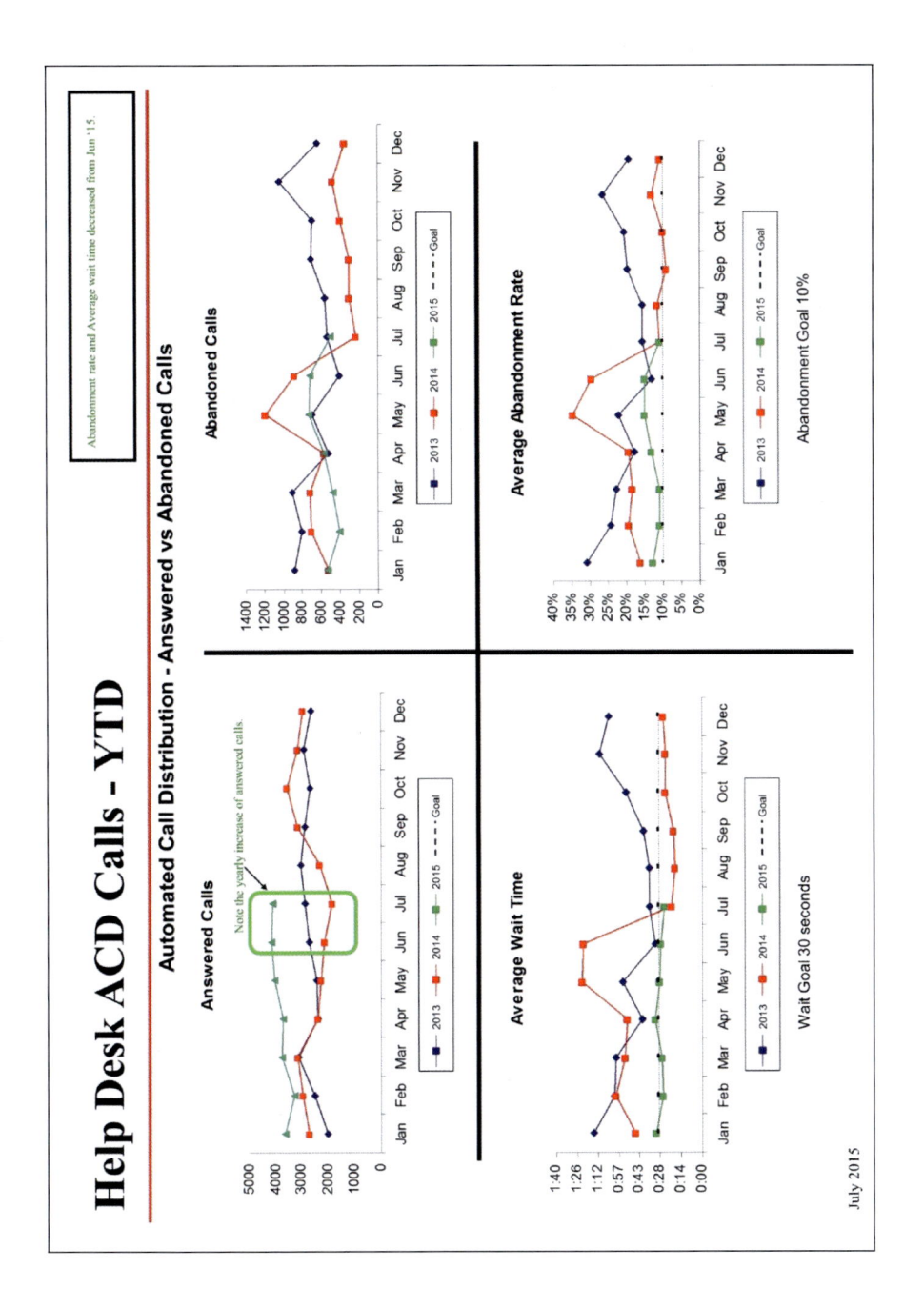

Help Desk ACD Calls - YTD

Abandonment rate and Average wait time decreased from Jun '15.

Automated Call Distribution - Answered vs Abandoned Calls

July 2015

Volume of Tickets / Call Closure

Beyond all of the deep statistics related to user incidents and call closure, there is a need to view what is happening at a very high-level. This chart presents the total volume of tickets that were closed by the Help Desk across multiple years. It further breaks down this aggregate number into those that arrived via the ACD, resulting in a phone call; those that arrived via an EMAIL to the Help Desk; and those that were received by the user leaving a voice mail on the help desk line.

Volume/Tickets Generated/Closure

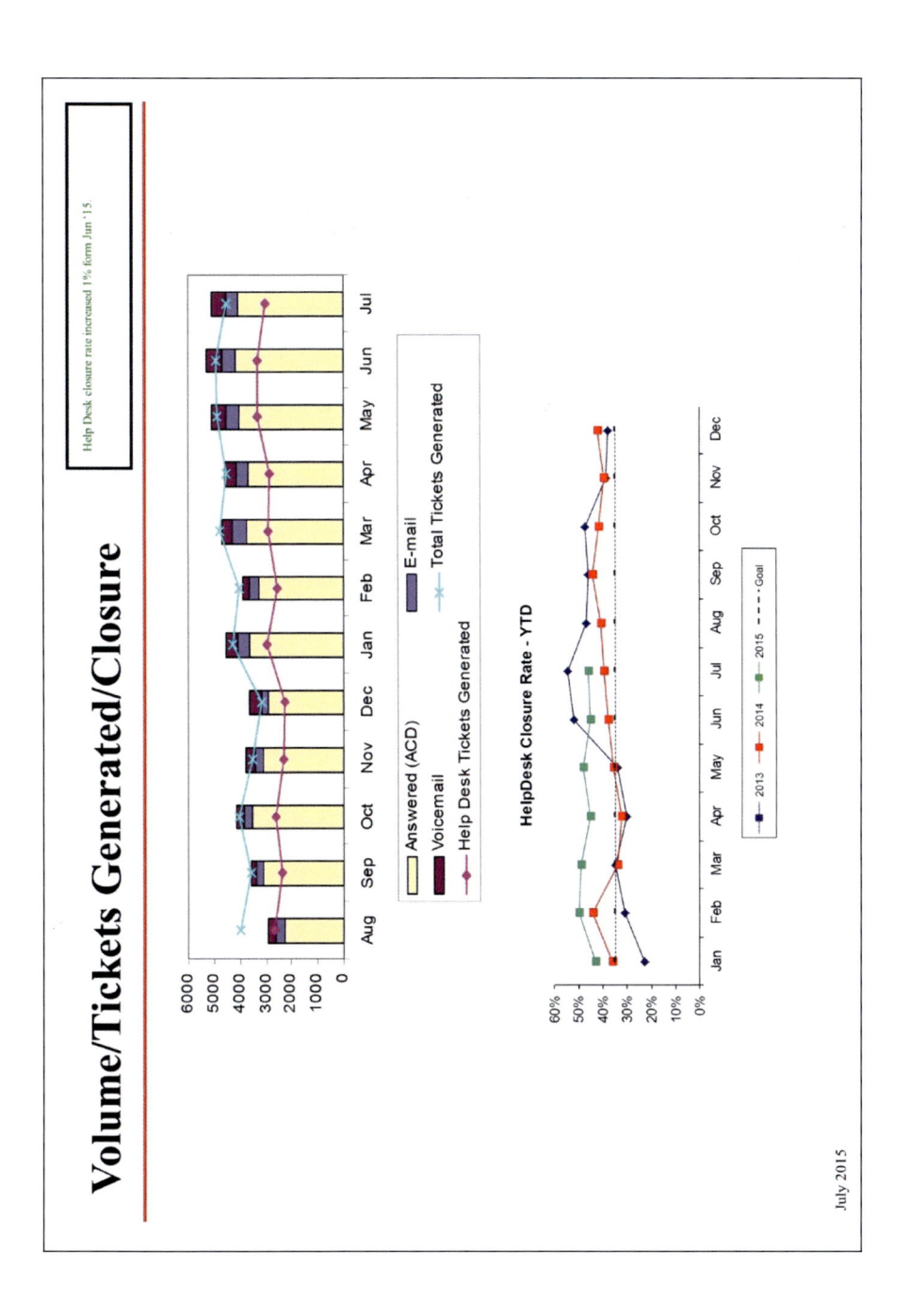

Help Desk closure rate increased 1% form Jun '15

Legend:
- Answered (ACD)
- Voicemail
- E-mail
- Help Desk Tickets Generated
- Total Tickets Generated

HelpDesk Closure Rate - YTD

- 2013
- 2014
- 2015
- Goal

July 2015

Usage Statistics

Another area of reporting is the size of the environment being supported. The number of users is one good indication, however, in many types of companies many of the users can have more than one workstation – Financial Traders may have two or more computers at their desk. Many employees have both desktops at the office and a laptop for at home and on the road. This makes reporting on the number of workstations a more accurate indicator of the size of the environment that End User Support and the Help Desk is supporting.

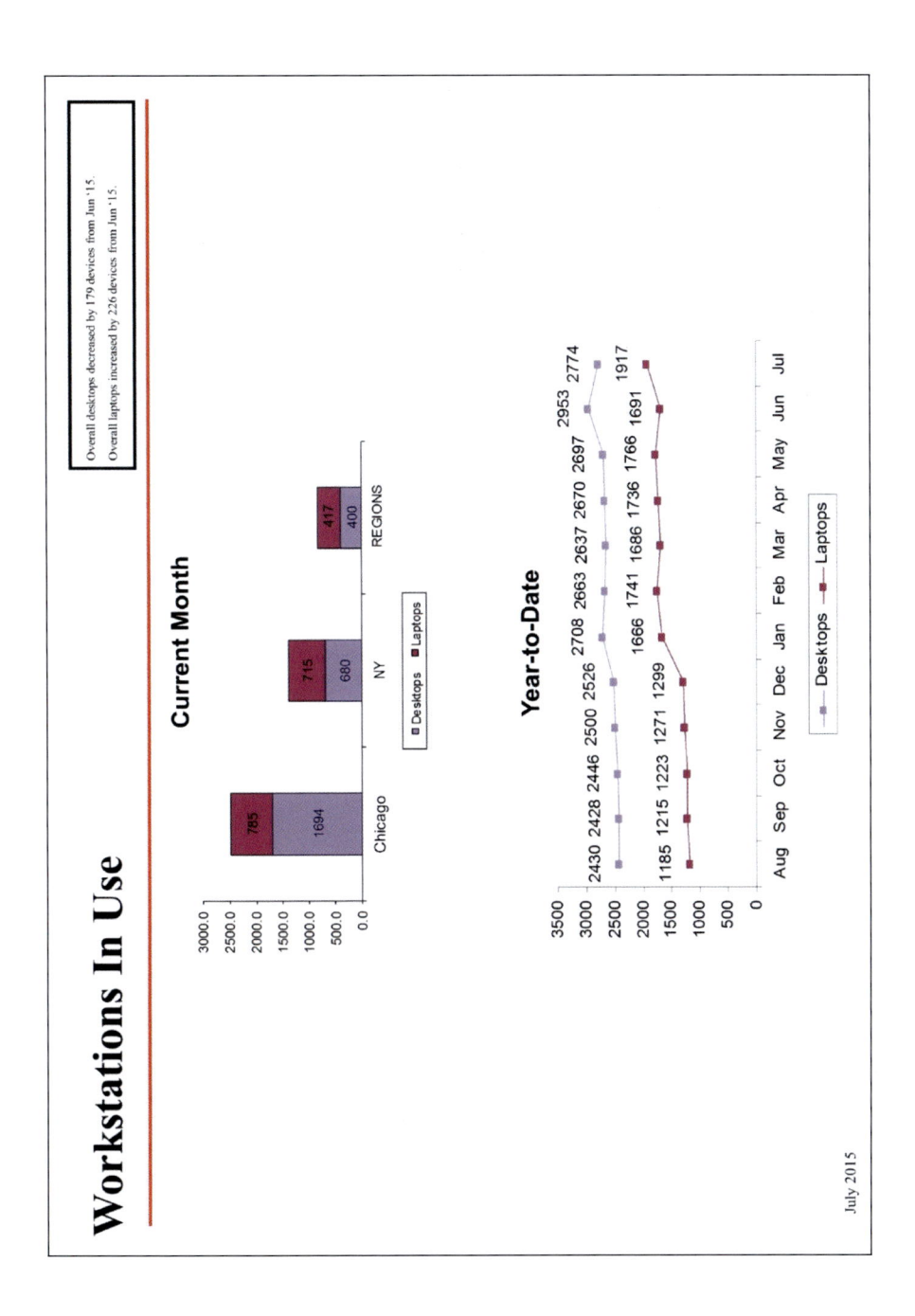

Workstations In Use

Overall desktops decreased by 179 devices from Jun '15.
Overall laptops increased by 226 devices from Jun '15.

Current Month

Region	Desktops	Laptops
Chicago	785	1694
NY	715	680
REGIONS	417	400

Year-to-Date

Desktops: 1185, 1215, 1223, 1271, 1299, 1666, 1741, 1686, 1736, 1766, 1691, 1917

Laptops: 2430, 2428, 2446, 2500, 2526, 2708, 2663, 2637, 2670, 2697, 2953, 2774

Months: Aug, Sep, Oct, Nov, Dec, Jan, Feb, Mar, Apr, May, Jun, Jul

July 2015

Remote Access Services

Remote Access Services – Another measure of the services being delivered is the number of users that are entitled to attach to the systems remotely. In addition, the number of active sessions over the preceding reporting period would also be a helpful measure.

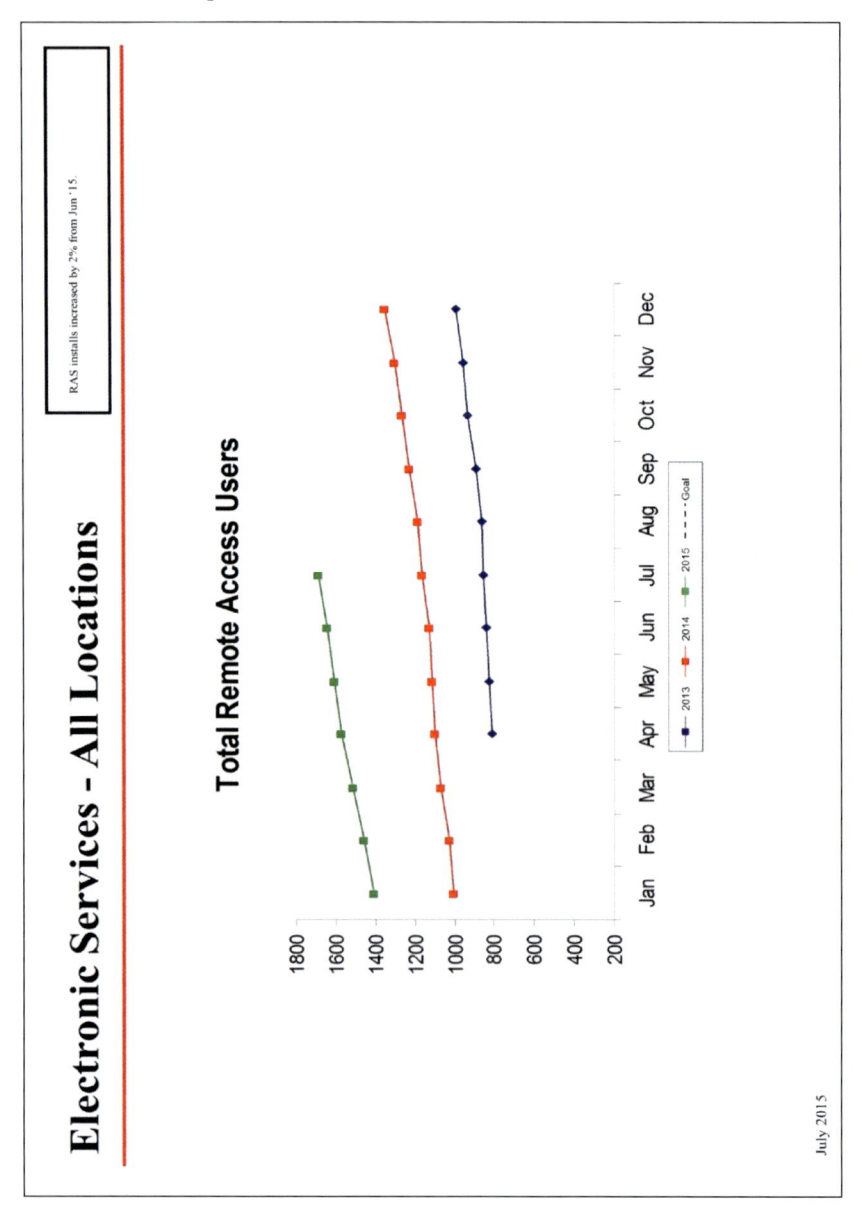

Electronic Services - All Locations

Total Remote Access Users

RAS installs increased by 2% from Jun '15.

July 2015

Messaging Services

Messaging has become one of the most critical IT services being delivered to the users. Understanding the activity and how that activity is growing is critical to delivering a reliable environment. This chart provides usage statistics over the preceding reporting period. It breaks the message activity down into Internal (user to user), external (between the internal user and an outside account), text messages, and Fax messages.

Messaging Services - Monthly Activity

All services are increasing steadily, for the year they are on track to show 50% increases in volume.

Internal Mail

Internet Mail

Text Messages

Fax Messages

July 2015

Messaging Usage Trended over 3 years – Again, this chart provides a trend of the TOTAL message usage over three years and is used for capacity planning and resourcing purposes.

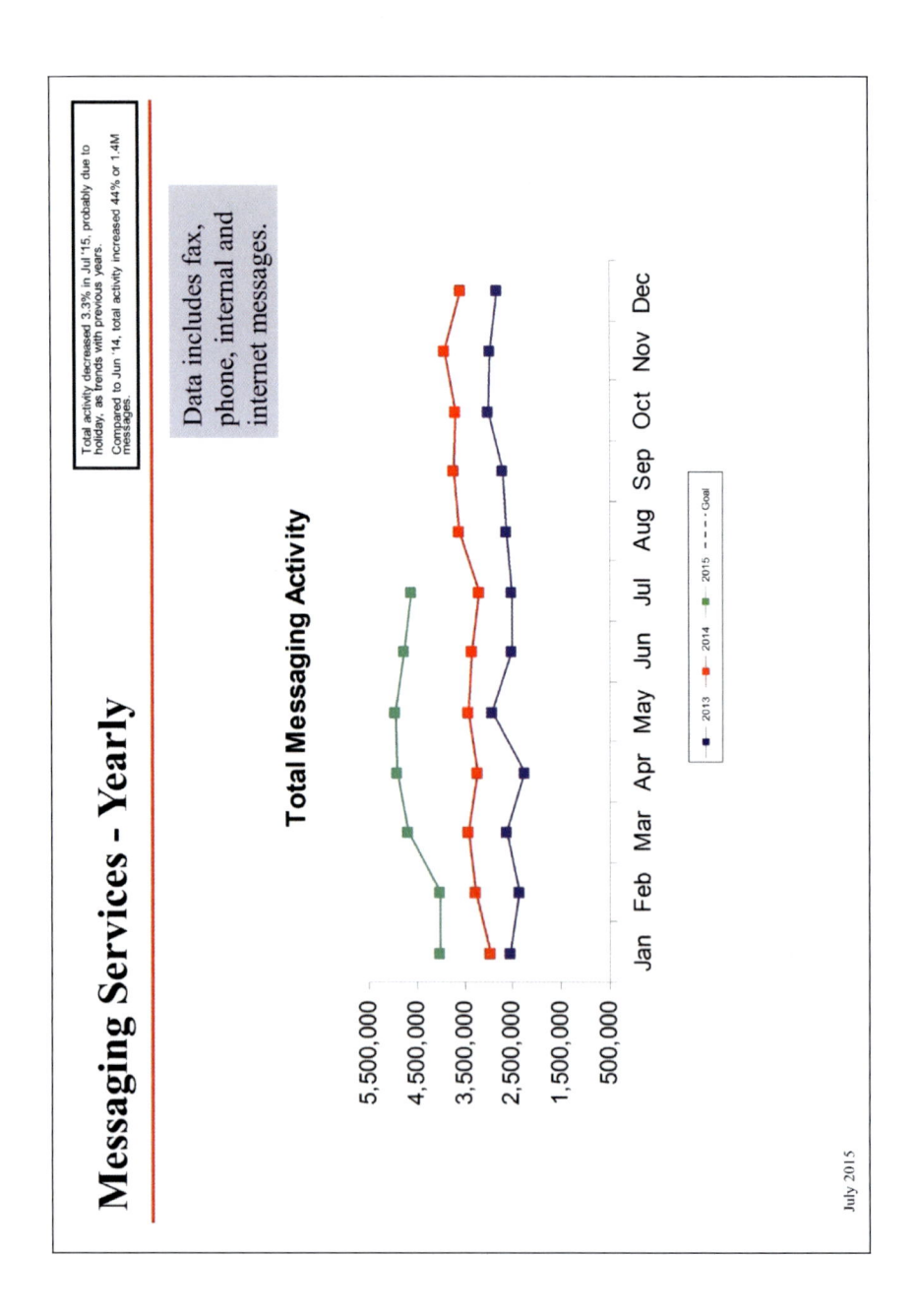

Messaging Services - Yearly

Total Messaging Activity

Total activity decreased 3.3% in Jul '15, probably due to holiday, as trends with previous years.
Compared to Jun '14, total activity increased 44% or 1.4M messages.

Data includes fax, phone, internal and internet messages.

July 2015

230

Messaging Usage Trended over 3 years – This chart presents message volume by message type over three years and is also used for capacity planning and resourcing purposes

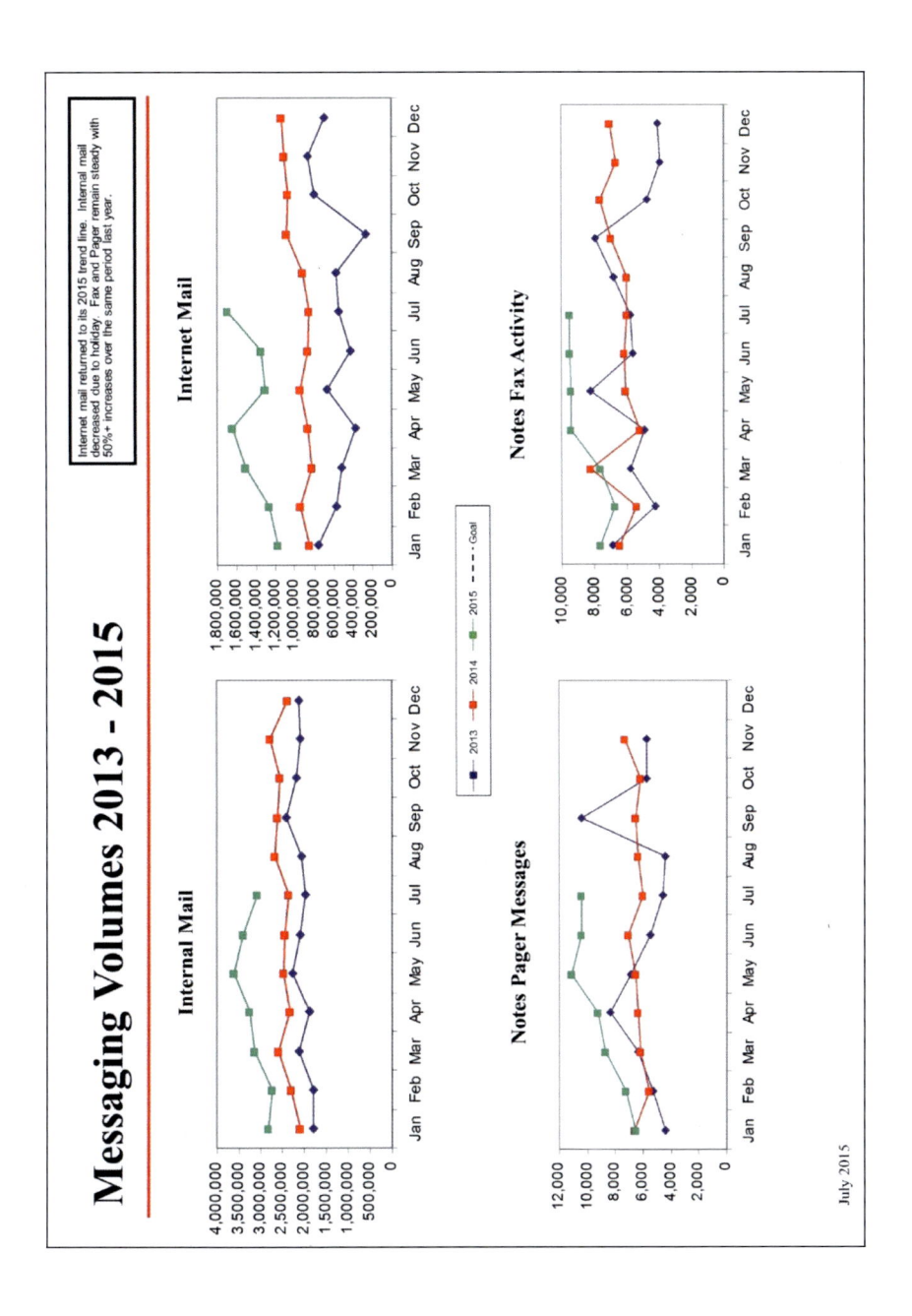

Messaging usage by site – This chart presents the total message activity by site and further averaged in those sites by user. It is used for capacity planning purposes.

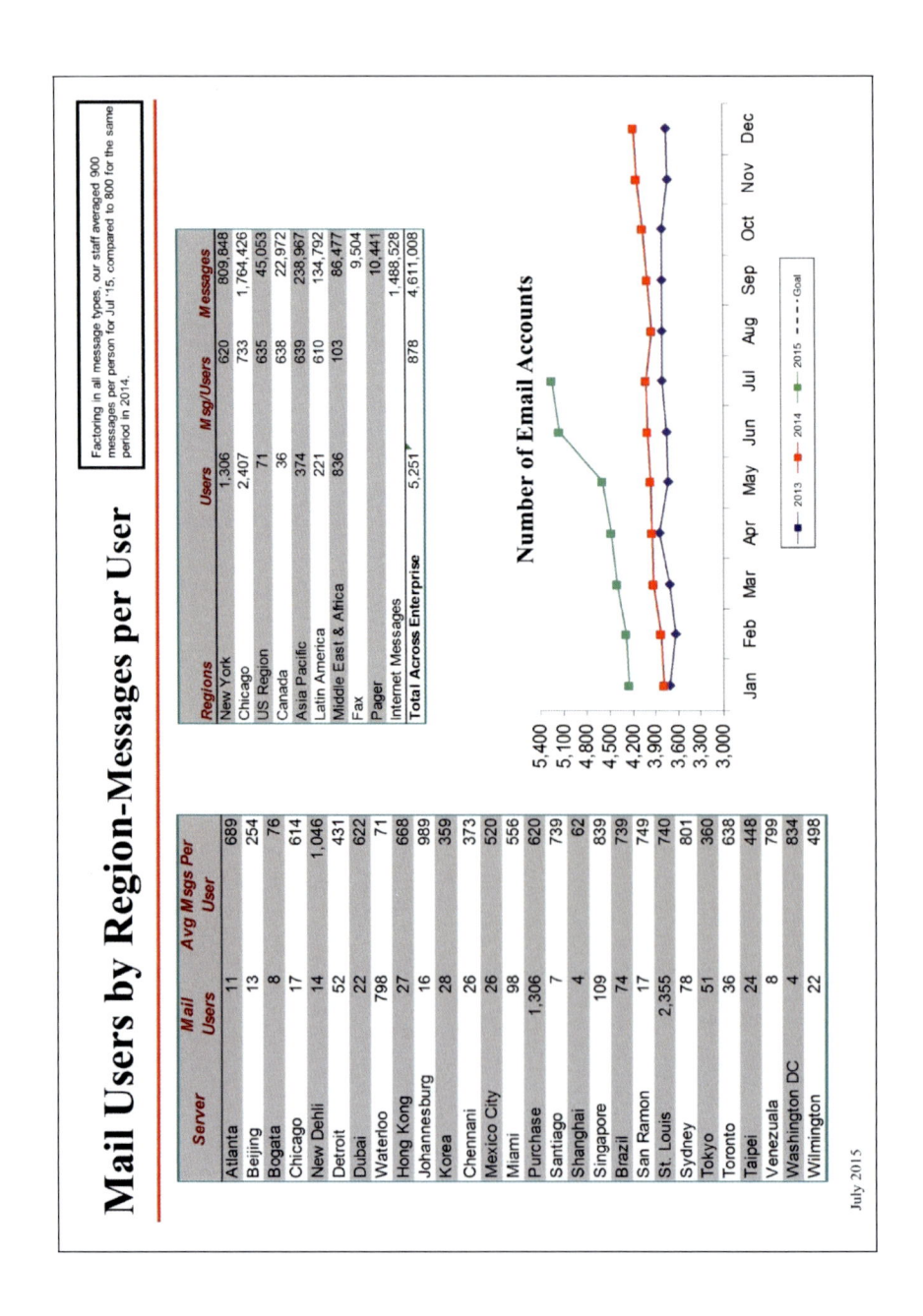

Mail Users by Region-Messages per User

Server	Mail Users	Avg Msgs Per User
Atlanta	11	689
Beijing	13	254
Bogata	8	76
Chicago	17	614
New Dehli	14	1,046
Detroit	52	431
Dubai	22	622
Waterloo	798	71
Hong Kong	27	668
Johannesburg	16	989
Korea	28	359
Chennani	26	373
Mexico City	26	520
Miami	98	556
Purchase	1,306	620
Santiago	7	739
Shanghai	4	62
Singapore	109	839
Brazil	74	739
San Ramon	17	749
St. Louis	2,355	740
Sydney	78	801
Tokyo	51	360
Toronto	36	638
Taipei	24	448
Venezuela	8	799
Washington DC	4	834
Wilmington	22	498

July 2015

Regions	Users	Msg/Users	Messages
New York	1,306	620	809,848
Chicago	2,407	733	1,764,426
US Region	71	635	45,053
Canada	36	638	22,972
Asia Pacific	374	639	238,967
Latin America	221	610	134,792
Middle East & Africa	836	103	86,477
Fax			9,504
Pager			10,441
Internet Messages			1,488,528
Total Across Enterprise	5,251	878	4,611,008

Factoring in all message types, our staff averaged 900 messages per person for Jul '15, compared to 800 for the same period in 2014.

Number of Email Accounts

(Chart showing monthly data Jan-Dec for 2013, 2014, 2015, and Goal, with values ranging from 3,000 to 5,400)

232

Server Availability

Clearly one of the key metrics that needs to be accumulated and reported on is the availability of the various technology environments. Server Availability by type is one such measure. In this chart, the various types of servers have their availability statistics reported on. It is important to note that the tools that accumulate server availability statistics should also provide alerting in the event a server is not responding. This chart does not define the reasons for "unavailability", just the overall statistics of availability.

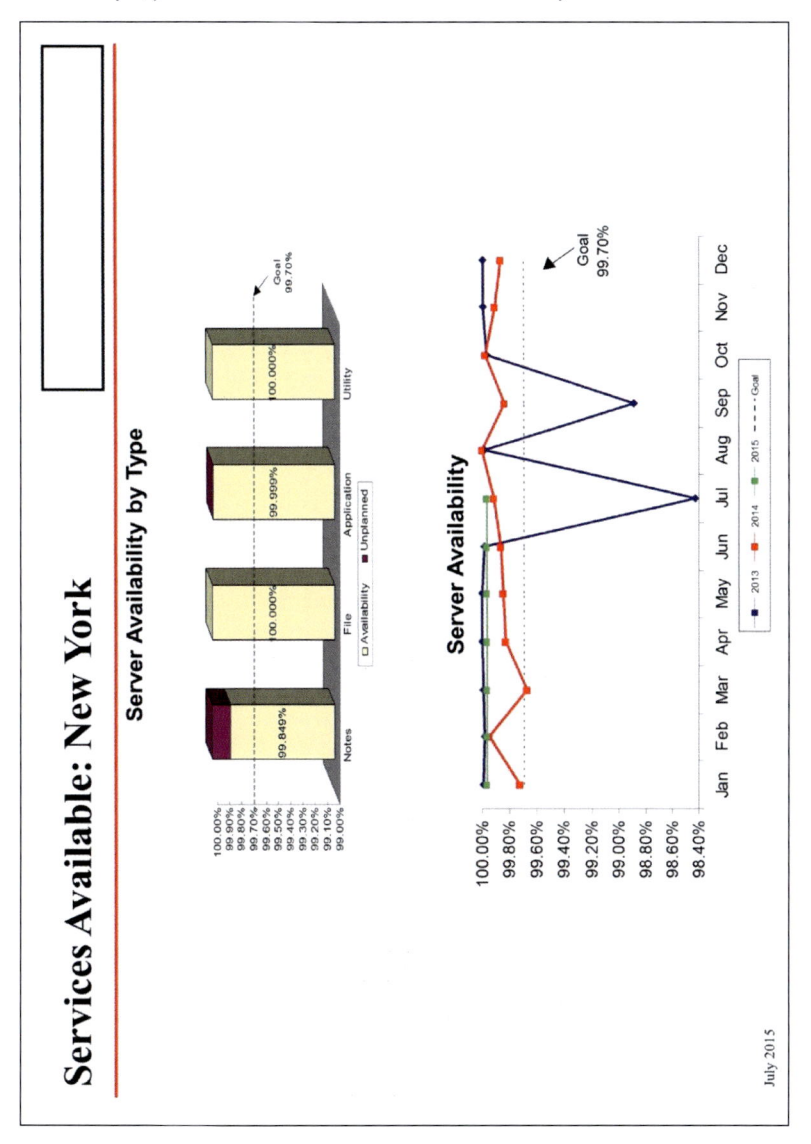

Storage Availability

Storage Availability is designed to look at how much Storage space is still available. This is used for capacity planning purposes. A well-designed storage monitoring facility will monitor the overall storage availability, as well as the availability of storage allocated to the individual servers.

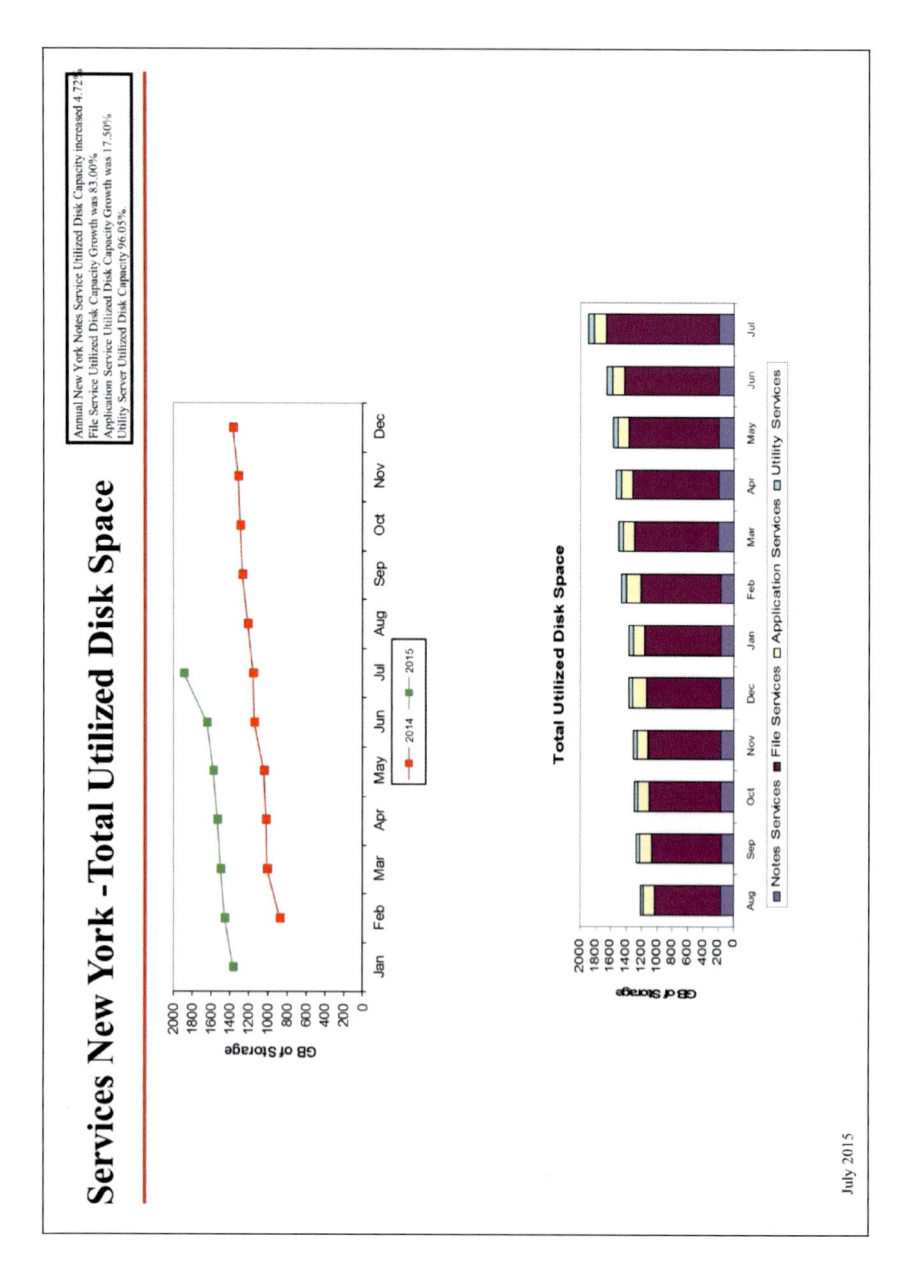

Network Availability

Similar to Storage Availability, Network Availability will provide the overall statistics on any downtime that was experienced over the last reporting period. Ideally, this availability measurement should be presented for each circuit individually. Along with Network Availability come measurements of Network Utilization. Again for capacity planning purposes, it is important to understand how much of the available bandwidth is being consumed. This will help you address any future capacity issues before utilization goes too high. It will also allow you to understand if you have oversized circuits in

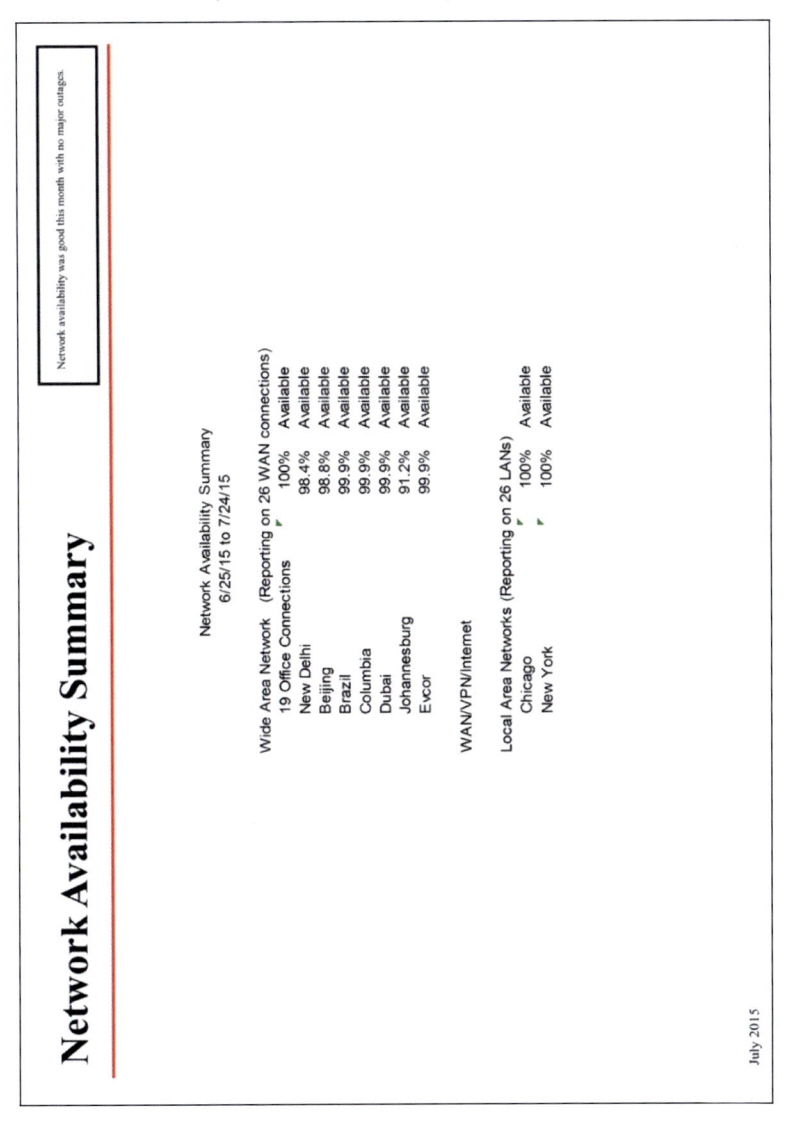

Network Availability Summary

Network Availability Summary
6/25/15 to 7/24/15

Wide Area Network (Reporting on 26 WAN connections)

19 Office Connections	100%	Available
New Delhi	98.4%	Available
Beijing	98.8%	Available
Brazil	99.9%	Available
Columbia	99.9%	Available
Dubai	99.9%	Available
Johannesburg	91.2%	Available
Evcor	99.9%	Available

WAN/VPN/Internet

Local Area Networks (Reporting on 26 LANs)

Chicago	100%	Available
New York	100%	Available

Network availability was good this month with no major outages.

July 2015

Mobile Devices

The final area of metrics tracking that will be examined is the Mobile Device environment. While there are many different metrics that we can develop for this area, we will simply define a chart that measures the absolute number of devices.

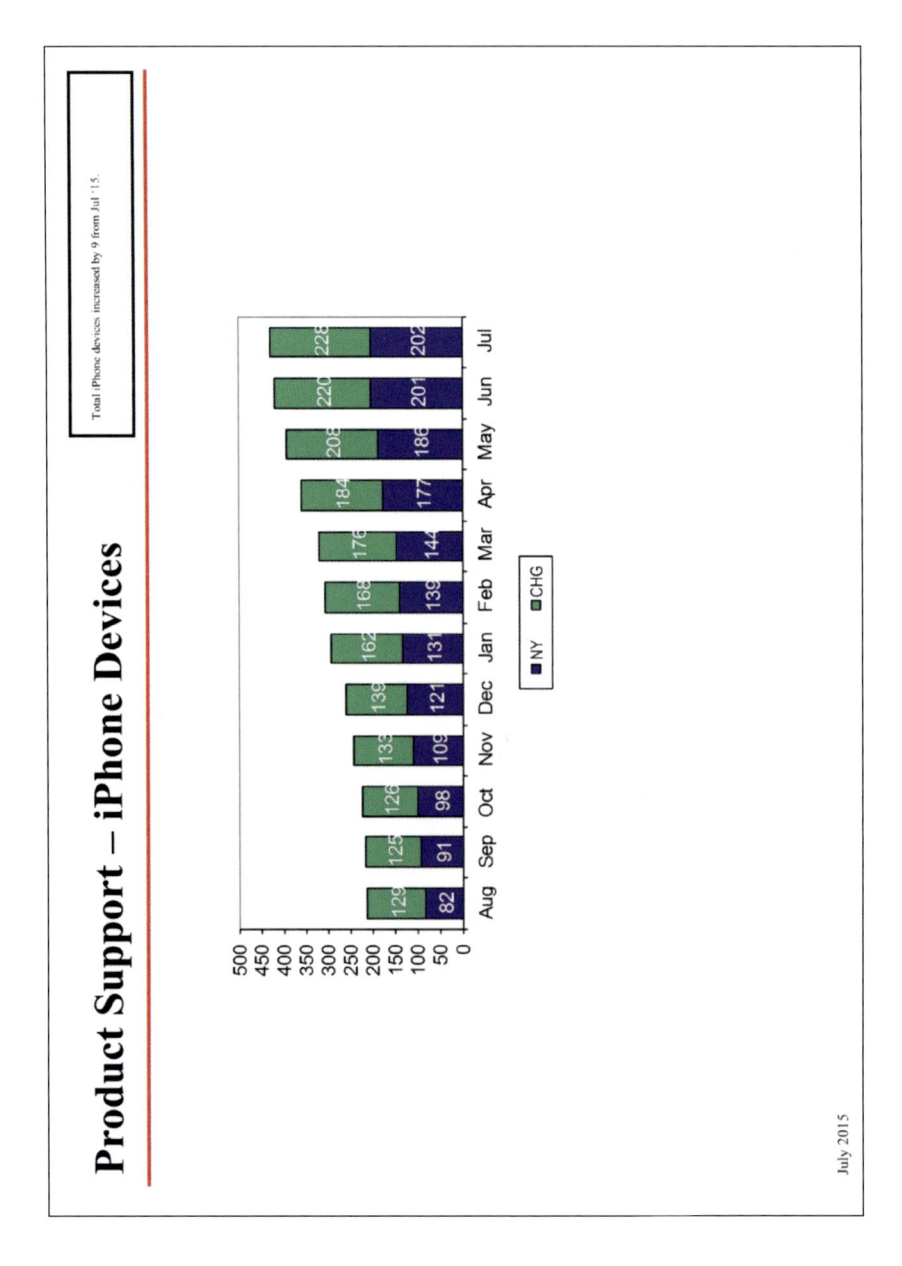

Chapter 16

Developing your IT Strategy

This book has focused mostly on the tactical or operational aspects of running an IT Infrastructure organization. In order to ensure you are providing maximum long-term value to the business, you must break from viewing your organization in a tactical day-by-day fashion and instead look at how your portion of IT is creating long-term value to the business. This is the realm of the IT Strategy.

This subject of IT strategy is huge and is the subject of many very large books (and countless thousands of articles). This book will provide an introduction to the subject in an effort to get your thinking to expand into the more long-range end-state goals.

What is an IT Strategy?

In one article I read the author started with the statement "Hope is not a strategy". He hit the nail on the head with that thought. Too many IT shops operate without a defined, written IT Strategy that links the investments IT makes and the activities IT performs to the goals of the business. They "Hope" they are doing the right things.

An IT Strategy is a comprehensive plan that the IT Management team uses to guide their organizations. It is a document that clarifies what the IT organization and technical environment is today and what it will become. It is a forward-looking plan that often focuses on or defines the end state of a transformation effort, the ultimate goal being an alignment of IT with the goals of the business. It is not a static plan, but evolves along with the business – it is a process, not a point in time.

The IT Strategy is often crafted either in partnership with the business or with substantial business guidance and approval. The most successful IT Strategy is where the capabilities of both the business and IT drive each other – rather than the business driving IT with nothing happening in the other direction. It should have demonstrable and measurable links to the business strategy.

The IT Strategy sets the direction for the IT function in an organization. It ensures that the greatest number of IT dollars is spent on activities that create maximum value for the business

An IT Strategic plan will address the following areas:

- Cost Management
- Human Capital Management
- Risk Management
- Asset Management
- Vendor Management
- Hardware Management
- Software Management
- Network Management

The IT Strategy is designed to ensure that IT is delivering the greatest possible value to the business. It must take into consideration the business' priorities, such as cost reduction, global expansion, digitization and so on; it must support the business' needs, such as providing the right tools and applications; it must be flexible to adjust along with changes to the business environment and it must also provide the tools to measure value and progress in a demonstrable way, providing the feedback to keep both the technology and business activities on track to meet goals. Your IT Strategy, therefore, should answer the following questions:

- Are we doing the right things with technology to address the organization's most important business priorities and continuously deliver value to the clients?
- Can our IT Strategy support current and future business needs?
- Is the IT environment sufficiently agile and flexible to continuously support a successful organization?
- Are we making the right technology investments?
- Is the IT environment well managed, maintained, secured, able to support the clients, and is it cost effective?
- Do we measure what is the real value that technology brings to the organization?

Most new IT managers have a difficult time adjusting to the strategic thinking required in their new role. If you recall in the section discussing issues which can derail you in your new job, an inability to think strategically is one of the items on the list.

Again, you become the person that must ensure the technology you deploy is well aligned with the long-term goals of the organization. Those long-term company goals drive your definition of the long-term target architecture for your environment. You must ensure that your organization's activities are all designed to evolve the technical environment into that long-term vision.

The Process of Defining an IT Strategy

Before you can start down the path of defining an IT Strategy, you need a good understanding of the current state of IT. You need to complete your IT assessment first, understanding the strengths and weaknesses of the organization, the current state of customer satisfaction, etc.

You also need to clearly understand the goals of the business and what they need to get there. Once you understand what your team is providing and what the business needs you will most likely realize two things: (1) Your group is not providing everything the business needs to meet the business goals and (2) The business does not fully understand how to leverage IT to get the maximum value for the business.

From a process standpoint, creating your IT Strategy consists of following a few well-defined steps:

1. Understand the business' strategic drivers

2. Understand the current state of IT
3. Identify gaps, risks, and opportunities for improvement
4. Define the future state of IT
5. Measure, provide feedback and adjust your direction

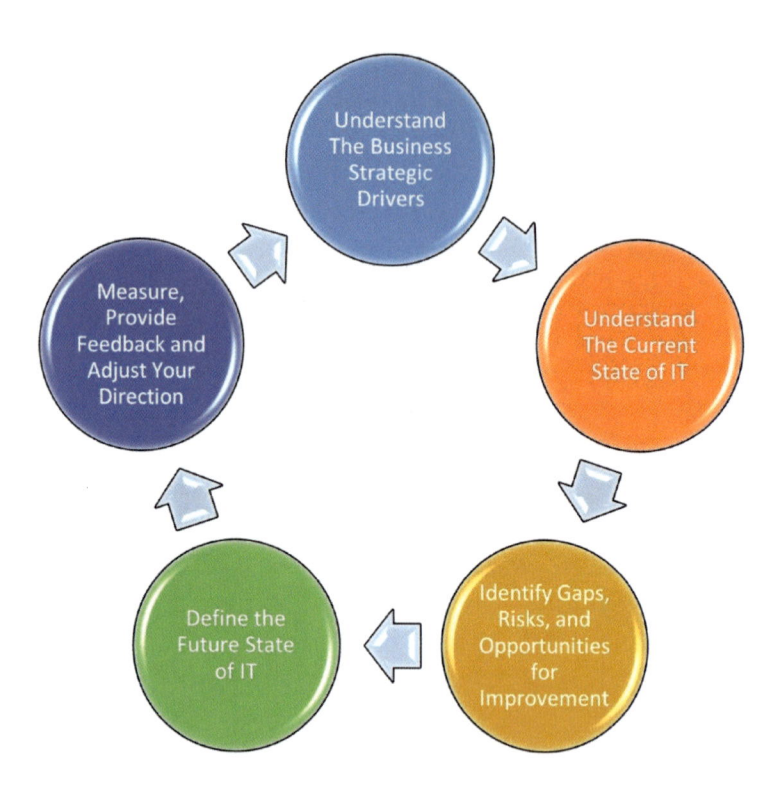

Developing an IT Strategy

Engaging with the Business

IT alignment with the business goals and strategy - you hear it in every discussion of IT strategy. How will you accomplish that? Most companies define their strategic objectives in terms of revenue growth, cost reduction, customer satisfaction, social media presence, global expansion, mergers and acquisitions, and the like. Strategically mature companies will cascade the enterprise plans down to the functional units and business units of the company. In so many cases today the business plans do not so much depend on IT for the success of its plans, but actually define plans that are completely built on and dependent on IT as the underlying platform for the business. Put another way that business would not / could not exist without a specialized IT platform that makes it function. As a result, IT needs to weave itself into the narrative of each of those plans.

Two examples I will give of such an environment is Quicken Loans and Credit Card companies.

Quicken loans have a fully exposed digitized workflow platform onto which all documents and decisions flow. Applications and other necessary documents are completed via their website; supporting documents are uploaded to their website and communications between customers and Quicken staff occurs within the site. Inside the company, the approval process uses the platform to provide workflow across the various approval steps. While the company might not be completely out of business without this environment, its ability to respond almost instantly to customer applications provides a huge competitive advantage. It is, in fact, the value proposition and differentiator that Quicken Loans advertises to its potential customers.

Credit card companies have evolved from what started as transaction switches between the vendors and the issuing banks and have evolved over time to deliver a wide range of services to their customers, who for the credit card companies (as in MasterCard and Visa) are the Banks, not the individual consumer. Consumers and Merchants are the customers of the Banks that issues the cards and provide the merchant accounts. In the case of the credit card companies, while the main product is moving transactions between vendors and banks through the transaction switch (as well as brand marketing, of course), key products include Analytics – they are wide and they are deep.

In both of these cases, the monumental level of success could not have been achieved without a very close alliance between the business and IT.

Ideally, IT will be a partner in the definition of the business strategy since that is how the company will derive the greatest value from IT. Whether or not that is true in your company, as an IT leader your goal will be to engage with the business to understand what products and services you can deliver to maximize the value of IT to that organization.

Part of the process of partnering with the business includes ensuring that the business considers itself as having a voice in the actual initiatives that IT undertakes. The most successfully way of achieving this is to have an IT steering committee that provides guidance to Information Technology's direction. This group should consist of senior business leaders from across the business.

When developing your IT strategy, your discussions with the individual business units should not be about technology solutions, but instead about business needs, opportunities, and challenges. From your perspective as an IT leader, IT should be tasked with identifying the solutions to the business unit's needs, once there has been a clear definition of what those needs are.

Once discussions with the business units are complete, the next step is to develop a list of initiatives that will provide the support for the business unit goals.

As an example of this process, let's take the example of the credit card company that decides it wants to begin offering analyses of the transaction data that is flowing through the transaction switch. This capability becomes one of IT's Strategic Goals.

If the company is new to analytics, there are a number of initiatives that will be required to make this goal a reality. First, the underlying infrastructure will need to be put into place to create a data repository. This will include sourcing the data (extraction), transforming the data into some standardized format (transformation) and loading the data into a database (loading) or ETL. There will obviously need to be the infrastructure for the data warehouse itself and then systems to slice and dice the data and deliver the reports that will be the actual products that will be offered to the clients. Depending on the analyses and reports, there may be a need for external data feeds and historical information.

In order to deliver this environment, it becomes clear that there are a number of specialized skills that do not currently exist within your organization. In addition, there are a number of IT tools that would be needed and the storage environment is far too small to support the quantities of data that this new initiative will produce. Implementing this may require expansion to data center space and the need for additional network capabilities.

This business need will be clearly represented within the IT Strategy. This does not mean that you represent this project in the next year's budget as a line-item that costs $3 million. Instead, this means that within your IT strategy it is represented as a multi-year initiative that defines an endpoint based on the current understanding. It defines incremental steps that will each provide incremental business value along the way.

The representation in the business strategy will define what the gap is between what is needed to be successful at this initiative and where you are today. It will be represented in the Human Capital Management, Hardware and Software sections of the Strategy document.

Since you will be performing this alignment process with each of the business units you will likely end up with many potential initiatives that the business' would request or require. This is where you will utilize the Project Prioritization process that was outlined earlier in the book. Using this process you will calculate a comparative value of each project to the business itself, based upon a common framework of criteria.

Identify the Gaps Using a SWOT Analysis

SWOT stands for Strength, Weakness, Opportunity, Threat. A SWOT analysis will guide you to identify the strengths and weaknesses as well as broader opportunities and threats of a situation. This analysis will provide the clarity of the situation necessary for both strategic planning and decision-making.

Assuming you have started your new job (or at any time after reading this book) with an extensive review of your organization, you will have the information to conduct this analysis. Put most simply, this SWOT analysis will expose the gaps between where you need to be and where you are now. It will also expose risks that can derail your projects.

Taking a look at each of the components of a SWOT analysis, you should think of them in terms of an initiative you will be adding to your IT Strategic Plan.

Strengths

- What advantages does your organization have? (skills, agility, well-defined processes, platform, cost management)
- What do you do better than anyone else? (customer satisfaction, data center convergence)

- What unique resources can you draw upon to be successful at the initiative?
- What do people in your company see as your strengths?
- What technology is in place that will make you successful?
- What are your organization's unique skills or organizational strengths that make your potential for success likely?

Weaknesses

- What needs to be improved? (staff size, staff morale, technical processes, policy compliance)
- What should you avoid?
- What are people in your company likely to see as weaknesses? (skill sets, IT communications, technology platform, etc.)
- What factors have resulted in past project failures?

Again, consider this from an internal and external basis: Do other people seem to perceive weaknesses that you don't see? Are your company's competitors doing anything better than you? It's best to be realistic now, and face any unpleasant truths as soon as possible.

Opportunities

- Are there any new or emerging technologies that can have a significant impact? (Software Defined Networking?)
- What interesting trends that you can leverage to improve IT services to the business? (BYOD?)
- Useful opportunities can come from such things as:
    - Changes in technology and markets on both a broad and narrow scale.
    - Changes in government policy related to your field.
    - Changes in social patterns, population profiles, lifestyle changes, and so on.
    - Local events

Threats

- Increased Risks and exposures, such as Information Security issues, lack of Disaster Recovery, etc.
- Is changing technology threatening your position?

- What obstacles do you face, such as lack of user awareness to Info Security?
- What are your competitors doing? (technical leaps by competitors)
- Are quality standards or specifications for your job, products or services changing?
- Is there a lack of available budget to address issues
- Could any of your weaknesses seriously threaten your business?

The Actual IT Strategic Plan Document

You've compiled a significant amount of information that will drive the strategic plan. Now it's time to turn it into a real document. The IT Strategic Plan can be in the form of a document, a Presentation or both. Generally accepted limits are that the document should be less than 15 Pages and a presentation should be less than 25 slides.

Some of the sections of the document you will need to think about are:

Mission Statement – The mission statement is designed to define the business of each organization. If you are managing the IT Infrastructure organization, your mission statement will be similar to:

"The mission of the IT Infrastructure group is to provide a reliable, flexible and agile IT infrastructure environment to Business and Application Development groups."

Vision Statement – The vision statement should not be your classic "build an IT organization to deliver the best services to the organization" statement – one that invokes either laughter or frustration. It should instead be one that paints a clear picture of where the IT organization is headed.

The Vision is a statement of the ideal way in which IT decisions will be made and the IT organization will operate. It includes values statements that reflect the desired organizational culture, management style, and client service perspectives.

Strategic Guiding Principles – These are statements that define the norms, ethics, and values that will guide your decision-making process irrespective of the circumstances. Some examples are:

- Investment decisions tied to mission impact

- Support for: transparency, engagement, collaboration
- Ubiquitous and universal access
- Common, interoperable, and enterprise-wide solutions
- Management visibility into IT
- Impact on the Business' mission
- Decreasing environmental footprint

Goals and Objectives – This section will define the goals that resulted from your discussions with the business. You should define the overall goal, the objectives that support achieving that goal and the Key performance Indicators that will provide the measures of your progress toward achieving the goal. Ideally, you can include a table that looks like the following.

Goals	Objectives	Key Performance Indicators
Goal 1	Objective 1.1 Objective 1.2 Objective 1.3	Indicator 1.1 Indicator 1.2 Indicator 1.3
Goal 2	Objective 2.1 Objective 2.2 Objective 2.3	Indicator 2.1 Indicator 2.2 Indicator 2.3
Goal 3	Objective 3.1 Objective 3.2 Objective 3.3	Indicator 3.1 Indicator 3.2 Indicator 3.3
Goal 4	Objective 4.1 Objective 4.2 Objective 4.3	Indicator 4.1 Indicator 4.2 Indicator 4.3

Drivers of the IT Strategic Plan – In this section you will define those aspects of the business strategy and IT environment that drove the elements of the strategy. These will most likely be business unit goals and needs and IT activities to improve efficiency and effectiveness.

Strategic Gaps – This is similar to the Drivers section, however, this is a broader statement of what's missing to achieve the Strategic Business and IT goals than a definition of what you will be doing to fill those gaps.

IT Strategic Plan – Sample Table of Contents

- Executive Summary - This is a summary of the IT strategy
- High-level Scope and Organizational Benefits
- IT Vision
- Goals and Objectives
- Drivers of the IT Strategic Plan
- Strategic Gaps
- Relationship to overall Business Strategy
- Resource Summary
  - Staffing
  - Budgets
  - Summary of key projects
- Metrics

- The Information Technology Department
- Mission Statement
- Core Values of Information Technology Organization
- Expectations of Information Technology
- IT Organization Structure and Governance
- IT organization roles and responsibilities
- IT role description
- IT Governance
- IT SWOT Analysis
- Goals, Objectives, and Strategies
- Major Themes
  - Theme 1
  - Theme 2
  - Theme 3
  - Theme 1

- - Goal
    - Strategy
  - Theme 2
    - Goal
    - Strategy
  - Theme 3
    - Goal
    - Strategy

IT Strategy Summary Thoughts

Developing an Information Technology Strategy is not a simple or quick task, however, there is so much riding on the proper investment in IT and the activities that IT undertakes that it is an essential process.

If you are a mid-level or lower level manager in IT, you may not need to develop a comprehensive strategy or be asked to participate in the development of the overall IT strategy, however you should still consider going through the process to clarify your thinking on where you will take your department, what you will spend your budget on and what resources you will need in the future to meet the overall goals that have cascaded down to you.

Chapter 17

Managing the Politics of IT Infrastructure

If you're managing an Information Technology environment you will find yourself dealing with political challenges almost on a daily basis. These almost always start with the unspoken (and sometimes actually spoken) message that "I'm more important than you are so I will tell you how we are going to handle this situation"

My advice will usually include at least two rules;

(1) *Listen to what the person has to say* - Clearly your first reaction will likely be to tell the person to go pound sand, but that can wait. It's better for you if, when they escalate above your head, they have to say "he listened to what I was asking for and then just told me to go pound sand" than if they say "he wouldn't even listen to what I was asking for. He just told me to go pound sand". Occasionally, you may find that the person makes sense in some fashion and you will be glad you listened.

(2) Document everything – However any discussion goes make a note that describes what was discussed and what your responses were. Follow-up the conversation with an EMAIL to the person you had the discussion with clarifying the discussion. This is essential. Political challenges almost always get escalated to more senior management and when you're dealing with a

political player, you can almost always count on their NOT telling the truth. Have that document trail to protect yourself and your organization.

Political challenges will come from so many places in so many forms it would be impossible to list even a small fraction of them here, but some of the more standard ones will include:

The Standards Rejecter

This is a person who, you guessed it, rejects the company standards you have put into place. In the vast majority of the cases, this is just someone who could easily have their technology requirements fulfilled using the standard systems and applications you have defined. It's a power play short and simple. That said; hear the person out (rule 1). You may find that there is actually a very specific need that cannot be fulfilled by the standards. An example may be someone that does very specific types of image work. That person may need a very specific piece of software that will need a more powerful computer than your standards include.

The Resource Hog

This political situation will come in the form of a person that wants something you have – your budget, your open headcount, some responsibility that your organization owns. In order to defend against this type of attack, you need to have a firm plan in place that clearly defines how you are spending your budget and what you have been doing to fill open headcount. If you have an open headcount for six months and haven't been interviewing to fill the spots you deserve to lose it.

The CYA Finger Pointer

This is someone in the organization (usually on the business side) that hasn't done their job. When they get called on it, they blame the technology. This is, unfortunately, a VERY common situation. An example is helpful here:

There was a Senior Vice president of one of the larger companies I worked for that went on a trip to South Africa. While he was away he didn't check his EMAIL or call into the office for almost a week. When he got back to the office his boss was just furious. This guy – let's call him Steve – simply said *"I tried every day to use the EMAIL systems but they just do not work in the South Africa office. Everyone down there was complaining about the technology they hate it and have zero confidence in our technology group*". I, of course, had messaging systems as one of the functions in my organization.

I ended up having to launch an investigation into what happened. I had to have people from my team call every single one of the staff members in South Africa, go through a general satisfaction survey that was designed for this review and get their attestation as to the quality of the technology they were using. It wasn't a huge office, but they are 7 hours ahead of us in New York, so this essentially had to be done during the overnight hours, while we were still managing all of our daily responsibilities. It took about a week to complete.

In the end, our technology was vindicated, but the cost to me and my team in terms of lost hours and grief was immense. This event drove changes to our monthly metrics program. Having the metrics in place that defined the availability statistics of the EMAIL servers and the number of messages in and out of every office kept this sort of claim from happening again. Metrics are immensely important to protecting yourself against false claims.

The Complainer

A subset of the CYA Finger Pointer is the Complainer. This person may not have a huge issue they need to cover up, just marginal to poor performance. " It's the computer", "The Printer doesn't work", "the network was down", "I took 8 hours for someone to stop by and fix whatever". The list will be endless and you can't let this stuff get out of hand. You need to make sure your desktop people close calls immediately when they are done so that you have accurate metrics of performance. Be able to go back to that person and say "your call came in at xx AM, was responded to in 20 minutes and was resolved within 35 minutes of your first call". Once that happens to a few people the rest will be careful not to blame your team for their poor performance.

The Non-Team Player

It's hard to know exactly what to call this type of person, but most everything I can come up with doesn't belong in print. This is the person that is part of a broader team and just will not play nice with the other members of the team. Most recently this was a facility manager on a new Headquarters buildout. In the distant past, I also had a Telecom Manager that just would not buy into being part of a consolidated IT Project team. Whoever the non-team player is, they will make your life miserable and put the success of the project at risk.

Some examples work here. In the headquarters build-out project, the Facilities manager was the overall PM on the project. He was simply incompetent and a liar. He would not share information and when he did, he would just give you what he felt you needed to know. He is also the person I referred to that wanted all discussions and decisions to be verbal agreements between the two of us, nothing written and distributed.

Naturally, the absolute first item we agreed to he reneged on and claimed there was no such conversation. To address this we did two things (1) Escalate the issue and our concerns about him to Senior Management and (2) document everything on the project an order of magnitude more than we would document other activities. It quickly became clear to Senior Management that this guy was a problem, but the opted to do nothing about it during the project. The net result – a $40 million facility build-out became a $70 million build-out. Too bad. IT came in under-budget on this project.

My telecom situation was a difficult challenge too. The Telco manager (otherwise known as the phone guy) just wouldn't accept any collaboration with me. Here is one dialog I will never forget; Me - "So when are the PRIs scheduled to be installed?" Him – "I don't know, when are the PRIs scheduled to be installed". Me – "When do you expect your equipment to be delivered?" Him – "I don't know, when do I expect my equipment to be delivered?" So it went. You can imagine the self-control I had to exhibit dealing with this guy.

One night I had a huge delivery of IBM Mainframe equipment coming in. It was several tractor trailer loads of equipment. The building was still under construction, so we needed to bring the equipment up the outside of the building using the hoist (outside elevator). It just so happened that on this very night the Elevator Operator's Union decided to go on strike. We paid the hoist operator a huge amount of money to help us get through the night, but he would only work until 1 AM, which just might do it for my equipment. After we started bringing in equipment for an hour or two, two additional tractor trailers show up with telephone equipment. The Telco guy comes down in a huff and says, "I need to get my stuff up to the data center floor".

I finished what I had to get up first and then started on his. Best I could do was get about a quarter of it up to the data center floor and the rest we just moved onto an empty floor since we were about to lose the hoist. The next morning when he came in and found his equipment wasn't all upstairs he was just FURIOUS. He went to my boss, my boss's boss and just said every terrible thing he could about me.

Luckily, I had documented all of his transgressions along the way, which just totally explained the situation. I was able to explain this very simply – "Sorry, this is just the TSS" (Tough-Sh!t Scenario).

Last-Minute and It's YOUR Fault

This political situation involves that customer that just ignores the standard policies and processes, fails as a result and then blames you for their failure. Think this is far-fetched? If you do, you shouldn't be running an IT Infrastructure group.

As an example, one of my peers ran an Application Development group. He just couldn't be bothered with the policies we had in place. If you needed an additional server for your new application, we had a policy that stated we needed a certain amount of advanced notice. At the time I believe this was measured in some number of weeks. One afternoon I get a call from this manager and he said: "Is my server going to be ready tonight?" I asked "What server?" He had never asked for a server.

We reported to the same manager and were in staff meetings together and this initiative never even came up. By pulling out all stops I was able to get him a server in three days – pushing literally everything else aside, but he still missed his date to the business. He simply told the business that I could not get the server to him on time (blaming me). The Business now says that because of this slip (of a few days), they would be delayed by three weeks in delivering the functionality they had promised.

So here is what I was up against. He didn't put in a request for a server, but instead, he told people *I* didn't do my job. The business used the opportunity to take this 3-day slip in getting their server and using it to justify a 3-week slip in delivering the functionality to their users. Unbelievable!

The sad fact is that this sort of thing is absolutely NOT an isolated situation. The saving grace for me was that I had an online change management process that was the definitive location where all requests were made. That said, everybody was upset with me and my team that we didn't cover their mistake.

Again, Document everything and have solid processes that you enforce to protect yourself in these situations.

The Change Management Failure

When someone requests a change and the Change Management Process rejects the change for whatever reason, the requestor will always point to YOU as the reason something did not get done, Expect this person to scream loud and to anyone that will listen – how dare you do your job!

The only way to address this situation is through documentation. The Change Management process MUST capture the date/time when anything was done. When was the change first requested? When was completed documentation received? Did the request fit into the standard schedule windows or if not did it qualify for the Emergency Change Process? If the change was rejected, what were the reasons for the rejection?

You must have that information at your fingertips and not need to dig through piles of papers to find it. Don't be afraid to let those to whom he has used you as an excuse know what the reality of the situation is.

Some People Are More Equal Than Others

The policy that is most often published states that all user calls are handled equally on a first come/first served basis. Now, I assume (and hope) that everyone reading this book that is managing an infrastructure group understands clearly and unequivocally that that is absolutely not true. Just as there is a hierarchy of event severity (technical severity), there is a hierarchy of who get service when.

I am confident that this statement will invoke horror, dismay, and revulsion in the purists that consult and teach how to manage an IT department – but never have actually done it themselves. Any of you that have been in the hot seat will agree wholeheartedly with this model.

The hierarchy is relatively simple to understand:

1. *Large Revenue Producers* - Your first priority will usually be a person or group that has a real and substantial impact on revenue on a real time basis. I'm talking Traders and likely Portfolio Managers here. This is someone where (1) an outage of their workstation can

cause a significant loss of a trade is not completed and (2) cannot move to another workstation to do his/her work. I'm certain there are other folks that will fall into this same category, but you get the picture

2. ***Senior Management*** – Assuming that there are no user issues in the first group, when a senior manager calls, they automatically are moved to the head of the list (or top of the pile of you prefer). In the organizations I managed, I have always defined the senior management into a separate group. They are flagged for special response. I have always designated one or two of the technicians as the people that would support these individuals.

If a call came in from one of the senior managers, that issue would be immediately assigned. The technician would be called on the telephone and would be instructed to make the senior manager's call the next one on the list. Also, depending on how senior the person is, a member of the management team would meet the technician at the senior manager's office to ensure everything went smoothly and that any questions or concerns were either immediately answered or taken back and escalated to the Infrastructure management team to be answered or resolved.

Now you may find that your manager, or members of the senior management team, may respond to your obvious over-the-top response with some humble statement like "thanks for this incredible response, but I don't want to be treated differently than everybody else." Yeah, right! I will submit to you that this is absolutely no different than your wife or girlfriend (or husband or boyfriend) telling you "I don't want you to do anything special for Valentine's Day! Don't spend a lot of money on flowers, jewelry, and chocolate". Hopefully, you know to ignore what your significant other says and you do actually show up with something . . . significant. The same is true here! Try treating senior management like everybody else, and then let us know how you like your next job.

3. ***Everybody Else*** – Yep, the last category is everybody else. This is where the actual Help Desk process takes over and functions according to a First-Come/First-Served in the context of the Severity assignments

Some People Are Not

This is the person that absolutely thinks he or she deserves special treatment and threatens to cause you all sorts of agony if you don't provide the special attention they demand. These folks are often the assistants of Senior Managers. They are characterized by calling the Head of Infrastructure or CTO for the simplest of Help Desk Calls. "My printer needs a new cartridge" or "I don't like the direction that my PC faces and want someone to move it". Usually, you can slowly manage these folks into the mainstream of support, especially if you are able to mention it to the person that they believe they derive their power from. Sometimes you cannot.

As an example, I ran Infrastructure for a Global Financial Services Company where one of the president's direct reports had a secretary that I will call Karen. Karen wasn't a particularly exceptional person by any measure but felt like she ruled the roost so to speak. She would call me for every stupid issue that popped into her head. I tried to be as helpful as possible but always said "Karen, I will have to call the Help Desk and ask them to come by to help you. It would be so much quicker and more effective if you just call them directly. I promise they will be exceptionally responsive" (especially since I would tell the help desk I didn't want them to give her any reason to call me and complain). Her response was always the same: "Art, do you know who I am?"

At first, I was annoyed, very annoyed, but I just gave in and said "fine, what do you need?" After the calls went on for months this changed into mild resistance, at which point I said "OK, I'll get to this as soon as I can, but it would be so much quicker if you called the Help Desk directly" Eventually I became tired of the calls so when she said "Art, do you know who I am?" I responded by just taking the phone away from my ear and saying loudly (to no one in particular) "Hey, do any of you guys know who Karen is? She keeps forgetting!" I then told her to call the Help Desk. That of course, got her angry and I dealt with it directly with her boss. She wasn't with the firm much longer.

The moral of this story is to deal with these sorts of pain in the butt directly and quickly. Don't wait until you're acting like a jerk too. Understand you need to be selective here. In some companies, the Assistant to the President is to a large measure a Senior Manager. They will handle their bosses business when he or she is unavailable and are fully empowered to make the required decisions. That person needs to be treated like a Senior Manager.

Home Setups

Home setups have just become a way of life for Infrastructure Managers. Again, I am not going to discuss the technology or even the policies in this part of the book. I am going to discuss the political aspect of providing home setups.

What is considered a Home Setup can vary across the spectrum. At one end of the spectrum, it can be as simple as a user's machine that can connect to the business network with certain controls. At the far other end of the spectrum, it can be a complete home system, including desktop workstation, printer, etc.

There are two aspects of how this is impacted by the politics of the situation.

1. First, there is the issue of who you give these units to. You will be expected to provide support for any in-home units, so think through any policies or decisions well.
2. The bigger political landmine is the interaction with whoever is at home when your technician arrives. Since most of these full setups go to the more senior management I will assume you know to send your most professional technician to the home. The technician needs to dress properly and conservatively and be ultra-polite. (yes sir or madam)

You will need your technician to completely prepare for the visit. Anything that they feel they may need should be brought along for the visit. As an example, in one situation one of the most senior managers at a company I worked for had a home setup. He purchased a printer himself to add to the computer. The request was simply to install the printer.

When the technician arrived he found that there was no cable to attach the printer to the computer included in the printer box. He needed to schedule another visit to come back with a cable. The manager's wife (who was there to supervise the visit) turned into one of the most abusive individuals we ever had to deal with. She insulted our technician; she called the office to insult me and my entire team and then called her husband to complain. Remember, we were asked to install something that he had purchased personally. We considered this visit a favor to the senior manager. All this being said, this issue could have been avoided if our technician had slipped a few cables into his bag before he went to the manager's house.

Your people also need to leave their work area in absolutely immaculate condition when they complete a home visit. Any packaging should be consolidated and removed. If it cannot be thrown out in the trash at the home, they should take it with them.

Beyond these two issues, you will undoubtedly need to contend with home setups being used primarily for home purposes. This means everything from benign surfing on the part of family members to online gaming and other uses that will clearly leave all sorts of Viruses and Malware on the machine. These should be addressed in your policies (appropriate use policies) as well as by having the most substantial local protection utilities on the machine.

Chapter 18

Final Words

Well, we sure did cover quite a number of items in this book, frankly far more than was originally planned. That's how it is when managing infrastructure, you think you have a clear view of everything that needs to be done, but then find there is some corporate or compliance requirement that dramatically expands the size of the effort.

Within the chapters of this book, we discussed a plan for how to approach starting a new position.

That plan started by gathering as much information about the current state of the department as possible, staff info, budgets, outstanding issues, major projects or other activities in flight, etc.

Following that information gathering, you will perform a deep dive assessment of the organization, including the technologies, policies, processes, customer relationships and so on. This provides your baseline against which any improvements are measured.

From that assessment, you will derive the list of transformations you will need to make to create a first-rate IT Organization. That list will drive both your IT Strategy and the Roadmap you define that will get you from your current state to your desired Strategic end point.

We focused quite a bit on the major activities and management processes you need to ensure exist in a form that meets your objectives. These include such areas as Asset Management, Risk Management, Technology Management, Project Management, Vendor Management and Operational Management. Remember that in most all of these management domains there is a wide continuum of the size or scope of the implementations. You need to choose how complete or complex a process fits the company you work for. All of these major processes should be represented in your IT strategy.

Being a successful Head of IT Infrastructure is so much more than getting the Technology and Processes right – so much of it depends on your ability to navigate the attacks and company politics and we've talked about that too.

Throughout this book, I've sprinkled some of the cynical "real-world" issues that you will face. I've read countless books on IT and IT management and most can put me to sleep from 50 feet away. An easy observation is that I have never seen a single book or article address these real-world situations – and that's a problem.

Over the years quite a few new or junior managers have come to me and asked how to handle a problem situation they are dealing with. In most of those cases, the answer was clear and simple to me, but that's only because I've been doing this for such a very long time. When I started down this path I was completely clueless – however learning IT management in the financial services industry is the definition of Baptism by Fire.

That's one of my big messages here, it does get easier, much easier, as time goes on. As I have said throughout this book, one of the more important keys to success is to develop the ability to know who is your friend and who is not. Who is a liar and who tells the truth? Who is competent and who is not. Most importantly, you must understand how to react in each of those situations.

Develop the necessary competencies to run a first-rate IT shop. Be strong, be confident, don't take a lot of abuse, but don't be an arrogant jerk either. You will be astounded how quickly people come to respect confident success.

I hope you have enjoyed reading this book and most importantly that you have gotten some real value from it. Don't forget to complete a review of the book on Amazon. You can submit your review at the following link:

http://www.amazon.com/review/create-review/ref=cm_cr_dp_no_rvw_e?ie=UTF8&asin=B01DIF7I9E&channel=detail-glance&nodeID=133140011&store=digital-text

Remember – 5 stars and feel free to sprinkle the work "Genius" in your written review!

Appendix A

Made in the USA
Columbia, SC
03 August 2019